The Regulation of Sport in the European Union

The Regulation of Sport in the European Union

Edited by

Barbara Bogusz
Nottingham Trent University, UK

Adam Cygan and Erika Szyszczak
University of Leicester, UK

Edward Elgar
Cheltenham, UK • Northampton, MA, USA

Published by
Edward Elgar Publishing Limited
Glensanda House
Montpellier Parade
Cheltenham
Glos GL50 1UA
UK

Edward Elgar Publishing, Inc.
William Pratt House
9 Dewey Court
Northampton
Massachusetts 01060
USA

A catalogue record for this book
is available from the British Library

Library of Congress Cataloguing in Publication Data

The regulation of sport in the European Union / edited by Barbara Bogusz, Adam Cygan, and Erika Szyszczak.
    p. cm.
    Includes bibliographical references and index.
    1. Sports—Law and legislation—European Union countries. I. Bogusz, Barbara. II. Cygan, Adam Jan. III. Szyszczak, Erika M.
    KJE6063.R44 2007
    344.24′099—dc22
                                                                    2007001390

ISBN 978 1 84720 363 2

Typeset by Cambrian Typesetters, Camberley, Surrey
Printed and bound in Great Britain by MPG Books Ltd, Bodmin, Cornwall

Contents

Contents

Contributors

Luca Barani, Institut d'études européennes, Bruxelles

Barbara Bogusz, Senior Lecturer in Law, Nottingham Trent University

Adam Cygan, Senior Lecturer in Law, University of Leicester

Jennifer Davis, Newton Trust Lecturer, Wolfson College, University of Cambridge

Estelle Derclaye, Lecturer in Law, University of Nottingham

Richard Disney, Professor of Labour Economics, University of Nottingham

Tim Kerr, 11 King's Bench Walk Chambers

Erika Szyszczak, Jean Monnet Professor of European Law, Professor of European Competition and Labour Law, University of Leicester

Stephen Weatherill, Jacques Delors Professor of European Community Law, University of Oxford

Robin C.A. White, Professor of Law, University of Leicester

Preface

If he helped me out in training we would be bottom of the league and if I had to work in his world of big business, we would be bankrupt! (José Mourinho, on his relationship with Roman Abramovich)[1]

This collection is the outcome of a one-day seminar on the *Regulation of Sport in the European Union* held at the University of Leicester, 11 May 2006. The seminar was part of *The Modern Law Review* seminar series, bringing together academics, sociologists, practitioners, political scientists and economists within the context of whether sport, as a discipline, raises distinct regulatory issues by comparison to other social and economic activities. A thread running throughout the volume is the desire to address the issue of whether sport is special. The contributions in this book engage with this question and consider whether the time has arrived to recognize the existence of a distinct *lex sportiva*. The legal discipline of 'sports law' has become accepted both by academic writers and by practitioners who suggest that sports law is not just a composite description of other branches of law, such as competition law or intellectual property and how they are applied to athletes or sporting federations.[2]

The arguments which are put forward by the proponents of a distinct sports law are not without substance. Athletes are subject to the rules and regulations of sporting federations which have powers to make binding quasi-judicial decisions and ultimately terminate a sporting career. Such decisions are increasingly being confirmed by a global sports court, the Court of Arbitration for Sport (CAS) which is based in Lausanne, Switzerland. The jurisdiction of the CAS is recognized by most international sporting federations and it has developed its own jurisprudence and precedent. Yet despite these developments there appears to be an absence of enthusiasm within the European Union (EU), national governments and their regulatory agencies to afford sport a special status. Many, if not all, professional sports have, in recent years,

---

[1] Taken from the 'World According to Mourinho', March 2005. Available at http://news.bbc.co.uk/sport1/hi/football/teams/c/chelsea/4392444.stm.
[2] See for example M. Beloff, T. Kerr and M. Demetriou, *Sports Law* (Oxford: Hart Publishing, 1999); M. Beloff, 'Is there a *Lex Sportiva*?', 2005 (3) ISLR, 49; J. Nafziger, *International Sports Law* (2nd edn, Ardsley, NY: Transnational Publications, 2004).

become first and foremost economic activities. Consequently, a prevailing view in governance circles is that sport should be regulated as such, which in practice means the application of competition rules, state aid rules and other established legal principles which are consistently applied across areas of economic activity.

The regulation of sport fills not only the back page, but often the headlines and business pages, in newspapers as the line between amateur sporting activity and professional sporting activity becomes increasingly blurred. One identifiable reason for this is that modern sport, as the quotation by José Mourinho suggests, is based upon a complex relationship between financial and on-field success. Many sports in the twenty-first century have acquired obvious commercial characteristics and sporting success is no longer the *only* goal of athletes, clubs or sporting federations. The increase of public interest in sports such as football, motor racing and, most recently, cricket has fuelled the development of these sports into commercially lucrative activities which bear little resemblance to those of the Corinthian days of amateur sport. Sport has been transformed into an important economic activity which involves large sums of money, acquired primarily from the sale of television rights, and through commercial exploitation of sporting brands and associated personalities. Yet, despite these changes, sport remains an important aspect of national and international cultural identity, as well as a leisure activity, and the idea of 'sport for all' or 'sport in the community' is a new mantra promoted by governments and the EU.

The growth of sport as an economic activity has, in recent years, led to the involvement of regulatory authorities and courts at both the national and EU level, often as an alternative route to the autonomous regulatory structure of sport. Increasingly, as sporting activity is caught by European Community (EC) Treaty provisions relating to competition law, cultural policies and citizens and workers' rights, it is the EU level which has become the focus for the regulation of sport and promotion of sport as a cultural pursuit. The 'Europeanization' of sporting activity has therefore produced identifiable implications for the regulatory structure of sport, its institutional structure and the enforcement of the rules, as well as the exploitation of sporting rights.

The purpose of this volume is to examine in an integrated manner, from a European Union perspective, the numerous developments which have taken place in the regulation of sporting activity in the last decade. It places the regulation of sport in the context of the EU regulatory structure which is emerging in a piecemeal fashion and this underlies the interdisciplinary approach which is adopted. The book is divided into three parts which reflects the current policy, legislative and judicial discourse that exists in the regulation of sport.

PART 1:   THE REGULATION OF ECONOMIC ACTIVITY
IN SPORT

The first part of the book addresses the legal and economic aspects of sport as a commercial and cultural activity, analysing the application of the free movement and competition rules to individuals and the implications for labour markets. The central legal issue explored by the contributors is what sporting or sport-related interest amounts to an 'economic activity' which requires formal regulation. In turn, this raises questions of whether certain kinds of activity can be sheltered from the application of the free movement and competition rules or, if caught, whether special exemptions and justifications should apply. The latter point is argued before national courts and the European Courts on an increasingly frequent basis and these key judgments are considered by the authors.

In Chapter 1, Erika Szyszczak analyses why sport is being portrayed as special in the EU regulatory processes analysing the political, economic and sociological arguments that are being used to inform the regulatory discourse. The chapter examines how a 'European model of sport' is being created through political and institutional processes in the EU. Through an analysis of the case law of the European Courts the chapter considers how, to what extent and why sport is accorded special treatment in the application of the Internal Market and the competition law rules. The chapter organizes the question 'Is sport special?' around two themes. The first is the belief that sport is special and that it has a role to play in creating a European polity. The second theme analyses *how* the idea that there is a 'European model of sport' has been created and how this idea is used to justify and underpin arguments for giving sport special treatment in regulatory processes.

In Chapter 2, Robin C.A. White considers the fundamental question of free movement and sport and how the European Court of Justice has applied the free movement rules to sport. This chapter finds that three principles have been clearly established by the case law of the Court in the fields where the free movement of individuals meets the regulation of sport. First, the rules of the EC Treaty on free movement of workers, freedom of establishment and the freedom to provide and receive services are fundamental rules of the Community constitution which apply to sporting activities of an economic nature. Secondly, sport enjoys no special status in the Treaty which exempts it from the prohibition of discrimination on grounds of nationality in relation to the free movement of sports professionals. Thirdly, rules of sporting regulatory bodies which are capable of restricting access to the labour market for sports professionals are permissible only in so far as they do not fall foul of the prohibition of discrimination, and are capable of justification on non-economic grounds. Finally, the chapter concludes by arguing that the approach of the

Court has been correct in its refusal to recognize a specific sporting justification to the free movement rules and that furthermore this has been recognized politically as well as legally. These political issues arising from the regulation of sport are taken up by Luca Barani in Chapter 6.

In Chapter 3, Stephen Weatherill considers the application of competition rules to sport since the *Bosman* judgment and how athletes have sought to use the Treaty, for example, in the recent cases of *Meca-Medina and Igor Majcen*, as a sword to fight disciplinary action by a sports governing body. Weatherill considers what comes within the scope of the Treaty rules and focuses on the question of what amounts to an economic activity for the purposes of competition law. He rejects the need for a special justification for sport in the Treaty and instead puts forward an argument based upon a holistic evaluation of the activities of the sporting authority. He concludes his analysis by suggesting that it will be most appropriate that the EC rules, both on free movement and on competition, should only take effect in circumstances following an overall assessment of the rules, including their objectives and whether the consequences of those rules go beyond that which is necessary to achieve those objectives.

Adam Cygan considers in Chapter 4 how legal principles have been applied to the regulation of Formula One motor racing. The chapter considers this issue in the context of the way EC law and national law have sought to regulate other sports, and addresses two key questions. Firstly, how is an activity such as Formula One motor racing most appropriately regulated given that it exhibits as many, if not more, characteristics of a commercial undertaking rather than that of a sport? Consequently, the essay poses the question of whether *all* sports are indeed special, and, if not, what this means for their legal regulation. Secondly, the chapter examines the specific question of regulation of Formula One motor racing and whether established principles such as the free movement and competition rules developed by the European Court of Justice are a more appropriate mechanism through which to regulate this activity, rather than through the creation of a specific regulatory system intended only for sport.

PART 2: THE REGULATION OF 'LABOUR' MARKETS

In Part 2, the contributions concentrate on dispute resolution in sport, how and through what methods this is best achieved. Thy explore how regulatory institutional forms are emerging and the consequences of such forms for individual rights. A theme running throughout this part is the need to examine the relationship between the athlete and the sports governing body and what options are available for dispute resolution when this relationship breaks down.

In Chapter 5, Tim Kerr examines how the individual conduct of athletes is regulated by sports governing bodies and what scope there is for independent review of disciplinary decisions of sporting federations through public law. Kerr thus examines the pivotal role being played by the Court of Arbitration for Sport (CAS) in Lausanne and its growth into a World Sports Court which has the power to make binding decisions. The chapter considers how sports governing bodies and the CAS implement disciplinary procedures, the role of CAS in both a national and EU context, and how decisions of CAS are viewed by traditional judicial bodies. It is this latter relationship which proves to be causing most controversy as the recent judgments by the European Court of Justice in *Meca Medina* and *Igor Majcen* illustrate. In an increasingly litigious and rights-oriented society, sportsmen and women, as well as their agents, promoters and sponsors, are frequently challenging disciplinary measures taken against them. One reason which can be identified for this is the increasingly short-term nature of many sporting careers and the rewards which are available. The outcome of such proceedings may have far-reaching economic consequences, not only for the individuals concerned, but also for any teams they perform for, investors and the international reputation of their nation state. Kerr highlights this issue and puts forwards the proposition that, as the regulation of sport raises many unique problems, the time has indeed arrived for the creation of a *lex sportiva*.

Luca Barani, in Chapter 6, examines the regulation of sport by considering key political questions relating to regulation. Barani focuses on the politics of sports' regulation at the EU level and examines the present choice of regulatory avenues and the adoption of policy solutions in a context of what he considers are imperfect regulatory alternatives. The chapter is especially concerned with issues arsing from the interaction between courts, markets and sport bodies to determine the most appropriate solution for regulatory problems arising from sporting matters. It begins by examining the political ramifications of the regulatory conundrum of sport and the imperfect alternatives that have been proposed to solve this conundrum, for example a political declaration in the shape of Treaty exception for sport. Barani considers the interplay between markets, courts and sport bodies, and how deregulation (that is, courts and markets) and re-regulation (that is, sport bodies) bring together law and policy. He argues that, while not offering a perfect solution, the current approach does at least provide a workable regulatory method. Finally, the author concludes by considering the lessons that have been learnt from the politics of sport regulation at the EU level and what this has contributed to the broader development of an EU polity.

In addition to a traditional understanding of disciplinary issues, a key feature of the regulation of labour markets concerns an athlete's ability to exploit his or her talent and receive adequate remuneration for this. The key question which Richard Disney explores in Chapter 7 is why some athletes are paid what they receive and what implications this may have for the regulation of sport. For example, post-*Bosman*, one factor identified is that the centre of gravity in terms of control of wages has shifted from the clubs to individual players. With an increase in such market power, how has this affected the ability of sports governing bodies to retain full control over their sport? The chapter describes how the competitive model of sports remuneration, which suggests that pay is largely determined by preferences, abilities and the 'personal scale of operations' of sports stars, has implications for the allocative efficiency of the sports labour market in the presence of alternative regulatory structures and distributions of property rights, and for the incidence of 'punishments' levied on players, clubs or leagues.

PART 3:   SPORT IN THE MULTI-MEDIA AGE

In Part 3, the authors consider the economic and cultural exploitation of sport. They analyse *how* and with *what effect* existing intellectual property, free movement and competition rules are being applied to sporting activities. A key thread which runs through these contributions is an analysis of the way the growth of technology, particularly audio visual advancement, has both assisted and hindered the commercial exploitation of sport. The contributions address the special problems posed to sport by new technology, including public accessibility of visual and factual data, creating the environment for a competitive market in the sale of sports rights and the ability of individual sportsmen and women to control the exploitation of their own image rights. The authors raise questions of ownership of sporting and related rights and consider judicial responses in relation to the exploitation of such rights and whether there are any public interest or cultural justifications for the exploitation of such rights.

In Chapter 8, Barbara Bogusz examines the tripartite relationship between sport, culture and commercial freedom. She considers the contribution made by the EU to the promotion of sport as culture and whether within the digital media age sport should be considered as first and foremost a commercial activity, with the cultural aspect relegated to a secondary importance. Central to this discussion is access to sporting events through the media and whether, and to what extent, regulatory bodies should interfere with the decisions of sporting federations to sell media rights for their sport to the highest bidder. The chapter considers how EC competition and free movement rules have been applied in such cases and whether the result has achieved a fair balance between the need for broad access and the commercial freedom of sporting federations. Finally, this discussion is broadened to evaluate the position of athletes as economically active individuals and how judicial protection has allowed successful athletes to exploit their image for commercial gain. This is a development which has led to athletes becoming 'cultural icons' of the twenty-first century and viewing this as an integral part of their sporting careers.

Jennifer Davis explores, in Chapter 9, how individual athletes and sporting organizations have used intellectual property law to exploit and protect what they consider to be legitimate economic interests. The focus of this chapter is the exploitation of individual image rights by sports stars and how the courts, in the UK, Europe and globally, have reacted to such claims. In addition to the traditional protection offered through breach of confidence and trademark protection, Davis examines how privacy laws are being used to protect economic rights. The chapter adopts a comparative perspective on this issue and examines the contribution to this development by the European Court of Human Rights and whether privacy laws are more developed in continental legal systems than those in the United Kingdom.

Chapter 10 focuses on intellectual property questions raised through the use of sporting data and information. Estelle Derclaye examines how the sport industry has been indirectly regulated by EC law through the interpretation of an intellectual property right, the *sui generis* right protecting databases (also referred to as the 'database right'). In 2004, the European Court of Justice interpreted the right in four related cases concerning football and horse racing fixtures (information relating to the dates, times, places, teams playing in the matches or horses running in the races). Organizers of important sport events such as the Olympics, football, rugby, cricket, tennis matches and horse races are therefore affected by law in their ownership rights on information relating to such events. This chapter explains the main features of the database right as interpreted by the European Court of Justice and examines the effect of the database right on sporting organizations. The analysis illustrates that, in most cases, the database right offers only limited assistance to sporting organizations, although, in some cases, sporting organizations can be very well protected. In such cases, Derclaye argues that issues of fair competition can occur if the organization has a monopoly, which will trigger EC competition rules. She concludes by addressing what the sporting industry can do to tackle these problems and outlines the prospects for future developments in the area.

The editors would like to thank the *Modern Law Review* for its generosity in funding the seminar on *The Regulation of Sport in the EU*. The seminar and this volume have brought together practitioners and academics to produce a timely piece of work. In addition to the contributors, the editors would like to thank Tania Rowlett for the administrative organization of the seminar and Anthony Berry for ensuring that all the audiovisual technology worked on the day. We are also indebted to Edward Elgar for agreeing to publish the volume and, in particular, Luke Adams and Nep Elverd for their commitment and enthusiasm to the project, and Dan Towse at the World Sports Law Report for his assistance in promoting the seminar.

B.B.
A.C.
E.S.

PART 1

The regulation of economic activity in sport

1. Is sport special?

Erika Szyszczak

INTRODUCTION

This chapter has three broad themes. The first theme analyses how sport is being portrayed as special in the European Union's (EU) emerging regulatory processes, analysing the political, economic and sociological arguments that are being used to inform the regulatory discourse. The second theme analyses how a European model of sport is being created through political and institutional processes in the EU. The third theme examines the case law of the European Courts to show how, and why, claims are made that sport should be accorded special treatment in the application of the Internal Market and the competition law rules. The chapter organizes the question, 'Is sport special?', around two broad ideas. The first idea is the belief that sport is special and that it has a role to play in creating a European polity. The second idea analyses how the idea that there is a 'European model of sport' has been created and how this is used to justify and underpin arguments for giving sport special treatment in regulatory processes.

WHY IS SPORT SPECIAL?

Increasingly, sport-related issues are emerging in litigation before the European Courts. Claims are made that sport is special in that it poses different questions for the EU regulatory processes and, it is argued, requires different solutions. The EU is struggling to find a role for sport to play in the emerging European polity as arguments are put forward that sport is not the same as other forms of economic activity brought within EU competence. However, being 'special' appears to be a general, and not a unique, claim today: health care, modernizing social protection, pensions, liberalized industries, new media platforms and services of general economic interest all lay claim to requiring special treatment under regulatory processes emerging from the EU regulatory structure. It is argued that the EU is facing a number of regulatory challenges, attributable to the changing role of the State in the modern economy, liberalization and globalization of financial markets, the rise in private power and the increased role played by autonomous and quasi-autonomous regulators. The EU also faces regulatory challenges from the competence perspective. The creation of economic and monetary union (EMU) and the development of an Internal Market led to the spillover of EU competence into new policy areas. Added to this, the adoption of the Lisbon Process focused EU attention upon a number of policies which needed coordination at the EU level. The regulatory gaps which consistently appear have led the EU to experiment with new forms of economic governance[1] to complement the conventional Community method and also to extend ideas of the *responsibility* of public power to other actors who exercise economic power in the market. Thus, at one level, the regulatory issues posed by sport to the EU governance and regulatory processes are not special. They are merely one part of a wider, fragmented, picture which highlights the limitations of the outdated regulatory processes in Europe in the modern era.[2]

THE CREATION OF AN IDEA: THE EUROPEAN MODEL OF SPORT

Sport as a concept is used in this chapter in a generic sense to cover a wide range of competitive and non-competitive, economic and non-economic activity[3] which has contributed to the ideas involved in defining a European Model of Sport. This section explores some of these ideas.

Separation of Amateur and Professional Sport

The separation of professional ('economic') activity from amateur ('non-economic') activity is an idea which permeates the European regulatory

---

[1]   E. Szyszczak, 'Experimental governance: the open method of co-ordination' (2006), **12**(4), *European Law Journal*, 487.

[2]   Complementing the variable geometry, which has increased in significance since the Maastricht Treaty 1991, in relation to Member State participation, and opt-outs, to new areas of competence for the EU.

[3]   Cf. Article 2 of the Council of Europe's European Sports Charter which defines sport as 'all forms of physical activity which, through casual or organised participation, aim at expressing or improving physical fitness and mental well-being, forming social relationships or obtaining results in competition at all levels'. 'A 'sport' may be defined through recognition by a competent authority, particularly a regulator, at either a national or international level, or through recognition of special treatment, for example as a charity, eligibility for public funding or special status, such as a tax exemption, limited (or a different) application of normal legal rules, for example the law of tort, public law in disciplinary cases or the competition and State aid rules.

approach to sport. Yet this is an idea which is easy to dismantle, and it is an argument which is difficult to sustain. Ancillary arrangements at *all* levels of sport belie the myth that the actors engaged in sporting activity merely 'live the dream'. The financial arrangements for the World Cup or Olympic Games are merely the pinnacle of commercial franchising, sponsorship and advertising chains which stretch down to the local sponsorship logos on the amateur Sunday League football shirts.

Regulatory disciplinary rules are routinely challenged for the effect an adverse finding may have upon future reputation and economic, as well as sporting, careers. This in turn has intensified the scrutiny of how regulatory bodies are established, their composition and rules of procedure, and questioned how far such bodies may deviate from the normal judicial process in adjudicating sporting claims. The European Convention on Human Rights and Fundamental Freedoms, particularly Article 6 which guarantees that, in the determination of civil rights, or of any criminal charge, a person is entitled to a fair and public hearing within a reasonable time by an independent and impartial tribunal, questions a number of practices carried out by sports' regulatory bodies. How far should disciplinary proceedings for sports-related misdemeanours take place behind closed doors? Or how far should disciplinary panels be independent[4] and how far should such experienced sports men and women be seen to be the best judge of sport-related disciplinary offences? Should there be appeals to independent bodies in order to secure compliance with Article 6 ECHR?[5]

The economic organization of sport has altered dramatically as a result of economic and technological changes during the 1990s. Merchandising, broadcasting rights and the sports 'star' status of high performing athletes (and also their managers and agents) has led to a 'winner-takes-all' market. In brief, consumers and investors are interested primarily in winners, and to be a winner intensifies the market position of the athlete, the club, or the team. This in turn may alter the national and international competitive structure of a particular sport, creating super leagues for the successful clubs or individual sports stars.[6] It may also lead to breakaway groups of successful champions wishing to exert more power in the market.[7] Not only does this affect the operation of the market, it magnifies the role of governance of such a market.

---

[4]   See *Modahl* [2002] 1 WLR 1192.

[5]   See *Bradley* v *Jockey Club* [2005] EWCA Civ 1056; *Wilander and Novacek* v *Tobin and Jude* [1997] 2 Lloyd's Rep 293; *R (Mullins)* v *Jockey Club* [2005] EWHC 2197.

[6]   For example, the Champions' League, the G14, the breakaway professional skaters in the Netherlands from the KNSB. Boxing is also governed by two federations.

[7]   For example, the G14 grouping of leading football clubs in Europe.

The European Pyramid

An idea has emerged that the European regulatory model and the market for sport is distinct from the American Model of Sport. In Europe this is a conceptual construct, invoking parallels with the concepts of a 'European Social Model' and a 'European Social Space' which have been used to create ideas of a European polity.

A distinctive feature of the European Model of Sport is the way in which sport is organized into a pyramid structure. The base of the pyramid is composed of the amateurs, local clubs and sports men and women. National federations organize sports competitions and select national teams. There is strong interdependence between amateur and professional sport in Europe. These federations in turn are members of European and international federations. Although the concept of a pyramid brings with it ideas of hierarchy, the European Model is informed by the idea of participation and representation at each layer of authority in the hierarchy.

The idea of a pyramid reveals immediately one of the weaknesses of the European Model from a regulatory stance: the use of one federation for each sport creates a monopoly and a dominant position for the regulatory body governing each sport. This raises questions of the application of competition law, the Internal Market rules and social/employment law. Issues arise about alternative dispute resolution (or, rather, the lack of it): how far European labour laws, for example, on equal pay and fixed-term contracts should apply to the employment relationship. Often an athlete, manager, agent or official of the game such as a referee must use internal grievance mechanisms and be subject to the disciplinary rules of a federation, creating a monopolist position for the regulatory body. Moreover, there is a general and widespread belief that sports issues should be heard by specialists with a knowledge and understanding of the sporting community and not tried by the courts. Recently, conflicts of interest have emerged where the regulatory body becomes involved in the commercial exploitation of sport. The use of one federation for each sport in each Member State of the EU organizes sport along national lines, dividing and fragmenting the Internal Market and creating barriers and obstacles to free movement.

In contrast, the American model of sport is organized around an overtly commercial basis with clear recognition of the commercial entertainment value of sport. As Richard Disney shows in Chapter 7, the differences between the European and American models account for the differences in the labour *markets* and the regulatory *structures* for sport and for sports professionals in the US and Europe.

The differences have consequences for the application of EU law to sport, especially the rules of competition. In the US, a clear and strict division is maintained between amateur[8] and professional[9] sporting activity. In the professional arena closed competition structures are accepted, based upon economic, rather than sport-based, entry barriers. Intervention is allowed to ensure that there is a competitive balance between clubs and there is a clear emphasis upon profit-maximization. In contrast to Europe, there is little individual mobility for participants in the league and few conflicts of interest between team participation and national participation. This in turn has led to a greater sense of solidarity between members of a particular league, allowing self-regulation to flourish.

In the EU market, such horizontal interdependence and collusion would be seen to be contrary to Article 81 EC and possibly infringe Article 82 EC, where it can be shown that the conditions for collective dominance exist.[10] The Court of First Instance in *Piau*[11] accepted that collective dominance may be found in the regulatory organization of sport and the regulatory structure of the FIFA football players' international release scheme is currently under judicial scrutiny as to its compatibility with EU law.[12]

---

[8] Amateur sports are mainly university sports governed by NCAA52. The term 'amateur' is used in a different sense from its meaning in Europe since American universities provide financial incentives (sport scholarships) and have big budgets to cover sporting activities. Success on the playing field can enhance a particular university's 'academic' reputation and encourage investment and contributions from alumni. In contrast to the European pyramid structure, the American model does not regulate amateur sport.

[9] Professional sport is organized around four major sport leagues: MLB, NFL, NBA, NFL. As Manchester United fans have discovered, membership of a league is regarded as a franchise which is owned by commercial actors (individuals or commercial undertakings) and run as a commercial activity with the aim of maximizing profit. The controlling body of each league not only organizes the competitive element but also engages in marketing the league with a view to maximizing profit.

[10] The conditions are set out in the merger ruling: Case T-342/99 *Airtours* v *Commission* [2002] ECR II-2585.

[11] Case T-193/02 *Laurent Piau* v *Commission*: Case C-171/05 P *Laurent Piau* v *Commission*, Order of the President 23 February 2006.

[12] Case C-243/06 SA *Sporting du Pays de Charleroi and Groupement des Clubs de football européens, pending*. This dispute is supported by the G14 football group which has demanded compensation payments for players called up to play at the international level. The call up is mandatory; clubs do not receive compensation for loss of their players fulfilling international obligations. Charleroi are arguing that one of their key players, Abdelmajid Oulmers, was injured for eight months after playing for Morocco; Charleroi finished fifth in the Belgian league and claim the loss of Oulmers was a contributing factor. The G14 are also backing a French club, Olympique Lyon, in a similar action regarding defender Eric Abidal, who broke his foot during a France friendly match. One argument is that FIFA commits an abuse of a dominant position under Article 82 EC. The outcome of the case will explore a number of economic and governance issues. See S. Weatherill, 'Is the pyramid compatible with EC law?' (2005), **3**(4), *The International Sports Law Journal*, 3.

US antitrust law is tolerant of the pro-competitive nature of the US model of sport organization. Regulators have acknowledged the special economic nature of sport and will allow exemptions from the application of antitrust law to certain sporting activities. In contrast to the regulatory issues which pose problems for Europe, a number of restrictive practices are *encouraged* to ensure the competitive and commercial nature of league sports. Amongst these, a restrictive transfer clause, roster limits, salary caps, revenue sharing, collective bargaining, payroll taxes and even a draft system (allocating new talent to poorly performing teams) are used to counter natural market power.

The apparent, self-regulatory, success of the US Model could be used as support for a 'sport exemption' in the EC Treaty. Under EU law, the exemption could be used where sporting bodies can show that the alleged anti-competitive sport regulation or practice benefits competition: to redistribute, or rebalance, the benefits to encourage competition. This draws parallels with the concept of solidarity developed by the European Court of Justice (ECJ) to exclude, or exempt, social functions of the State which may have been delegated, such as healthcare or pensions from the full thrust of the competition and Internal Market rules.[13] Solidarity is a flexible legal tool since the European Courts have deployed a variety of indicators which can be used to show that solidarity is present, and as a concept solidarity can exist in varying degrees. In relation to the multifaceted nature of sport, solidarity appears to be a useful conceptual idea which could be transplanted.

However, a tenable reason for arguing that sport should be given special treatment in competition law must be put forward. It could be argued that sport performs a wide range of functions, involving educational, public health, social, cultural and recreational functions. On the other hand, sport does not occupy the same kind of public policy role that, say, the protection of the environment, a consumer policy, creating employment and combating unemployment enjoy in the acceptable derogations from the Internal Market and competition policy. The difference with sport is that it is still not an area where the EU has competence, or a policy, and this weakens the case for saying that sport is a legitimate derogation from the fundamental economic constitutional clauses of the EC Treaty.

The argument which could be made is that *some* forms of sport regulation have an inherent form of vertical solidarity. This is seen in the inter-dependence between the various levels of sporting federations in Europe and what is described as 'the double pyramid' theory:

---

[13]   See, for example, Case 238/82 *Duphar* [1984] ECR 523; Cases 159/91 and C-160/91 *Poucet and Pistre* [1993] ECR I-637; Case C-7/95 *Sodemare* [1997] ECR I-3395; Case C-67/96 *Albany* [1999] ECR 984; Joined Cases C-180/98 *Pavlov* [2000] ECR I-6451.

The relationship between elite sports and the grassroots level is described in the 'double pyramid theory'. According to this theory thousands of amateur athletes generate a few Olympic champions (feeding), while these champions inspire thousands to participate in amateur sports (inspiring).[14]

Transient Value of Sport

Sport as an economic activity often has a transient value. This fact interacts with other changes in technological development as well as societal and cultural mores. The transient nature of economic activity related to sport applies to the organization of sport, at the individual/club/national level. For example, the active professional life of many sportsmen and women is often short, and can be cut short by injury or a run of bad luck resulting in poor performance or underperformance. Similar factors may also apply to sports managers or trainers. During this sport-active period a professional sportsperson must not only maximize his/her earnings, but also keep the image clean, since many sports people derive their earnings from ancillary economic activities, creating new forms of property rights. Non-active sports stars may go on to have a second career related to sporting activity: for example, coaching, leisure centres, managing clubs, or individuals, journalism/broadcasting, advertising and also political activity,[15] and as ambassadors for sport. Allegations of doping, game/race fixing must be dealt with swiftly and decisively, removing any taint of illegal behaviour. Otherwise, in contrast to supermodels, the current and future earnings potential of a sports star will be tarnished.

Sport-related economic activity, such as the broadcasting of major sporting events, must occur 'as it happens': 'live' sport is the mantra of sports media exploitation. Similar ideas permeate the *selling* and *advertising* of sports wear, especially replica football kits. In relation to the exploitation of media rights in sport, competition law has intervened, treating some aspects of sport media exploitation as special.[16] For example, the fragmentation of commercial rights to avoid the foreclosure of markets which the monopsony–monopoly sports market creates is seen in the UEFA Decision of the Commission on the joint selling arrangement for the sale of commercial rights of the UEFA Champions League.[17] The Commission found that a joint selling arrangement restricted

---

[14]   *The EU & Sport Matching Expectations*, Consultation Conference with the European Sport Movement on the Social Function of Sport, Volunteering in Sport and the Fight Against Doping, Brussels, 14/15 June 2005, 27.

[15]   For example, Lord Sebastian Coe would not have such a high political and popular profile if he had not created a 'clean' image on the track.

[16]   See D. Geradin, 'Access to content by new media platforms: a review of the EC Competition Law problems' (2005) **30**(1), *ELRev* 68.

[17]   OJ 2003 L 291/25.

competition between the football clubs because it coordinated pricing policy (and all other trading conditions) on behalf of individual clubs. The agreement could be granted an individual exemption, however, because it provided the consumer with the benefit of media products focused upon the Champions League through a single point of sale. The broadcasting of the football matches could not be produced or distributed efficiently by individual clubs selling the rights to each match. The initial agreement posed particular problems in that it could lead to foreclosure of markets because of the bundling arrangements of free-TV and pay-to-view TV to a single broadcaster in each territory over a period of years. Thus a number of adjustments were made in order to receive the exemption and these are the blueprint for subsequent Notices by the Commission under Article 19(3) of Regulation 17/63[18] and later under Article 27(4) of Regulation 1/2003.[19]

THE ROLE OF SPORT IN THE EUROPEAN POLITY

Sport was not included within the competence of the EEC. In the 1950s, sport was viewed as an amateur activity and not practised as a *significant* economic activity. Sport as a regulatory issue has been brought to the attention of the EU as a result of individual litigation, a proactive response from the Commission and the lobbying of political actors using primarily the vehicle of the European Parliament. This activity has been both negative and positive in character, creating new opportunities, as well as new constraints, for sport to find a role in the European regulatory and political system. The utility of using the EU law is found in the simple fact that EU law takes supremacy over conflicting national law and the regulatory rules of organizations. EU law has the power to create individual rights and impose duties upon individuals as well as autonomous sporting associations. The transnational nature of the EU allows new political actors and processes to emerge, occupying new political sites.

Sport is special because, it is argued, at a professional level, sportsmen and women are subject to much tighter regulation than ordinary professionals and the regulatory structures and procedures governing their professional practice often do not have the equivalent procedural and legal safeguards accorded to other, comparable professions. In recent years we have seen the increased use of the latent regulatory space offered by EU law to tackle regulatory activity using the free movement and competition rules. This in turn has provoked a reaction from the professional bodies that see their autonomy chipped away by this opportunistic litigation. As a result, through lobbying, sport is often

---

[18]   FA Premier League, OJ C 2004 115/3.
[19]   German Bundesliga, OJ C 2004 229/13.

portrayed as occupying a special space in the EU regulatory process. Sport appears to operate as a regulatory sub-system created by what are portrayed as polarized views: firstly, those who want sport to be regulated in the same way any other economic activity is regulated in the EU; secondly, a school of thought which sees sport as special, wanting to protect its unique qualities by keeping it out of the EU regulatory grasp, or, in the alternative, by applying a special pleading to sport.

The EU has struggled to find the appropriate role for sport in the integration process. As we shall explore, the two arguments are not too polarized and can be seen to occupy a common space within the EU regulatory map. This is achieved by analysing the creation of a role for sport through soft governance processes in the emerging European polity and, secondly, by analysing the creation of a European Model of Sport through litigation processes.

THE REGULATORY MODEL DERIVED FROM SOFT FORMS OF GOVERNANCE

Lobbyists and the institutions of the EU have been resourceful in drawing upon EC Treaty provisions which may be of relevance to sport issues. Article 149 EC, which addresses 'Education, Vocational Training and Youth', was used as the legal base to designate 2004 as the 'European Year of Education through Sport'. Article 151 EC, addressing Public Health, was used as the EU legal base for policy on anti-doping.[20] Through soft law processes the Commission and the European Parliament have created the notion of a European Model of Sport which does not operate under the same conditions as other industries and calls for recognizing the specificity of sport. This led to recognition of EU competence for sport as a 'supporting measure' in Article III-282 of the Constitutional Treaty.

Soft Approaches

Since the 1980s the EU has struggled to find its own identity and the Fontainebleau Summit of 1984 created the Adonnino Committee whose remit was to propose measures which were designed to strengthen the image of the EU.[21] One of the ideas which emerged was to create EU policies on youth

---

[20] Discussed in Case T-313/02, *David Meca-Medina and Igor Majcen* v *Commission* [2004] ECR II-3291.

[21] Commission of the European Communities, *A People's Europe, Reports from the ad hoc committee*, COM (84) 446 final, para. 5.9.

education, exchanges and sport and this led to a number of EU-led initiatives during the 1980s.

A review of the Adonnino initiatives in 1991 led to an expanded funding and communication role for the EU and in particular the creation of a European Sports Forum. More money was committed to initiatives creating European sporting initiatives and sport took on an expanded role to implement socio-cultural activity of the EU. This expanded role was cut short by the ruling in *UK* v *Commission*.[22] Sport, quite obviously, did not have a legal base in the EC Treaty and the Commission was not competent to commit expenditure in these fields. Thus the Commission was compelled to look for ways of integrating sport into other EU programmes: the integration of minorities and people with disabilities, introducing young people to ideas of active citizenship. Subsequent Conclusions of the Presidencies of the Council brought sport within a range of EU policies, increasingly linking sport with education, making use of the expanded competence of EU law in this field.

Bosman: No Going Forward

The *Bosman*[23] ruling is a turning point in the EU policy towards sport.[24] The weakness inherent in the *Bosman* ruling is that it emphasized the incompatibility of the previous football transfer regime with the fundamental economic provisions of the EC Treaty but provided no guidance on how to resolve the issues. Several European Parliament Reports addressed how sport could play a role in the European integration,[25] but the Commission was the main driver

---

[22]   Case C-106/96 [1996] ECR I-2729.
[23]   Case C-415/93 [1995] ECR I-4921.
[24]   For a discussion of the pre-*Bosman* politics of EU (non)-intervention see D.G. Dimitrakopoulos, 'More Than A Market? The Regulation of Sport in the European Union' (2006), **41**(4), *Government and Opposition*. One explanation for the EC Commission being reluctant to bring EU regulation into the football arena before *Bosman* is given by Dimitrakopoulos, who argues that 'Delors, a keen football fan with links to a number of top club and league officials believed that the EC had no powers to deal with this issue'. See also L. Barani, 'The role of the European Court of Justice as a political actor in the integration process: the case of sport regulation after the *Bosman* ruling' (2005), **1**(1), *JCER*, 42; R. Parrish, 'Football's place in the Single European Market' (2002), **3**(1), *Soccer and Society*, 1.
[25]   A3-0326/94 Part A (27/4/94) Part B (29/4/94), *Report on the European Community and Sport*, Rapporteur: J. Larive (The Larive Report 1994); A4-0197/97, *Report on the European Union in the Field of Sport*, Rapporteur: D. Pack (The Pack Report 1997); A5-0208/2000 *Report on the Commission Report to the European Council with a view to safeguarding current sports structures and maintaining the social function of sport within the Community framework – the Helsinki Report*, Rapporteur: P. Mennea (The Mennea Report 2000).

in addressing sport from a regulatory perspective, using its competence and powers in the field of competition policy.

After *Bosman* the Competition Commission Directorate received a complaint from a Belgian trade union (SETC) arguing that the FIFA regulations were in breach of the free movement of workers provisions (now Article 39 EC) and the competition rules contained in what is now Article 81 EC. This again focused EU law attention upon the FIFA transfer regulations and the Commission issued a statement of objections in 1998. The issue concerned the 'gentleman's agreement' not to poach players under contract without some form of remuneration. It was not until 2001 that FIFA and the EC Commission were able to agree on a new set of transfer regulations. This agreement was a special case and would presumably fall under the 'file closed' category of EC Commission competition law practice. It has not been approved by a formal Decision. Mario Monti is on public record as stating that this was 'the end of the Commission's involvement in disputes between players, clubs and football organizations'.[26]

FIFA has introduced new rules to encourage the development of young talent though home-grown players in football, the *Oulmers* case is pending before the Court of Justice and there is litigation in the Danish High Court addressing the potential incompatibility of FIFA's new Transfer Regulations regarding training compensation. The latter case also reflects on the question of whether collective agreements prevail over FIFA and Football Associations' rules. This may result in a reference to the Court.[27] It is unlikely that litigation will disappear.

From the political perspective, sport became 'special', created from a socially constructed, as well as institutionalized, idea. This not only legitimized the special pleading for sport in EC regulatory intervention but also constrained the way sport-related actors could act. Like the European Social Model, the European Sport Model became an *idea* generated by various stakeholders but not necessarily enjoying approval from the main EU institutional decision-making structures.

The Treaty of Amsterdam 1997 included a weak, non-binding Declaration on Sport, Declaration No 29:

> The conference emphasizes the social significance of sport, in particular its role in forging identity and bringing people together. The conference therefore calls on the bodies of the European Union to listen to sports associations when important questions affecting sport are at issue. In this connection, special consideration should be given to the particular characteristics of amateur sport.

---

[26] Cited by S. Weatherill, 'Fair play please!: recent developments in the application of EC law to sport' (2003), **40**, *CMLRev.*, 51 at 72.

[27] My thanks to Flemming Martinussen, for providing this information.

Further impetus for EU recognition of the special status of sport came in the Presidency Conclusions of the December 1998 Vienna European Council.

The Commission's Working Paper[28] identified sport as performing an educational, public health, social, cultural and recreational function. It recognized that sport could be used as a vehicle through which policy objectives in these fields could be pursued. The Commission followed up the Working Paper with a Consultation Document, *The European Model of Sport* and *The Helsinki Report.*[29] The European Council responded to *The Helsinki Report* in the Presidency Conclusions of Santa Maria da Feira, in June 2000, in which 'the European Council requests the Commission and the Council to take account of the specific characteristics of sport in Europe and its social function in managing common policies'.

The Treaty of Nice 2000 did not address the issue of sport as a new competence for the EU. Instead, the Nice Presidency Conclusions adopted a *Declaration on the Specific Characteristics of Sport and Its Social Function in Europe, of which account should be taken in Implementing Common Policies.* This Declaration emphasizes that the Community, acting under various Treaty provisions, 'should take account of the social, educational, and cultural functions inherent in sport and making it special, in order that the code of ethics and the solidarity essential to the preservation of the social role may be respected and nurtured'. This in turn paved the way for the inclusion of Article III-282 in the Constitutional Treaty.

With the deadlock over the ratification of the Constitutional Treaty the Commission has indicated that it will continue with its approach to mainstream sport through other EU policies. At a conference in November 2005, Pedro Velazquez, Deputy Head of the Sports Unit, DG for Education and Culture argued that a European sports policy would be continued by intensifying collaboration with Member States and the building of networks, strengthening dialogue with stakeholders and increasingly mainstreaming sport into other EU programmes. However, the use of a mainstreaming concept is a different one from the *legal* duty to mainstream equality/non-discrimination and environmental issues found in the EC Treaty.

A White Paper on Sport is anticipated in 2007. It is expected to address a number of governance issues in sport, alongside the growing litigation in this area.

---

[28]   Commission of the European Communities, *Developments and Prospects for the Community Activity in the Field of Sport*, Commission Staff Working Paper, DG X, 1998.

[29]   COM (1999) 644 final of 10 December 1999.

THE EU REGULATORY MODEL DERIVED FROM LITIGATION

The lack of a legal base to create a sport policy at the EU level has led to the regulation of sport through processes of negative integration as a result of litigation. A determining question as to whether sport can be caught by EU law is the issue of whether it involves economic activity which is defined by Articles 2 EC and 3 EC and the European Courts' case law.

Different jurisprudence and rules have evolved in sports-related cases as a result of whether the Commission and the Courts decide to use the Internal Market, or the competition rules, to determine an issue. Many cases which start at the national level and use Article 234 EC to get the issue into the European judicial arena raise the Internal Market and competition rules concurrently. The European Court of Justice appears to choose between the legal bases which may apply, rather than apply the two areas concurrently. While academics[30] write about the increased convergence, complementarity and interrelationship of the Internal Market and competition rules, the Court appears to continue to keep the rules apart,[31] with Advocate General Poiares Maduro in *FENIN* arguing that different rules and criteria can apply for the different heads of EU competence/jurisdiction.[32] Recently, competition issues relating to sport have received greater prominence as a result of the Court of First Instance (CFI) receiving appeals from two EC Commission Decisions. The Commission and the Court have identified rules and practices in sport which are viewed as non-economic and therefore remain outside the scope of EU regulation. The Commission is able to create a normative dimension to the regulation of sport by formal investigations and prosecutions as well as using less formal and coercive strategies such as the use of soft Communications and Notices. In contrast the European Courts are less in control of their agenda. They must address issues which arrive in Luxembourg on an ad hoc basis, usually raising legal issues within a specific national context. As a result the case law is casuistic.

---

[30]   K. Mortelmans, 'Towards convergence in the application of the rules on free movement and on competition?' (2001), *CMLRev;* E. Szyszczak, 'State intervention and the internal market', in T. Tridimas and P. Nebbia (eds), *European Union Law for the Twenty-first Century*, vol. 2 (Oxford: Hart, 2004).

[31]   In contrast to the much fuller analysis by the Advocates General of the questions raised by national courts, see Advocate General Lenz, in *Bosman*, Advocate General Cosmas, in *Deliège*, Advocate General Alber, in *Lehtonen*. See now Case C-519/04P *Meca-Medina and Majcen*, judgment of 18 July 2006.

[32]   Case C-205/03 P *FENIN* Opinion of 10 November 2005, [2006] ECR I-6295.

In order to understand, and tease out the problems with the Courts' analysis of sport the case law can be analysed under three distinct categories based upon the outcomes of the Court's reasoning: firstly, sports issues which are *non-economic* in character and are not affected by EU law; secondly, sports issues which are caught by the EC Treaty because they are *economic* in nature but deserve special treatment through exemptions or justifications; thirdly, sports issues where the practice/regulation is incompatible with EU law.

Sport Activity which is Outside the EU Regulatory Grasp

In his Opinion of 10 October 2005, Advocate General Poiares Maduro in *FENIN* provides a useful summary of the European Courts' case law in deciding whether or not an activity is caught by the EC competition rules:

> In order for an entity to be subject to Community competition law, it must be classified as an undertaking. Although the EC Treaty makes frequent reference to the concept, it does not define it and it has instead been clarified in case law, which gives it a functional content. It has been established that an entity engaged in an economic activity is an undertaking for the purposes of Articles 81 EC to 86 EC, irrespective of its legal status and the way in which it is financed. While it is accepted that certain tasks in the public interest such as the maintenance and improvement of air navigation safety and the protection of the environment are not economic in nature, it is less easy, where activities are linked to the operation of the national social security system, to determine when they may be classified as noneconomic, since the case law in this field undertakes a case-by-case analysis, and asks whether the principle of solidarity requires that the application of the Community competition rules be excluded. *It is difficult to specify the circumstances in which that principle will result in an activity being classified as non-economic in nature.*[33]

The sensible methodology for determining the issue of whether there is EU competence to determine a sports-related issue is to address a number of questions which are a series of hoops for the facts of the case to jump through.

The first issue is to examine whether the activity is *economic*. Then, if the answer is in the affirmative, look to see if the activity infringes EU law. The final issue is to ask, could the activity be justified? Sometimes the Court rolls up this analysis into a one-stage test, looking to see if the justification can exempt the application of the Internal Market rules, using a balancing process and deploying proportionality. The three-step approach is one of the clearest methodologies in the context of creating a clear line between activity which is caught by the EC Treaty, and activity which is not. Yet, if we examine the Court's case law, we see that the Court rarely follows up this methodology in a rigorous way.

---

33   Ibid., n. 32, para. 1. My emphasis, footnotes omitted.

Walrave involved nationality restrictions on the composition of national teams: a pace maker and a stayer in cycling had to be of the same nationality according to the rules of the AUCI.[34] In *Walrave* the Court stated: 'the practice of sport is subject to Community law only in so far as it constitutes an economic activity within Article 2 of the Treaty'.[35] In the context of the free movement of workers and services provisions the Court went on to say that economic activity has 'the character of gainful employment or remunerated service'. Further, in paragraphs 7 and 8, the Court refines the rule in relation to economic activity and in situations where the non-discrimination on grounds of nationality rule does not apply:

7. In this respect the exact nature of the legal relationship under which such services are performed is of no importance since the rule of non-discrimination covers identical terms in work or services.
8. This prohibition however does not affect the composition of sport teams, in particular national teams, the formation of which is a question of purely sporting interest and has nothing to do with economic activity.

Subsequent cases, *Bosman*,[36] *Lehtonen*,[37] *Deliège*,[38] found the sport activity to be economic in nature and caught, to some degree, by EU law, but the sense of a clear methodology to determine *why* this is the case appears to be lost. The lack of a rigorous approach is seen in *Donà*.[39] The issue concerned a dispute over the non-payment of fees to a football scout. The Chairman of the Italian football club, Rivigo, refused to pay for an advertisement placed by Donà in a Belgian newspaper advertising that he was recruiting players. Under the rules of the Italian Football Federation only Italian nationals could be affiliated to the Federation and affiliation was a precondition of eligibility to play in the Italian League. This kind of rule is a form of *direct* nationality discrimination, covered by what is now Article 12 EC. The Court ruled that Article 12 EC applied to sport rules, 'unless such rules or practice exclude foreign players for reasons which are not of an economic nature'.[40] The Court did not examine first whether the activity was economic in nature but jumped at the idea, through a negative reasoning: that certain kinds of rules may be used to justify the application of the EU-non-discrimination principle. Furthermore, the Court did not engage in an analysis of the *justifications* for the Italian rules. This balancing of what might be termed an exception to EU law is seen in other cases, especially in the application of Article 86 EC.

---

34 Case 36/74 *Walrave* v *AUCI* [1974] ECR 1405.
35 Para. 4.
36 Case C-415/93 [1995] ECR I-4921.
37 Case C-176/96 [2000] ECR I-2681.
38 Case C-191/97 [2000] ECR I-2549.
39 Case 13/76 *Gaetano Donà* v *Mario Mantero* [1976] ECR 1333.
40 Para. 19.

In *Bosman*[41] the Court does not follow the *Walrave* approach but instead the Court jumps two steps, to begin the analysis of whether sport is caught by EU law by determining whether the nationality clauses gave rise to an obstacle to one of the fundamental, economic, Internal Market freedoms and if the obstacle could be justified. The Court uses the language of 'non-economic grounds' to apply a justification for a rule/practice which *prima facie* infringes EU law. Non-economic grounds are also linked directly to sport:

> It must be recalled that in paragraphs 14 and 15 of its judgment in *Donà*, cited above, the Court held that the Treaty provisions concerning freedom of movement for persons do not prevent the adoption of rules or practices excluding foreign players from certain matches for reasons which are not of an economic nature, which relate to the particular nature and context of such matches and are thus of sporting interest only, such as, for example, matches between national teams from different countries. It stressed, however, that that restriction on the scope of the provisions in question must remain limited to its proper objective.
> Here, the nationality clauses do not concern specific matches between teams representing their countries but apply to all official matches between clubs and thus to the essence of the activity of professional players.[42]

In this case the Court found that the non-economic grounds were not 'limited to [their] proper objective' and therefore they were considered as not satisfying the principle of proportionality.[43]

Deliège addressed the extension of *Bosman*, in scope and in substance, to the rules of the Belgian judo federation relating to selection criteria of judokas to participate in international tournaments in the semi-professional sport of judo.[44] The case concerned the participation of a judoka in an international competition where the judoka would not be paid. The Court referred to the ruling in *Bond*,[45] which held that activities may be caught by the free movement of services provision even where the services 'are not paid for by those for whom they are performed'. This opens the issue of how far advertising and sponsorship of amateur and international competitions in sport may draw sport into the net of EU competence. A parallel might be drawn with the education case of *Wirth*[46] and later cases discussing the issue of not-for-profit activity in relation to healthcare issues.[47]

---

41   *Supra*, n. 36.
42   Paras 127–8.
43   See S. Weatherill, 'Fair play please!: recent developments in the application of EC law to sport' (2003), **40**, *Common Market Law Review*, 51, 56.
44   Case C-191/97 *Deliège* [2000] ECR I-2549.
45   Case 352/85 *Bond van Adverteerders e.a.* v *Netherlands* [1988] ECR 2085.
46   Case C-109/92 [1993] ECR I-6447.
47   See the discussion of V. Hatzopoulos, 'Health law and policy: the impact of the EU', in G. de Búrca (ed.), *EU Law and the Welfare State* (Oxford: OUP, 2005).

The ECJ left the question of whether participation in an international competition was an economic activity within the meaning of Article 2 EC, but, consistent with its case law in the Internal Market and competition field, ruled that the classification by an association of its members as 'amateurs' did not affect the application of the Internal Market rules. The Court ruled that Article 49 EC might apply to the situation but also looked to a justification for the rules: selection rules were necessary and an inherent aspect of participation in high-level international tournaments.[48]

The *Walrave* and *Bosman* rulings examined only the Internal Market rules. In *Meca-Medina*, the Court was asked to address the issue of whether the same principles should also apply in relation to the competition rules of the EC Treaty. The case, which has attracted a lot of media attention through the protests used by Meca-Medina, concerned sanctions imposed for doping offences in sport.[49] Two long-distance swimmers tested positive for nandrolene and were suspended for four years by Fédération Internationale de Natation (FINA) (reduced to two years on appeal to the Court of Arbitration for Sport) for breach of the anti-doping regulations set by the IOC.

The swimmers brought a complaint to the EC Commission alleging the International Olympic Committee (IOC) was in breach of Articles 81, 82, and 49 EC. The swimmers alleged firstly, that the anti-doping rules were anti-competitive within the meaning of Article 81 EC; secondly, the setting of a limit for the amount of permissible nandrolene was a concerted practice between FINA, the IOC and the accredited network of testing laboratories; thirdly, the dispute settlement system established by the IOC was anticompetitive.

The Commission rejected the complaint.[50] The Decision is of interest since the Commission states that the IOC may be classified as an undertaking, and an association of undertakings, within the scope of Article 81 EC. But the Decision is not fully reasoned. The Commission decided that the rules and alleged concerted practices which were complained about did not fall within the scope of the 'economic' activities of CIO and FINA. The Commission departed from its case law on sport and the Internal Market and instead relied upon the *Wouters*[51] case, accepting that, while the anti-doping rules may limit a swimmer's freedom of action, the rules are 'intimately linked to the proper conduct of sporting competition'. In the Report for the hearing before the Court of First Instance (CFI) the Commission admits that the reference to the *Wouters* case is for the sake of completeness, the Decision being based upon

---

[48] Para. 64.
[49] Case T-313/02, *Meca-Medina and Macjen* v *Commission*, judgment of 30 September 2004; on appeal, Case C-519/04 P [2006] ECR I-6991.
[50] COMP/38.158.
[51] Case C-309/99 [2002] ECR I-1577.

Walrave, Donà and *Deliège*. Rather oddly, the Commission does not refer to its own soft law, *The Helsinki Report*,[52] where this idea, derived from the ruling in *Walrave*, is set out.

On appeal to the CFI, the Court begins by discussing the *Walrave* ruling and states that Articles 39 and 49 EC may apply when the activity in question 'takes the form of paid employment of a provision of remunerated service'. The Court refers to the Court's case law where sporting activity has been found to be *economic* in nature but then states that the EC Treaty does not affect 'purely sporting rules', referring to *Walrave, Donà* and *Deliège* as examples and adding 'rules of the game', for example rules which affect the length of matches. The CFI then states that the principles which have been developed from the Internal Market case law are 'equally valid' when applied to Articles 81 and 82 EC.

The CFI examines the nature of the anti-doping rules but, unlike the EC Commission, does not begin by asking if the regulatory bodies, FINA or the IOC, are an undertaking within the meaning of the competition rules, in line with the case law set out by AG Poiares Maduro in *FENIN*.[53] The CFI departs from the traditional discussion of whether the activity is an economic activity and focuses immediately upon the question as to whether the anti-doping rules adopted by the IOC are based upon 'purely sporting considerations' and have nothing to do with economic considerations. The CFI refers to *The Helsinki Report* and the EU's policy on anti-doping in sport to endorse its position.

Under the previous approach, this was the ground for a *justification* of the measure, not the initial question of whether the rules were caught by the EC Treaty. The CFI also introduces the concept of discrimination, finding that the anti-doping rules are not selective.[54]

The discussion of the application of *Wouters* to sport regulation stresses the differences between the *Meca-Medina* situation and the professional services' regulation but the CFI does not find grounds to annul the Decision. Similarly, the CFI cannot find grounds to annul the reasoning based upon the application of Article 49 EC.

Weatherill[55] is critical of the CFI's reluctance to apply the competition rules to this sporting situation, hoping that the ECJ will set aside 'the CFI's disdain for orthodox competition law analysis as a means to deal will sporting practices . . .'. The essence of his argument is not that anti-doping rules

---

[52]   COM (1999) 644 final of 10 December 1999.

[53]   *Supra*, n. 32.

[54]   Cf. *Donà, supra*, n. 39, where the non-discrimination principle was held to apply, the rules were clearly directly discriminatory on the grounds of nationality, and selective, but capable of justification because of their sport-related nature.

[55]   'Antidoping rules and EC law' (2005), **26**(7), *ECLR*, 416.

are 'non-economic' but rather that 'they are part of the very core of the nature and purpose of the activity in question. Protecting that core is a task validly performed by sports federations'.

Wouters provides sports bodies with a wide latitude. The exact scope and the content of the ruling is open to interpretation. The Court appears to base its test on the *reasonableness* of the multidisciplinary practice ban imposed by the Bar Regulation.[56] This is not based upon any absolute, or objective assessment of what might be seen as necessary to ensure the proper practice of the legal profession but instead relies upon the test of what the professional body itself could believe to be a reasonable rule. On appeal the Court of Justice repeats its established case law from *Walrave*. Where sporting rules are of purely sporting interest, and as such have nothing to do with economic activity, they are not caught by the EC Treaty.

In the light of the increased commercial interest in sport it is difficult to think of rules which fall into this category, outside of the limitations imposed upon the membership of national teams in international competition and established rules of the game, for example the off-side rule in football. Other examples which are put forward, for example the length of matches, 'comfort' breaks, criteria for equipment (the size and shape of balls, tennis racquets and so on), the size of pitches, height of goalposts and the rest, and even accredited tests and laboratories for doping tests can have an economic connection; for example, approved sports equipment may favour one supplier over another, and the venue, length and timing of sporting events may be organized around broadcasting coverage, obtaining maximum audiences at live events, sponsorship and advertising.

In relation to the difficult task of severing the economic aspects from the purely sporting aspects of a sport, the Court refers to its ruling in *Donà*[57] and states that rules are justified on non-economic grounds where they relate to the particular nature and context of certain sporting events, but these rules must be limited to their proper objective and cannot be relied upon to exclude the whole of a sporting activity from the scope of the EC Treaty. The Court ignores the Opinion of Advocate General Léger who advised that the appeal should be dismissed because, although the commercial context of sport creates an economic interest in anti-doping rules in sport, this is a purely secondary interest and cannot deprive the rules of their 'purely sporting' character.[58] In rejecting this approach, the Court is able to address the issue of the application of Community law to sport in a functional economic context.

---

[56] Para. 110.
[57] *Supra*, n. 39.
[58] Para. 28 of the Opinion, 23 March 2006.

The Court rules that the competition rules and the Internal Market rules must be examined separately. The fact that the Internal Market rules are not infringed does not preclude the application of competition rules. The CFI was found to have made an error of law in finding that purely sporting rules which are linked to economic activity and therefore do not fall within the scope of Articles 39 and 49 EC are also excluded from the scope of the competition rules. The Court does not expand upon this interpretation of the relationship between the fundamental economic rules of the EC Treaty. Litigators have raised the possibility of concurrent infringements of the free movement *and* the competition rules with the Court usually showing a preference to decide cases under only one of the claims.[59] This may be because, until recently, the free movement provisions provided a wider set of derogations and justifications for the Member States than the competition law provisions, read literally, are capable of providing. The emergence of a wider set of justifications as to why the full force of the competition provisions should not be applied to the State and regulatory bodies has been influenced by the developments under the free movement provisions, leading to tendencies towards, if not the *convergence* of, the rules,[60] at least an understanding of the *complementarity*[61] of the two sets of fundamental EC Treaty provisions. There are strong arguments for suggesting that, in relation to the justification for sporting rules, there should be a complementarity between the two sets of provisions; that is, justifications which are acceptable under the free movement provisions should not be trumped by a finding of incompatibility with the competition law provisions, and vice versa.[62]

The ECJ concludes that the CFI made an error of law by finding that the rules were purely sporting rules and could be excluded from the application of Article 49 EC without determining first whether the rules fulfilled the specific requirements of Articles 81 and 82 EC. Thus the contested judgment was set aside.

The Court takes the unusual step of relying upon Article 61 of the Statute of the Court to give a judgment on the substance of the case, rather than referring the case back to the CFI. The Court most probably did this because of the

---

[59]   See E. Szyszczak, 'State intervention in the market', in T. Tridimas and P. Nebbia (eds), *Eurpoean Union Law for the Twenty-First Century: Rethinking the New Legal Order, volume 2* (Oxford: Hart, 2004).

[60]   See K. Mortelmans, 'Towards convergence in the application of the rules on free movement and on competition' (2001), **38**, *CMLRev.*, 613; R. O'Loughlin, 'EC competition rules and free movement rules: an examination of the parallels and their furtherance by the ECJ *Wouters* decision' (2003), **24**, *ECLR*, 62.

[61]   Szyszczak, *supra*, n.59.

[62]   See also S. Weatherill, 'Anti-doping revisited – the demise of the rule of "purely sporting interests"?' (2006), **27**(12), *ECLR*, 645.

growing importance of the issue and the fact that the role of competition law in relation to pure sporting rules has not been addressed squarely.

In examining the first plea the appellants had contended that the Commission was wrong not to treat the IOC as an undertaking for the purposes of Article 81 EC. The Court pointed out that this was an incorrect reading of the Decision and dismissed the plea. The second argument advanced by the appellants was that the Commission misapplied *Wouters* and had not looked at the proportionality of the doping rules. Here the Court held that it did not have enough detail to examine the merits of the claim.

The Court endorsed the application of Article 81 EC to the anti-doping rules, taken in the overall context of the support for an anti-doping policy in sport, the effects such a policy produced and, more specifically, its objectives. The Court, like the Commission, applied the *Wouters* case, looking to see if the consequential effects of the anti-doping rules were restrictive of competition. It then asked whether these effects were inherent in the pursuit of the sporting objectives pursued by the anti-doping rules and proportionate to them. The Court found that the anti-doping rules did not constitute a restriction of competition within the meaning of Article 81 EC since 'Such a limitation is inherent in the organization and proper conduct of competitive sport and its very purpose is to ensure healthy rivalry between athletes'.[63]

The appellants had not disputed this fact but had argued that the aims of the anti-doping rules went further, to protect IOC's own interests and thus were *excessive* rules taking them outside of the proper conduct of competitive sport and within the scope of Article 81 EC. The Court accepted that the proportionality restrictions must be limited to what is necessary to ensure the proper conduct of competitive sport since the penal nature of anti-doping rules, combined with the magnitude of the penalties, could result in adverse effects for competition. If the penalties were not justified an athlete's unwarranted exclusion from sporting events could impair the conditions under which the sporting activity takes place. Anti-doping, and similar sporting rules, could be excessive by virtue of, first, the conditions laid down for establishing the dividing line between circumstances which amount to doping in respect of which penalties may be imposed and those which do not and, secondly, the severity of the penalties.

The appellants had contended that the level set for the presence of nandrolene was excessively low but the Court held that they had not surmounted the higher hurdle of showing *how* or *why* the Commission had made a manifest error of assessment in finding the rule to be justified. The Court accepted that anabolic substances may improve an athlete's performance and therefore the

---

[63] Para. 45.

ban was justified in the light of anti-doping rules. While the Court would not be drawn into substituting its own views of what should be the acceptable level of illegal substances in an athlete's body, the Court examines the scientific evidence in some detail, accepting that there is a problem with anti-doping rules in that nandrolene may be produced endogenously. The appellants contended that, from 1993, the IOC should have been aware that nandrolene could be present in an athlete's body as a result of other factors. The Court held that the scientific studies had no bearing on the *Commission's* Decision. The appellants had not specified at what level the threshold in question should have been set at the time of the IOC decision. Furthermore, the appellants had not argued that the penalties imposed were excessive, or established that the anti-doping rules at issue were disproportionate.

On the appellant's last point of appeal, that the CFI had committed an error of law because it rejected the argument that the IOC rules infringed Article 49 EC, the Court pointed out that this was a mistaken application to the CFI since the appeal process related to the Commission's use of powers under competition procedures. Thus any judicial review application must be limited to the competition rules of Articles 81 and 82 EC and cannot be extended to other provisions of the EC Treaty.[64]

The Court, following the Opinion of AG Léger, accepts that 'each professional rule must be examined on a case by case basis, depending on its subject matter, context and purpose'.

The issue of how much autonomy sports federations should be allowed in order to create rules for a particular sport is most likely to be the centre of much of the future litigation and the Court's approach of taking each rule on a case-by-case basis offers up the opportunity of litigation in each context in which a sport-related regulatory rule is applied. Academic critiques of *Wouters* have argued that the case applies a rule of reason approach to Article 81(1) EC, while others see the case as an application of the ancillary restraints doctrine.[65] Whish[66] sees the case as a major departure from the Court's previous case law. Controversially, it opens up a wider range of exemptions, not inherent within Article 81(3) EC.[67]

---

[64]   A similar problem occurred in Case C-171/05 P *Piau*, Order of 23 February 2006, para. 58.

[65]   For discussion, see E. Loozen, 'Professional ethics and restraints of competition' (2006), **31**, *ELRev.*, 28.

[66]   R. Whish, *Competition Law* (London: Butterworths, 2004, 4th edn), pp. 120–23.

[67]   The ideas contained in *Wouters* can be traced back to the submissions of Germany in *Gebhard* (Case C-55/94 [1995] ECR I-4165). See also AG Cosmas in *Deliège, supra*, n.38 and AG Alber in *Lehtonen, supra*, n.37 in examining the nature of the sporting rules under Article 81 EC, relied on *Gottrup-Klim e.a. Grovvareforeninger*

It is in this respect that *Wouters* is important for the regulation of sports bodies, and other bodies which perform delegated public functions, for example the provision of social protection by non-State bodies. *Wouters* makes the link between a *generic public interest justification* which has developed for the State, and non-State bodies, developed in *Reisebüro Broede*,[68] under the free movement (Internal Market) rules and a generic public interest justification in relation to competition law.[69] In this respect it provides closure to the unanswered questions of *how* to apply the competition rules to non-state activity which is inherent within the rulings in *Bosman* and *Deliège*.

There is a jurisprudence from the European Court of Justice which distinguishes committees which act in the public interest and committees which act in members' interests.[70] This jurisprudence is problematic since the traditional doctrine of the ECJ is to look at the *effects* of economic behaviour, not the *form* of the body allegedly acting in a anti-competitive manner.[71] But Schepel points out that the test fashioned by the ECJ contributes towards the idea of a 'good governance' model for private regulation.[72]

The reason for self-regulation of the liberal professions is explained by a general trend towards de-centred governance using a variety of actors who are capable of drawing upon diverse resources to contribute to the governance of a particular regulatory space.[73] Within professional services the use of regulatory bodies satisfies the need to maintain an adequate level of professional ethics, specifically for each profession (a deontological purpose), and also as a consumer protection purpose: measures to protect consumers, who are usually less knowledgeable than the practioner, from abuses which may

---

v *Dans Landbrugs Grovvareselskab AmbA* (Case C-250/92 [1994] ECR I-5641), a rule of reason judgment that academics see as the predecessor of *Wouters*.

[68] Case C-3/95 [1996] ECR I-6511.

[69] Applied by the Commission in *ENIC* (COMP/37 806). Cf. the Opinion of AG Léger who argued that the introduction of a public interest justification would amount to a misconstruction of the *ratio legis* of the competition rules, 'liable to negate a great part of the effectiveness of [Articles 81(3) and 86(2)] of the Treaty' (para. 107).

[70] Case C-55/94 *BNIC* v *Clair* [1995] ECR I-4165; Case C-198/01 *CIF* [2003] ECR I-8055.

[71] Case C-41/9 *Höfner* v *Macrotron* [1991] ECR I-1979.

[72] H. Schepel, 'Delegation of regulatory powers to private parties under EC competition law: towards a procedural public interest test' (2002), **39**, *CMLRev.*, 31. See in the context of the free movement rules the creation of procedural good governance: E. Szyszczak, 'Golden shares and market governance' (2002), **29**, *LIEI*, 255.

[73] See, *inter alia*, J. Freeman, 'Private parties, public functions and the new administrative law' (2000), **52**, *Administrative Law Review*, 813; C. Scott, 'Analysing regulatory space: fragmented resources and institutional design' (2001), *Public Law*, 32; J. Black, 'Decentring regulations' (2001), *CLP*, 103; J. Black, 'Enrolling actors in regulatory systems: examples from the UK financial services regulation' (2003), *PL*, 63.

emerge when dealing with a highly specialized professional service provider and asymmetries of information are likely to occur. *Wouters* closes the gap between the legitimate defences which may be raised by the State to protect national interests and the acceptance that where States have delegated authority for self-regulation by the professions the members of regulatory bodies are in the best position to regulate a particular sector.

Wouters may be overtaken by the Commission's proposals for greater deregulation. In the most recent Commission Paper on the modernization of the regulation of the professions, the Commission emphasizes that the Member States must take the lead in reducing the anti-competitive effects of the regulation of a number of professional services, examining rules to see if they satisfy the principle of proportionality. The Commission does not rule out the use of Article 86 EC. The ECJ may accelerate this process as more cases are brought before it examining the validity of national regulatory rules in the light of the Internal Market and competition rules.[74] Note also that sport does not receive special status in the proposal for a Directive on Services in the Internal Market.[75]

Yet the *Declaration on Sport attached to the Treaty of Amsterdam* stresses the importance of the independence of sports organizations, underlining the importance of sports organizations' regulatory functions. The increasing interdependence between economic and non-economic activities will stretch the Courts' reasoning to achieve the right balance between market and non-market values.[76]

Other cases which have been found to fall outside of EU competence include rules preventing club relocation,[77] rules preventing multiple club ownership[78] and the use of state aid to sports club for educational purposes.[79]

---

[74]   Case C-35/99 *Criminal Proceedings Against Arduino* [2002] ECR I-1529; Case C-94/04 and 202/04 *Cipola*, Opinion of Advocate General Poiares Maduro of 1 February 2006.

[75]   Directive 2006/123/EC, OJ L376/26.

[76]   See Case C-90/76 *Van Ameyde* v *UCI* [1997] ECR 1091.

[77]   In *Excelsior Mouscron* a Belgian football club wanted to stage a home leg of a UEFA Cup tie at a larger stadium across the border in France. UEFA blocked the move, arguing that the home match must be played at the club's stadium and the rules were justified to protect the structure of UEFA competitions. The Commission rejected a complaint against the UEFA home and away rule, on the basis that this is a sporting rule that is a necessary part of the organization of sporting competitions and as such therefore falls outside the scope of competition law: IP/99065 9 December 1999.

[78]   The English National Investment Company controlled four football clubs (Glagow Rangers, Slavia Prague, Vicenza and AEK Athens). Its challenge to the UEFA rules which prevented two or more clubs directly or indirectly controlled by the same entity or managed by the same person from participating in UEFA club competitions. The Commission dismissed the complaint stating: 'The limitation of the freedom of

Within EC Competence but Capable of a Special Justification

The Court of Justice has used a number of techniques to regulate activity which may be caught by the EC rules but should be protected from the full thrust of the application of the rules.[80] If the sporting activity is economic in nature certain aspects of the regulatory environment may constitute a restriction on the free movement of persons, goods, establishment and capital or may infringe the competition provisions, contained in Articles 81–89 EC.

A weakness of the current EC Treaty is that the derogations, exemptions and justifications from the fundamental, constitutional economic freedoms are limited. The free movement provisions continue to focus upon the practices and regulations of the State which may impede free movement, despite the fact that a number of cases recognize that restrictions on free movement may be imposed by non-State actors,[81] for example, sports regulatory bodies. Thus the free movement rules must take on board a generic public interest defence. Maintenance of a competitive balance in sport, the preservation of the integrity of sport, encouraging the education and training of young players and protection of the national team are all seen as legitimate objectives. This is where the idea of sport being special, created through political processes, informs the legal process.

Piau raised the issue of the complementarity of the Internal Market and competition rules, this time in relation to rules regulating players' agents.[82] Piau brought a complaint to the Commission alleging that the FIFA rules on players' agents were contrary to Article 49 EC in that they prevented players and clubs from using agents not licensed by FIFA. It was also alleged that the conditions set by FIFA for the licensed agents were not proportionate. The Commission opened an investigation against FIFA after another complaint was brought by a Danish undertaking, Multiplayers International Denmark. A statement of objections was sent to FIFA and FIFA adopted a set of new

---

action of clubs and investors which the rule entails does not go beyond what is necessary to ensure its legitimate aim: i.e. to protect the uncertainty of the results in the interests of the public.' In this Decision the Commission appears to apply the reasoning from *Wouters*, as well as a necessity and proportionality test to create a 'sport integrity' justification in competition law, derived from the ECJ case law in relation to the Internal Market: COMP/37 806.

[79] French Professional Sports Clubs: aid was compatible with the EC Treaty where it was given to provide training resources for young players.

[80] E. Szyszczak, 'State intervention in the internal market', in T. Tridimas and P. Nebbia (eds), *European Union Law for the Twenty-First Century, volume 2* (Oxford: Hart, 2004).

[81] See *Walrave, supra*, n.34; *Bosman, supra*, n.23.

[82] Case T-193/02 [2005] ECR II-209; on appeal to the ECJ, Case C-171/05P order of 23 February 2006.

Regulations for player's agents, arguing that, if the Regulations were in breach of Article 81(1) EC, they would qualify for an exemption under Article 81(3) EC. At this point in time the Regulations should have been notified to the EC Commission under Regulation 17/62. The Commission closed the file in April 2002 and at the same time rejected Piau's complaint. Piau appealed to the CFI. The CFI rejected the appeal, finding that there was no manifest error of assessment by the Commission. The CFI found that the FIFA Regulations could qualify for an exemption under Article 81(3) EC. The CFI also argued that the Regulations did not eliminate competition because they apply *qualitative* selection criteria, not *quantitative* selection criteria. The Court of Justice upheld the CFI decision.

The CFI found that the national football clubs held a collective dominant position. It also held that national associations that constitute FIFA are undertakings, as well as associations of undertakings, within the scope of Article 81 EC. Referring to *Deliège*, the Court states that the legal classification of the association is not determinative and the fact that the association regulates both professional and amateur clubs does not detract from the status of being an undertaking for competition law purposes.

The CFI held that the services provided by players' agents are services of an economic nature which do not fall within the scope of the specific nature of sport. However, the Court does not address specifically the first question posed in *Walrave:* are the activities in Piau *economic* in nature? The CFI assumes they are, and that they cannot be excluded by the special sporting nature exclusion rule. The focus of the ruling is upon the nature of the Regulations drawn up by FIFA. The CFI finds that the Regulations adopted by FIFA 'fall within the scope of the freedom of internal organization enjoyed by sports associations'.[83]

The first question the ECJ should ask is whether the regulations/practices of 'purely sporting interest' are limited to their proper objective.[84] If the answer is in the negative then the issue will be whether the Internal Market rules apply because of the economic activity being carried out, and in relation to competition, whether or not there is an undertaking carrying out economic activity. This may focus the European Courts' attention to examine more closely the definition of an undertaking in relation to regulatory bodies in sport, the concept of economic activity in relation to sport and may prevent special pleading for economic activities related to sport which clearly have some commercial value.

---

[83]   Para. 74.

[84]   An application of this rule is seen in the ECJ, stating, somewhat controversially, in *Bosman*, that the nationality rules were of 'purely sporting interest' but they did not satisfy the principle of proportionality.

Even if caught by the EC Treaty rules there is the possibility for such activities to be exempted from the full thrust of EU Internal Market and competition law by the use of Article 81(3) or Article 86(2) EC[85] and the generic public interest justification, incorporating procedural guarantees of good governance, which is emerging especially in relation to free movement of services, establishment and capital.[86] This allows for scrutiny by regulators and courts, creating a level playing field across the EU.[87] An example of the application of this justification would be the Status and Transfer of Players, adopted by FIFA in July 2005 which are justified in attempting to ensure a degree of stability in what could be a dynamic and volatile football transfer market.

Examples of Regulatory Behaviour which is Prohibited by EU Law

In some cases the ECJ has handed down definitive rulings, finding the activity to be caught by the EC rules and in conflict with the rules. For example, nationality restrictions in the composition of club sport,[88] out-of-contract transfer payments[89] and discrimination on the grounds of nationality.[90]

The logical extension of the *Bosman* ruling was to extend its scope to other sportsmen and women who might gain rights using the direct effect of agreements made between the EU and non-EU states which contain free movement and competition clauses. A number of litigation issues arose at the national level, for example involving the Ukrainian footballer, Shevchenko, in Italy and the Estonian footballer, Karpin, in Spain, and in France the Administrative Court in Nancy held that a Polish-born basketball player could not be discriminated against by the use of quota restrictions based upon nationality.[91] In *Balog*[92] an attempt was made to extend the *Bosman* ruling to football players from Hungary. Balog, a Hungarian national, claimed that his rights to free movement were infringed because, when his contract with RSC Charleroi ended in 1997, he was prevented from moving to another football club because Charleroi demanded a transfer fee. The case was withdrawn in 2001 after a negotiated compromise with FIFA.

---

[85]   Case C-67/96 *Albany* [1999] ECR I-5751.
[86]   I can see problems emerging with this analysis where social law is being applied, since any opt-outs have to be agreed on adoption of the particular law. It is for this reason that football has been encouraged to negotiate a collective agreement using the social partners under Article 138 EC.
[87]   See S. Boyes, 'Caught behind or following-on? Cricket, the European Union and the *Bosman* effect' (2005), **3**(1), *Entertainment and Sports Law Journal*.
[88]   *Bosman, supra*, n.23.
[89]   Ibid.
[90]   See *Kolpak, Simutenkov*, discussed below.
[91]   *Malaja* v *French Basketball Federation*, 3 February 2000.
[92]   Case 264/98, withdrawn.

The first ruling from the ECJ came in *Kolpak*[93] which concerned a Slovakian who was the goalkeeper of a handball club, TSV Ostrigen, in Germany. He had been employed under a contract of employment from 1997. He objected to the rules of the German Handball Federation which generally did not provide equal rights for non-EU handball players and, more specifically, he challenged the rules which stated that his player's licence should have the letter 'A' on it, indicating that he was a foreign, non-EU player. Under the rules of the Handball Federation, clubs in the Budesesligia or Regionalligen were allowed to use only two 'A' listed players in each competition handball match. This restriction created economic consequences: it not only affected appearances for the team but also limited non-EU player mobility between clubs in Germany. In short, a non-EU player did not enjoy the same conditions under which he could fully exploit his potential. Kolpak used his employment status and the pre-Accession Association Agreement between the EU and Slovakia to gain rights to equal treatment concerning working conditions, remuneration and dismissal. The Court provides a broad interpretation of working conditions to find that, in the case of professional sportsmen, participation in competition matches is part of their working conditions. The Court finds the relevant provision of the Association Agreement to be directly applicable, thus taking supremacy and overriding the conflicting national regulatory rules. The Court is also able to make the connection between the employment contract and the discriminatory rules of the Federation.

Kolpak has a narrow application: it only addresses the *internal* dimension of discrimination in employment. It does not extend to access to the EU or cross-border mobility. *Kolpak* individuals do not achieve the more fundamental status of citizenship in EU law.[94] Article 17 EC continues to apply to EU nationals only. But the impact of the *Kolpak* ruling is wide. Even after the 2004 enlargement/accession a number of Member States have continued to restrict the free movement of workers from the Accession states and similar agreements exist with a number of would-be Accession states or states where the EU has negotiated special trading arrangements.[95] This impact is seen

---

[93]   Case C-438/00 [2003] ECR I-4135.

[94]   Case C-184/99 *Gryzelczyk* [2001] ECR I-6193, 'Union citizenship is destined to be the fundamental status of nationals of the Member States, enabling those who find themselves in the same situation to enjoy the same treatment in law irrespective of their nationality, subject to the expressions as are expressly provided for.'

[95]   Currently: Armenia, Azerbaijan, Belorus, Bulgaria, Estonia, Georgia, Kazakhastan, Kirgistan, Moldova, Romania, Russia, Ukraine, Tunisia, Algeria, Morocco and the ACP states.

immediately in *Simutenkov*,[96] which involved a factual situation similar to *Kolpak*.

The impact of the *Kolpak* and *Simutenkov* cases has been seen in the regulation of cricket. For many foreigners the rules of the game are a mystery and, indeed, cricket would not be seen to be a 'European' sport.[97] But the EU has a special relationship with the African, Caribbean and Pacific (ACP) states under the Contonou Agreement. Together, with immigration controls, the rules of cricket have been adjusted to allow county sides in England to continue to breed raw talent for international Test Series.

Continuing at the individual level, but in a different context, the use of discriminatory transfer deadlines for players[98] has also been found to be contrary to EU law. The ancillary services attached to sports are also included within the scope of EU law. Neither the mutual recognition of a qualifications Directive,[99] nor the Services Directive,[100] give sport a special pleading. Adaptation, aptitude and language proficiency are probably the main areas where sport could argue for a special case to be made for further training under the mutual recognition directives. If Member States want a special exemption for a sporting activity a derogation from the EC Commission must be obtained on a case-by-case basis and examples of this are seen in the 'piste wars' of the Italian, Austrian and German mountain and ski tour guides. France has also obtained a special derogation for parachuting instructors. But many examples of national protectionism go unchallenged. One of the earliest cases on mutual recognition, and one which involved a sports trainer, *Heylens*,[101] not only provided important criteria for the mutual recognition of qualifications, but also affirmed that free movement within the EU was a fundamental right and set out procedural guarantees, including access to judicial review, for asserting EU law-based rights.

---

[96] Case C-265/03 [2005] ECR I-2579.

[97] It is played at the professional level only in England, Ireland, Wales, Scotland and the Netherlands.

[98] *Lehtonen, supra*, n.37.

[99] Directive 2005/36/EC of the European Parliament and the Council of 7 September 2005 on the recognition of professional qualifications, OJ 2005 L 255/22. This directive consolidates earlier mutual recognition directives, entering into force on 20 October 2007.

[100] Directive 2006/123/EC, OJ 200L L376/26.

[101] Case 222/86 *Heylens* [1987] ECR 4097.

IS SPORT SPECIAL?

This chapter shows how the increased commercialization of sport has made it difficult to argue that sport is special and should be excluded from the regulatory processes of the EU. The generic application of the Internal Market and competition rules has made it difficult for sport-related issues to be given a complete or blanket exemption from the EU processes. In analysing the political processes of the EU, sport is seen as posing special problems and attempts to use the cultural, social and educational aspects of sport to form the basis of an EU policy continue to founder because of the inherently national organization of sport within the EU. It is claimed that sport is being mainstreamed into EU policies as a tool of integration but attempts to create a European policy on sport are still rudimentary and fragmented, with the focus on areas where there is consensus, such as anti-doping policies. Sport differs from other areas where new forms of experimental governance are being deployed, in that, while local level stakeholders are involved, the necessary EU level framework for coordination continues to be underdeveloped so long as sport is not seen as a high priority of the new governance agenda.

In legal processes attempts to take the regulation of sport outside the EC Treaty have received a sharp response from the Court of Justice in the *Meca-Medina* ruling.[102] If the Commission and the European Courts continue with the methodology set out in *Meca-Medina* for testing the compatibility of sport-related rules with the competition rules of the EC Treaty, sporting bodies are no longer able automatically to use a protective veil to create immunity from regulation by EU law. What the Court has done is to show that such rules are not necessarily incompatible with the EC Treaty. It has created a space in which regulatory bodies can continue to operate with a degree of autonomy. This bears a resemblance to the methodology used to draw lines in relation to other sensitive areas where there is a potential clash between the perceived residual sovereignty of the Member States and the functional impact certain national policies may have on market integration, the most obvious example being the application of competition law and Internal Market law to social protection issues.[103]

---

[102]   *Supra*, n.20.
[103]   See A. Winterstein, 'Nailing the jellyfish: social security and competition law' (1999), **20**, *ECLR*, 324.

2. Free movement of persons and sport

Robin C.A. White

INTRODUCTION

In any discussion of the interface between European Union law and sport, the perspective of the commentator is a key to the likely content of the argument which will follow. As many commentators note,[1] different actors in the system bring different values to the debate. Furthermore the Union itself has recognized that there are aspects of sport which give it characteristics which go beyond the market place. The Declaration on Sport attached to the Treaty of Amsterdam in 1997 noted:

> The Conference emphasises the social significance of sport, in particular its role in forging identity and bringing people together. The Conference therefore calls on the bodies of the European Union to listen to sports associations when important questions affecting sport are at issue. In this connection, special consideration should be given to the particular characteristics of amateur sport.[2]

Following the Commission's influential Helsinki Report on Sport,[3] there have been increasing references to the new approach to sport. This was followed by the rather bland declaration of the European Council at Nice in December 2000.[4] Following the Presidency Conclusions, Viviane Reding, the Commissioner responsible for education, culture and sport, announced that the declaration was a policy declaration only and did not set out to extend

---

[1] For example, R. Parrish, 'Reconciling conflicting approaches to sport in the European Union', in A. Caiger and S. Gardiner (eds), *Professional Sport in the EU: Regulation and Re-regulation* (The Hague: TMC Asser Press, 2000), 21; R. Parrish, 'The birth of European Union sports law' (2003), **2**, *Entertainment Law*, 20; and S. Weatherill, ' "Fair play, please!": recent developments in the application of EC Law to Sport' (2003), **40**, *CMLRev.*, 51.

[2] Declaration 29 annexed to the Treaty of Amsterdam [1997] OJ C-340/01.

[3] COM (1999) 644 final of 10 December 1999.

[4] Annex IV to the Presidency Conclusions, Declaration on the specific characteristics of sport and its social function in Europe, of which account should be taken in implementing common policies, http://ue.eu.int/ueDocs/cms_Data/docs/pressData/en/ec/00400-r1.%20ann.en0.htm (last visited 21 April 2006).

Community responsibilities.[5] Though there is now recognition that there is a social dimension to sport, it has not attained any special status within the legal framework of Community law. As Weatherill has noted, professional sport is a commercial activity which does not merit any 'protection provided by spurious claims to promotion of social inclusion'.[6]

Nothing was included in the Treaty establishing a Constitution for Europe which changed the legal status of sport, though in its section on education, youth, sport and vocation training, Article III-283 provides: 'The Union shall contribute to the promotion of European sporting issues, while taking account of the specific nature of sport, its structures based on voluntary activity and its social and educational function.'

There is accordingly no Treaty base for treating sport differently from cognate activities. My concern is with the free movement of persons and sport. Here we are in the territory of the fundamental freedoms in the EC Treaty. Certainly, in this area of Community law, the most compelling reasons would need to be adduced to treat professional sport as so special that the fundamental freedoms either do not apply or are modified in their application. My perspective is that of promoting the single market as envisaged in the EC Treaty, and interpreted and applied by the Court of Justice.

WHICH FREEDOMS APPLY?

Much of the literature focuses on the free movement of workers, but those engaged in sport may also be self-employed. Furthermore, sport is entertainment and so the provision of services is relevant from this perspective. The camp followers who support professional sport may well be workers or self-employed persons; they may also be service providers. Little turns on this, given the broad convergence of legal principles applicable to the free movement of workers, freedom of establishment and freedom to provide and receive services when the issue is consideration of obstacles to free movement.[7]

The effect of the case law is that national rules regulating economic activity will not breach Articles 39, 43 or 49 where they (a) apply equally to all engaged in the activity; (b) are justified by compelling reasons relating to the public interest; (c) are objectively necessary to safeguard that public interest;

---

5   Press release IP/00/1439 of 11 December 2000.
6   S. Weatherill, ' "Fair Play, please!": recent developments in the application of EC Law to Sport' (2003), **40**, *CMLRev.*, 51, 92.
7   See, generally, R. White, *Workers, Establishment and Services in the European Union* (Oxford: Oxford University Press, 2004), chs 10 and 11.

(d) are not already the subject of safeguards under rules applying in the home Member State; and (e) are the least restrictive necessary to secure the public interest.[8]

EXEMPTING SPORT FROM FREE MOVEMENT RULES

The starting point must always be the twin cases of *Walrave and Koch*[9] and *Donà* v *Mantero*.[10] It is pertinent to remember that these cases were decided at a time when the Court of Justice was determining what activities fell within the Treaty rules on free movement of persons.

In April 1974, the Court had handed down a judgment in infringement proceedings brought by the Commission against France.[11] The Commission had complained that the provisions of the Code du Travail Maritime were incompatible with what was then Article 48 of the EEC Treaty and certain provisions of Regulation 1612/68. One of the arguments advanced by the French Government was that the 'rules of the Treaty regarding freedom of movement for workers do not apply to transport and, in any event, not to sea transport so long as the Council has not so decided under Article 84(2) of the Treaty'.[12] The Court concluded that the rules on the free movement of workers applied to sea transport, because the establishment of the Common Market refers 'to the whole of the economic activities in the Community' and that the four freedoms as foundations of the Community 'can be rendered inapplicable only as a result of express provision in the Treaty'.[13]

In October 1974, the Court handed down its judgment in *Walrave and Koch*. This was a case in which both the free movement of workers and the freedom to provide services were in issue. The context was a prohibition on rules applicable to international motor-paced cycling competitions. Advocate General Warner helpfully describes the nature of the competition as:

---

[8] See Case C-55/94 *Gebhard* v *Consiglio dell-Ordine degli Avvocati e Procuratori di Milano* [1995] ECR I-4165; Case C-384/93 *Alpine Investments* v *Minister van Financiën* [1995] ECR I-1141; and C-415/93 *Union Royale Belge des Sociétés de Football Association, ASBL and others* v *Bosman and others* [1995] ECR I-4921.

[9] Case 36/74 *Walrave and Koch* v *Union Cycliste Internationale and Others* [1974] ECR 1405.

[10] Case 13/76 *Gaetano Donà* v *Mario Mantero* [1976] ECR 1333.

[11] Case 167/73 *Commission* v *France* [1974] ECR 359.

[12] Para. 8 of the Judgment.

[13] Paras 19 and 21 of the Judgment.

one between teams consisting of a man on a motorcycle, known as a 'pacemaker' or 'pacer', followed by one on a bicycle, known as a 'stayer'; or . . . between men on bicycles ('stayers') each of which is preceded by a man on a motorcycle (the 'pacemaker' or 'pacer'). What is undoubted is that the function of the pacemaker or pacer, who wears special clothing, is to create a moving vacuum for the stayer, who can thus achieve speeds – of up to 100 k.p.h. – that a man alone on a bicycle could never attain. Nor is it in doubt that both men require considerable skill.[14]

With effect from 1973, the sports governing body changed the competition rules to require the pacemakers to be of the same nationality as the stayer. Walrave and Koch were both professional pacemakers with Dutch nationality who had acted as pacemakers in particular for Belgian and German stayers. It seems that there was a paucity of world-class Dutch stayers. The new rules were seen as a threat to their livelihoods, so they challenged the compatibility of the new rules with Community law.

The Court responded to arguments that Community rules did not apply to the activity in question by saying:

> Having regard to the objectives of the Community, the practice of sport is subject to Community law only in so far as it constitutes an economic activity within the meaning of Article 2 of the Treaty.
>
> When such an activity has the character of gainful employment or remunerated service it comes more particularly within the scope, according to the case, of Articles 48 to 51 or 59 to 66 of the Treaty.[15]

The precise categorization of the activity of pacing either as employment or as service provision was irrelevant since the prohibition of discrimination on grounds of nationality applied equally to these two areas of Community law.

Though the Court does not address the question of nationality requirements in relation to the constitution of national teams, the Advocate General does. The Advocate General expressly states that rules of organizations concerned with sport that are designed to ensure that only nationals of a particular country compete in the national team of that country are an exception to the prohibition of discrimination on grounds of nationality, because that was a matter of common sense which did not need to be incorporated in the Treaty.[16] So three core propositions emerge from this case. First, the EC Treaty *only* applies to sport where it constitutes an economic activity. A detailed test for this is not provided. But the second proposition is that, where a person is engaged in sporting activities as gainful employment or a remunerated service, that is sufficient to constitute the sport an economic activity. Thirdly, the prohibition

---

[14]   [1974] ECR 1405, 1422.
[15]   Paras 4 and 5 of the Judgment.
[16]   [1974] ECR 1405, 1426.

of discrimination applies subject only to an exception for rules relating to the composition of national teams.

Some 18 months passed before the Court of Justice handed down its judgment in *Donà* v *Mantero*.[17] The challenge to nationality rules in national professional football competitions arose in an adjectival manner. Mario Mantero was the chairman of Rovigo Football Club in Italy. He engaged the services of Gaetano Donà, a football agent, to recruit players. Gaetano Donà placed an advertisement in a Belgian newspaper and subsequently sought reimbursement of his costs, which Mario Mantero resisted. In the legal proceedings which ensued, the compatibility with Community law of the rules of the Italian Football Federation requiring players to have an affiliation with that Federation in order to play in the Italian league, which was only open to Italian nationals, was raised. The key paragraph of the judgment reads:

> . . . rules or a national practice, even adopted by a sporting organization, which limit the right to take part in football matches as professional or semi-professional players solely to the nationals of the State in question, are incompatible with Article 7 and, as the case may be, with Articles 48 to 51 or 59 to 66 of the Treaty unless such rules or practice exclude foreign players from participation in certain matches for reasons which are not of an economic nature, which relate to the particular nature and context of such matches and are thus of sporting interest only.[18]

Advocate General Trabucchi expressly affirms the principles laid down in *Walrave and Koch* in the following terms:

> The judgment in *Walrave* has, in fact, a dual significance. The Court rightly stressed the value of sporting activity as such and the need to encourage it; at the same time, it reaffirmed the general principle of the right to freedom of movement for those who, in the world of sport, want to take part in it as a preponderantly economic activity of a professional nature.[19]

This might seem ancient history, but in the context of renewed claims for professional sport being a special case,[20] it may be important to reiterate some fundamentals of Community law. For more than 30 years, the principles established in *Walrave and Koch* and *Donà* v *Mantero* have provided the bedrock of the application of Community law to sport. The statements in these two cases have become something of a mantra in cases involving sport.[21]

---

17   Case 13/76 *Gaetano Donà* v *Mario Mantero* [1976] ECR 1333.
18   Para. 19 of the Judgment.
19   [1976] ECR 1333, 1344.
20   In 2005, UEFA proposed that there should be a minimum number of 'home-grown' players on match sheets for UEFA competitions. See http://www. uefa.com/uefa/news/Kind=128/newsId=276997.html (last visited 21 April 2006).
21   See, for example, C-415/93 *Union Royale Belge des Sociétés de Football*

OBSTACLES TO ACCESS TO THE LABOUR MARKET IN SPORT

The most famous sporting case is undoubtedly the *Bosman* case.[22] In this case, the Court of Justice applied the obstacles approach to the free movement of workers. At issue was the transfer system developed by national and transnational football associations. A football club which sought to employ a footballer whose contract with another club had come to an end had to pay the club from which the player came a transfer fee before the player could be registered to play for the new club. The transfer fee arrangements are collateral to the arrangements between the player and his new club concerning his personal terms. Bosman was playing for the third division Belgian club, Olympic de Charleroi, and wanted to move to the French club, Dunquerque. Bosman's argument was that the system of transfer payments prevented him from securing employment with the French club. The Court considered that it was dealing with a non-discriminatory rule which was capable of restricting the free movement of workers. As such, the system would only avoid breaching Article 39 EC if it could be justified as serving a legitimate aim required by pressing reasons relating to the public interest.

It was argued that the system of transfer fees was necessary to maintain a financial and competitive balance between clubs and to support the search for and development of new football talent. The Court accepted that these were legitimate aims but went on to apply the ubiquitous proportionality text. Here the means were not the least restrictive to meet the aim; there were other mechanisms which would achieve the aim without inhibiting the free movement of workers.

Though the Court's reasoning avoided such application, the case does raise the possibility that non-State actors might rely on the exceptions contained in Article 48(3) (now 39(3)) EC. Logically, if non-State actors are bound by the Treaty provisions on the free movement of workers, then, in principle, the derogations provided in the Treaty should also be available to them independently of any State action or regulations authorizing such derogations.

Association, ASBL and Others v *Bosman and Others* [1995] ECR I-4921, para. 73 of the Judgment; Joined Cases C-51/96 and C-191/97 *Deliège* v *Ligue francophone de judo et disciplines associées ASBL* [2000] ECR I-2549, para. 41 of the Judgment; Case C-176/96 *Lehtonen and another* v *Fédération royale belge des sociétés de basket-ball ASBL* [2000] ECR I-2681, para. 32 of the Judgment; Case C-438/00 *Deutsche Handballbund eV* v *Maros Kolpak* [2003] ECR I-4135, para. 53 of the Judgment; and Case T-313/02 *Meca-Medine and Majcen* v *Commission*, Judgment of 30 September 2004, para. 37.

[22]   C-415/93 *Union Royale Belge des Sociétés de Football Association, ASBL and Others* v *Bosman and Others* [1995] ECR I-4921, noted at (1996), **21**, *ELRev.*, 313 and (1996), **33**, *CMLRev.*, 991.

Fernández Martín, however, while indicating that further clarification is required, pertinently notes:

> That would constitute a far too radical application of the rationale of self-regulation and has no basis in previous case law nor in the Treaty or secondary legislation. Thus, an alternative interpretation would be that the Court intended to limit the use of Article 48(3) EC exceptions by private organisations to those cases where the latter are entitled, under national legislation, to regulate conditions of employment *in a collective manner* with respect to their areas of activity and perform therefore a semi-public function.[23]

The *Deliège* case[24] concerned a serious dispute between a Belgian judoka and her national sports federation. The circumstances were different from those in the *Bosman* case; the contested provisions did not determine access to the labour market and nationality clauses were not in issue. The dispute concerned participation in competitions which qualified the athlete for selection for a national competition. Matters came to a head during the run-up to the Atlanta Olympic Games. In order to qualify for this competition, nomination by the national federation was required. These eligibility rules had been agreed by the Union Européenne Judo, who were one of the parties to Case C-51/96. Christelle Deliège brought legal proceedings to secure her participation in qualifying competitions. It seems that she was regarded by the national federations as a difficult character. After reaffirming the earlier case law, the Court notes that it is not dealing with a case in which the composition of a national team is in issue. Nor, said the Court, is the classification by the sporting federation of its members as amateur athletes sufficient to preclude their being regarded in Community law as engaging in economic activity within the meaning of Article 2 EC. Christelle Deliège regarded herself as a professional athlete. She claimed that the federation rules were not compatible with the Treaty rules on the freedom to provide services. The Court's conclusion was one which left many matters to be resolved in the national court:

> A rule requiring professional or semi-professional athletes or persons aspiring to take part in a professional or semi-professional activity to have been authorised or selected by their federation in order to be able to participate in a high-level international sports competition, which does not involve national teams competing against each other, does not in itself, as long as it derives from a need inherent in the organisation of such a competition, constitute a restriction on the freedom to provide services prohibited by Article 59 of the EC treaty (now, after amendment, Article 49 EC).

---

[23] J.M. Fernández Martín, 'Re-defining obstacles to the free movement of workers' (1996), **21**, *ELRev.*, 313, 324 (emphasis in original).

[24] Joined Cases C-51/96 and C-191/97 *Deliège* v *Ligue francophone de judo et disciplines associées ASBL* [2000] ECR I-2549, noted at (2000), **25**, *ELRev.*, 554.

Advocate General Cosmas had been rather clearer in indicating that the contested measures were not in breach of Community law. His Opinion makes express reference to the non-economic grounds taken into consideration, including measures related to the organization of the selection of European national teams to take part in the Olympic Games and 'guaranteeing the representative nature of international matches as a constituent part of the balanced development of sport at pan-European level'.[25]

The next case also originated from Belgium and concerned the regulation of basketball.[26] The Court handed down its judgment two days after the *Deliège* judgment. The contested measures were time limits on transfers of players between clubs, if the player was to be eligible to play for the new club during the current season. The applicant, Lehtonen, is a Finnish basketball player, playing the sport professionally, who sought registration to enable him to play in the Belgian league. The Belgian federation refused to register his transfer because it was not within the relevant time limits.[27] He nevertheless played and his club won, but the Belgian federation penalized the club by awarding the match to the opposing team. The Court concluded that the time-limits for registration of new players were capable of restricting the free movement of workers, and so required justification on non-economic grounds. The Court accepted that 'ensuring the regularity of sporting competitions' was capable of being a legitimate aim.[28] The matter was again left for the national court to determine in the light of the following guidance relating to the different time limits for players inside and outside the European zone:

> At first sight, such a rule must be regarded as going beyond what is necessary to achieve the aim pursued. It does not appear from the material in the case-file that a transfer between 28 February and 31 March of a player from a federation in the European zone jeopardises the regularity of the championship more than a transfer in that period of a player from a federation not in that zone.[29]

It was inevitable that the tentacles of Community law would reach into perhaps less obvious areas once the direct effect of association agreements was established.[30] The *Kolpak* case[31] attracted nearly as much attention as the

---

25   [2000] ECR I-2549, 2594.

26   Case C-176/96 *Lehtonen and Another* v *Fédération royale belge des sociétés de basket-ball ASBL* [2000] ECR I-2681.

27   The deadline for players from a federation in the European zone was 28 February, while that for players outside the European zone was 31 March.

28   Para. 53 of the Judgment.

29   Para. 58 of the Judgment.

30   Most notably, the Europe Agreements with applicant Member States, but also agreements with other countries, such as the Cotonou Convention with African, Caribbean and Pacific countries.

31   Case C-438/00 *Deutscher Handballbund eV* v *Kolpak* [2003] ECR I-4135.

Bosman case. The case concerned a Slovakian handball player who was under contract to a German team. The rules of the sports federation drew a distinction between players who held the nationality of the Member State and those who did not. At the time, Slovakia was not a Member State. There was a limit on the number of non-European Union players eligible to play in a league or cup match. Kolpak challenged this provision on the basis that it constituted discrimination, which was not permitted by the terms of the Association Agreement between the Union and Slovakia.

The Court had already ruled that the corresponding provision of the Europe Agreement with Poland was capable of giving rise to direct effect,[32] from which it followed that Polish nationals employed in a Member State were entitled to equal treatment with nationals of that State. It was therefore entirely predictable that the same view would be taken of provisions of the Europe Agreement with Slovakia. It therefore followed that nationals of those countries with agreements with the Union were entitled to equal treatment with nationals of the Union once they were lawfully employed in one of the Member States. There is, of course, no Community right of entry to the country; that is a matter of national law. But, once admitted and in lawful employment, there must be no discrimination on grounds of nationality. The reverberations in the world of sport were significant, especially in England in relation to the composition of cricket teams in county competitions where there was a limit of two overseas players.[33]

The application of the *Kolpak* ruling to association agreements which were not with countries on the brink of membership was confirmed in the *Simutenkov* case.[34] This case concerned a Russian soccer player who was lawfully employed by a Spanish football team. There was a limit of three overseas players in the Spanish First Division. Simutenkov successfully claimed that under the terms of the Communities-Russia Partnership Agreement, he was entitled to be treated equally with nationals of the Member States in relation to his eligibility to play in the Spanish football league.

---

[32]   Case C-162/00 *Land Nordrhein-Westfalen* v *Pokrzeptowic-Meyer* [2002] ECR I-1049, para. 30 of the Judgment.

[33]   See, for example, http://news.bbc.co.uk/sport1/hi/cricket/3529413.stm (last visited 24 April 2006); and http://www.ecb.co.uk/ecb/publications/kolpak-ruling,BP.html (last visited 24 April 2006). Players from many Commonwealth countries would cease to be treated as overseas players under the *Kolpak* ruling. See also S. Boyes, 'Caught behind or following-on? Cricket, the European Union and the *"Bosman"* effect' (2005), *European Sports Law Journal*, No. 1, http:// go.warwick.ac.uk/eslj/issues/volume3/number1/boyes (last visited 25 April 2006).

[34]   Case C-265/03 *Simutenkov* v *Ministerio de Educación y Cultura and Real federación Española de Fútbol*, Judgment of 12 April 2005.

PROHIBITING DISCRIMINATION: PLAYER SELECTION RULES

There is no doubt that the prohibition of discrimination on grounds of nationality applies to the free movement of workers, to freedom of establishment and to freedom to provide and receive services. The current position is neatly summarized by Advocate General Stix-Hackl in the *Kolpak* case:

> It is apparent from the Court's case law that Article 39(2) EC precludes the application of rules laid down by sports federations under which, in competition matches which they organise, sports clubs may field only a limited number of professional players who are nationals of other Member States.

Where international agreements place nationals of associated countries in the same position in relation to the prohibition on discrimination, this prohibition will extend to such nationals.

RECOGNITION OF QUALIFICATIONS

A further area where the law on the free movement of persons is relevant to sport is the recognition of qualifications. It was the refusal of the French authorities to recognize the Belgian training qualification held by Georges Heylens which precipitated a key decision on the mutual recognition of qualifications.[35] Heylens was a Belgian national with a Belgian diploma entitling him to work as a football trainer. Football trainers in France could only undertake this activity if they held a French diploma. Heylens sought recognition of his Belgian diploma in France, but this was refused by the French authorities without their giving any reasons. Heylens took issue with this and the national court referred questions to the Court of Justice. The Court reaffirmed that, in the absence of harmonizing measures, the Member States were entitled to regulate the knowledge, skills and experience required to undertake particular activities. However, it was a general requirement of Community law that there must be a good faith assessment of the equivalence of qualifications obtained in other Member States. Reasons must be given for any adverse decision, and such decisions had to be subject to challenge in the national legal order. Without the articulation of reasons, the applicant would not be in a position to know whether the refusal was compatible with Community law. It is also, of course, the case that the requirement to articulate reasons acts as a check on decisions being made on improper grounds. Thus the Court imposed positive

---

[35]   Case 222/86 *UNECTEF* v *Georges Heylens* [1987] ECR 4097.

obligations on the Member States to assess in good faith the equivalence of qualifications. This case was decided in advance of the introduction of the horizontal directives on the mutual recognition of qualifications, which might well apply to such situations today.[36]

Because the horizontal directives on the mutual recognition of qualifications require individual decisions to be made, recognition is not automatic but frequently depends upon a good faith assessment of equivalence.[37] This has continued to give rise to infringement proceedings by the Commission against a number of Member States.[38]

Mutual recognition of qualifications is known to have been a problem for British ski instructors seeking to work as ski instructors in France. The best known case is that of Simon Butler, which resulted in a petition to the European Parliament.[39] Simon Butler owns a chalet in a French ski resort; his business is the provision of holidays and ski instruction for children. His British Association of Ski Instructors (BASI) Grade 1 ski instructor qualification was not recognized by the French authorities, which Butler claimed jeopardized his entire business. The Commission's response to his petition recognized the difficulty and referred to agreement reached among ski instructor associations. This had added a further ingredient to the BASI test[40] which must be completed by those wishing to seek recognition of their qualification in France. As the Commission response to the petition notes:

> The agreement is not a Community legislative act and it can therefore only influence conditions of recognition to the extent that it is implemented in national training programmes and recognition processes in individual Member States.

There is, however, nothing unusual or exceptional relating to sport in this context; it is merely an illustration of how the law in practice may be different from the 'law-in-the-books'.

---

[36] Note that the directives on the mutual recognition of qualifications have been consolidated into a single omnibus directive: Directive 2005/36/EC of the European Parliament and the Council of 7 September 2005 on the recognition of professional qualifications [2005] OJ L255/22, which enters into force on 20 October 2007.

[37] By comparison with the sectoral directives, where recognition is automatic if one of the named qualifications is held.

[38] See http://europa.eu.int/comm/internal_market/qualifications/infringements_en.htm (last visited 24 April 2006).

[39] Petition 929/2002 by Simon Butler, of British nationality, on the non-recognition of professional ski-ing qualifications by the French authorities, PE 326.197 of 17 February 2003.

[40] See http://www.basi.org.uk/basi/int_status.asp (last visited 25 April 2006).

COMMENTS

Three principles have been clearly established by the case law of the Court of Justice in the fields where the free movement of persons meets the regulation of sport. First, the rules of the EC Treaty on free movement of workers, freedom of establishment and the freedom to provide and receive services are fundamental rules of the Community constitution which apply to sporting activities of an economic nature. Secondly, sport enjoys no special status which exempts it from the prohibition of discrimination on grounds of nationality in relation to the free movement of sports professionals. Thirdly, rules of sporting regulatory bodies which are capable of restricting access to the labour market for sports professionals are permissible only in so far as they do not fall foul of the prohibition of discrimination, and are capable of justification on non-economic grounds.

All that said, the Court's case law on non-discriminatory obstacles is sufficiently flexible to take account of arguments on non-economic grounds justifying certain practices. It also seems that the closer the relationship of those rules to selection for international competition, the more likely it will be that the contested measures can be regarded as justified. In the *Bosman* case, the Court accepted as legitimate 'the aims of maintaining a balance between clubs, a certain degree of equality and uncertainty as to results and of encouraging the recruitment and training of young players'.[41]

Indeed, in the ensuing paragraphs, the Court indicates its agreement with some of the alternative ways which the Advocate General had identified[42] in which football associations might achieve the objectives in a manner which was less restrictive of the free movement of sports professionals. Furthermore, it is clear from the judgment in the *Deliège* case[43] that, where the contested measures are closely related to the selection of those sportsmen and women to compete in international competition, they may be regarded as justified.

Perhaps it has been an unexpected consequence of the network of association agreements that so many sports professionals now have to be treated equally with nationals of the Member States. In a special release dated August 2003 following the *Kolpak* case, Davenport Lyons, a law firm, reported that, of the 643 players registered to play in the Premiership, 232 were not from the United Kingdom. Of that 232, only 49 could be subjected to a foreign player quota, since the remainder were either nationals of the Member States or bene-

---

[41]   C-415/93 *Union Royale Belge des Sociétés de Football Association, ASBL and Others* v *Bosman and Others* [1995] ECR I-4921, para. 106 of the Judgment.
[42]   At paras 226ff of his Opinion.
[43]   Joined Cases C-51/96 and C-191/97 *Deliège* v *Ligue francophone de judo et disciplines associées ASBL* [2000] ECR I-2549.

ficiaries of the ruling in *Kolpak* which required them to be treated as nationals of the Union.

Much of the debate about whether the European Union has adopted the right approach to the regulation of sport underplays two significant developments in recent years: the globalization of sport[44] and the commodification of sport. It is estimated that eight out of ten people worldwide watched some part of the Soccer World Cup in the summer of 2006. That makes media broadcasting of huge significance. In this context, arguments about developing new players have less to do with the creation of sporting talent and more to do with increasing the market for a product.

At an extreme level, one could question why national teams cannot employ the best regardless of nationality. There are, after all, outstanding footballers who come from countries which are unlikely to generate a team with a real prospect of success. It can be questioned whether World Cup 2006 is merely 'of sporting interest only'.[45] Indeed, it seems that the coach of the Qatar national team sought to recruit foreign players to the Qatar national team in order to secure qualification for World Cup 2006.[46] There are frequently stories about nationality shopping or hopping by major sports professionals.[47]

FIFA itself reports that the 2000 season saw almost 15 000 men and women being transferred from clubs belonging to one association to clubs belonging to another association in another country. At club level, free movement of professional footballers is big business. The argument that this inhibits the development of national talent can be questioned. After all, the mobility of players worldwide means that the best players get the opportunity to play for the best clubs in the most competitive leagues in the world. This has probably

---

[44]   See, for example, A. Gupta, 'The globalization of cricket: the rise of the non-West' (2004), **21**, *International Journal of the History of Sport*, 257; and S. Boyes, 'Globalisation, Europe and the re-regulation of Sport', in A. Caiger and S. Gardiner (eds), *Professional Sport in the EU: Regulation and Re-regulation* (The Hague: TMC Asser Press, 2000) 65.

[45]   The phrase used in para. 19 of the Court's Judgment in Case 13/76 *Gaetano Donà* v *Mario Mantero* [1976] ECR 1333.

[46]   See http://www.payvand.com/news/04/mar/1032.html (last visited 24 April 2006); and http://www.fifa.com/en/news/feature/0,1451,101563,00.html (last visited 24 April 2006).

[47]   Notable examples are Zola Budd's transformation into a GB athlete: see http://www.afd.org.uk/general/budd.htm (last visited on 25 April 2006). See also '100 years of debates over player nationality and status', http://www.fifa.com/en/news/feature/0,1451,101563,00.html (last visited 24 April 2006). For more detail, see P. Lanfranchi and others, *100 Years of Football. The FIFA Centennial Book* (London: Weidenfeld & Nicolson, 2004). See also J. Paul McCutcheon, 'National eligibility rules after *Bosman*', in A. Caiger and S. Gardiner (eds), *Professional Sport in the EU: Regulation and Re-regulation* (The Hague: TMC Asser Press, 2000) 127.

resulted in the quality of international football being higher than it has ever been. It also provides an opportunity for those outstanding players from countries which will probably never be the top teams in international competitions to compete in their chosen sport at the highest level, and for unprecedented financial rewards both on and off the field.

One commentary on sport in the European Union examines the impact of the *Bosman* ruling, and concludes:

> The conclusion can be drawn that the changes taking place in the field of professional sports can primarily be attributed to the consistent economic orientation of this sector and that the existing EU legislation is merely limiting the scope available to sporting associations for restricting this development through their own regulations. The indirect EU sports policy is therefore only contributing secondarily to the changes taking place in professional sport in Europe and does not actually affect vast parts of the sports system.[48]

CONCLUDING REMARKS

There are no convincing arguments for exempting professional sport from the fundamental freedoms contained in the EC Treaty. The prohibition of discrimination on grounds of nationality, and the subjection of non-discriminatory obstacles to a test of justification, have been the right way forward in this area. As the Helsinki Report on Sport noted:

> ... the Community must ... ensure that the initiatives taken by the national State authorities or sporting organisations comply with Community law, including competition law, and respect in particular the principles of the internal market (freedom of movement for workers, freedom of establishment and freedom to provide services, etc.).[49]

Community law in the internal market field has shown the flexibility to permit an exception for national teams participating as representatives of their country in international competitions.

There will, no doubt, continue to be cases in the areas of the free movement of workers, freedom of establishment and freedom to provide and receive services which involve sport. However, the principles seem to be firmly established and well settled. Quite where the dividing line is between professional sport and amateur sport may need to be resolved, although successful participation in sport at the highest level can these days seldom be achieved if the

---

48   W. Tokarski, D. Steinbach, K. Petry and B. Jesse, *Two Players One Goal? Sport in the European Union* (Aachen: Meyer and Meyer Sport, 2004) 98.

49   COM(1999) 644 final of 10 December 1999, para. 4.

activity is pursued purely in a person's spare time. Most successful Olympic athletes are professional sportsmen and sportswomen.

For some the outcome of the application of the rules of the EC Treaty is controversial. For others, it is merely a new legal order subjecting established practices to justification in the modern world. Much of the current debate is little more than a reiteration of a much longer running debate between advocates of an amateur model of sport and of a professional model of sport.

3. On overlapping legal orders: what is the 'purely sporting' rule?

Stephen Weatherill

INTRODUCTION

This chapter examines the overlap of two legal orders. One is the legal order established by the EC Treaty. The other is the legal order which governs sport – a set of rules established by sports federations whose decisions have such profound consequences for the functioning of sport that it is not misleading to label them 'law' despite their formal source as private arrangements. Put another way, this chapter's concern is to explore the relationship between EC law as a basis for controlling sport from 'outside' and the network of governance which regulates sport from 'within'.

In practice, examination of this overlap has typically been inflamed by the anxiety of sports bodies to keep EC law (and other forms of public control) at bay. Appeals to respect sporting autonomy – meaning that there should no overlap of legal orders, but rather clean separation – are commonplace. And there is a basis in the EC Treaty for advocating such a division. The EC Treaty does not refer to sport at all. It is therefore not constitutionally competent to adopt legislation with the explicit aim of regulating sport. And yet the plea to keep sport free from EC law's intrusion is readily contested. The EC Treaty contains provisions that exert a broad control over the functioning of the economy – most significantly, the provisions on free movement of persons and services and the rules on competition. Since sport has an (increasingly prominent) economic dimension, these Treaty rules have been used to assert a basis for supervising sporting practices. In this way EC law has overlapped with 'internal' sports law.

But are there at least some practices which are 'purely sporting' in nature and therefore immune from EC law's overlap with sport? Where sports rules are found to fall within EC law's grip, how then to secure a reconciliation between the peculiar demands of sports governance and the economic objectives mapped out by the EC Treaty? How can EC law show sensitivity to the interests that motivate sports federations given that its foundational document, the Treaty, is barren of sports-specific policy articulation? These questions invite both constitutional and substantive inquiry. This chapter seeks to provide an account of the development of the practice of the Court and the Commission, and in particular it shows how the current approach is strongly to assert the unavoidable overlap between EC law and 'internal' sports law, but to ensure that the area of overlap is nourished by appreciation that in some respects 'sport is special'.

THE CHALLENGE OF THE 'PURELY SPORTING' RULE

In *Walrave and Koch* v *Union Cycliste Internationale*, the first case involving sport to reach the European Court,[1] the Court stated that the practice of sport is subject to Community law 'in so far as it constitutes an economic activity within the meaning of Article 2 of the Treaty'. This approach was followed in *Donà* v *Mantero*,[2] vigorously adopted by the European Court in *Bosman*,[3] and confirmed most recently in *Meca-Medina and Majcen*.[4] This is settled law and it is, in fact, no more than a reflection of the constitutionally fundamental point rooted in Article 5(1) EC that the EC enjoys no general regulatory competence. But what really does this mean? How does one determine whether a particular sporting practice falls or does not fall within the scope of the Treaty? And then, if it does, how does its compatibility with the Treaty fall to be assessed, given the absence in the Treaty of any explicit articulation of the intended relationship between EC trade law and sport?

Walrave and Koch set EC sports law's ball rolling and the judgment still deserves careful attention.[5] The case involved nationality-based discrimination, which one would normally assume to fall foul of (what is now) Article 12 EC's prohibition of such practices. However, the Court treated the composition of national sports teams as unaffected by the prohibition where their formation is 'a question of purely sporting interest and as such has nothing to do with economic activity'. In *Donà* v *Mantero*[6] the Court held that the Treaty provisions governing free movement do not prevent practices that exclude foreign players from certain matches for 'reasons which are not of an economic nature' and which are 'of sporting interest only'. In *Bosman*[7] the Court, citing its judgment in *Donà*, again adopted this formula, but, reflecting

---

1   Case 36/74 [1974] ECR 1405.
2   Case 13/76 [1976] ECR 1333.
3   Case C415/93 [1995] ECR I-14921.
4   Case C-519/04P [2006] ECR I-6991, para. 22.
5   Case 36/74 cited above, fn.1.
6   Case 13/76 cited above, fn.2.
7   Case C-415/93 cited above, fn.3.

the insistence found in the *Walrave* judgment and repeated subsequently that this 'restriction on the scope of the provisions in question must however remain limited to its proper objective', offered confirmation that the Court will patrol the limits of the autonomy granted to sports federations to set rules undisturbed by the demands of EC law. In *Bosman* the Court refused to accept that nationality-based restrictions in *club* football, as distinct from representative international football, constituted legitimate rules of sporting interest.[8] It concluded that they fell within the scope of, and violated the requirements of, the EC Treaty.

But precisely why was the Court prepared to find that selection policies for national representative teams escaped condemnation under EC law? In *Walrave and Koch* the Court referred to 'a question of purely sporting interest' which 'as such has nothing to do with economic activity'. This, however, is an awkward formulation. Perhaps there are some such rules which are beyond the reach of the Treaty – the detail of the offside rule perhaps, the height of the goalposts or the length of a match – but most rules of sporting interest are not purely of sporting interest, they also impinge on economic activity. In practice, the Court's consistent insistence that any restriction on the scope of the Treaty provisions in question must remain limited to its proper objective has helped to contain inflated claims to sporting autonomy via this unhappy 'purely sporting interest' formula. But *Walrave and Koch*, as the source of the Court's treatment of the overlap between EC law and 'internal' sports law, embedded into the jurisprudence an unfortunate suggestion of clean separation between rules of 'purely sporting interest' and rules with an economic impact. It is most of all the word 'purely' that is apt to mislead. In reality the two spheres commonly overlap, for most sporting rules are of sporting interest and they also exert an economic impact.

Subsequent case law and Commission practice have tended to reflect this unstable claim to a separation between the sporting and the economic sphere, while groping for legal formulae that would give space for sport to assert its particular requirements even where their promotion has detrimental economic consequences for individuals.

In this vein, in *Bosman* the Court shrewdly referred to 'the difficulty of severing the economic aspects from the sporting aspects of football', but then added – rather unhelpfully – that 'the provisions of Community law concerning freedom of movement of persons and of provision of services do not preclude rules or practices justified on non-economic grounds which relate to the particular nature and context of certain matches'. Although it is plain that

---

[8]   See also Case C-438/00 *Deutscher Handballbund eV.* v *Kolpak* [2003] ECR I-4135.

the Court is in general terms doing what it did in *Walrave and Koch* and accepting there is an area of sporting autonomy free of interference by EC law, in strict constitutional terms this statement is not easily understood. In particular, if the justification is non-economic, is this to say (with AG Lenz in his Opinion) that the matter falls outwith the scope of the Treaty altogether, in which case 'justification' is not the correct term? Or is that the rules have an economic effect and fall within the scope of the Treaty but are not condemned by it because they also have virtuous non-economic (sporting) effects, in which case the precise legal source of this justification could helpfully have been made plain?

Advocate General Warner in *Walrave and Koch* had it right when he asserted robustly that the permissibility under Community law of national sporting teams is no more than a simple matter of common sense. But in law, of course, we crave a more precise explanation of why the Treaty does not bite. In *Bosman* it was not forthcoming. Still, painstaking textual analysis is probably of only limited value and, to satisfy, would in any event require examination of the judgment in other languages, because the awkward course chosen by the Court is a reflection of the Treaty's own inadequacies in failing to set out how sport overlaps with EC trade law. More broadly still, the whole rich literature exploring the concept of EC sports law and policy strives to show how the institutions of the EU seek to piece together a coherent approach against a Treaty background which is barren of sports-specific material and reveals how EC law, by empowering a range of actors, tends to erode the self-regulatory paradigm which has for so long been dominant in sports governance.[9]

Deliège concerned selection of individual athletes (*in casu*, judokas) for international competition.[10] Participation was not open. One had to be chosen by the national federation. If one was not chosen, one's economic interests would be damaged. Could EC law be used to attack the selection decision? This was a classic case which brought the basic organizational structure of sport into contact with the economic interests of participants. The Court stated that selection rules 'inevitably have the effect of limiting the number of participants in a tournament' but that 'such a limitation is inherent in the conduct of

---

[9] For example, R. Parrish, *Sports law and policy in the European Union* (Manchester University Press, 2003); S. Greenfield and G. Osborn (eds), *Law and Sport in Contemporary Society* (London: Frank Cass Publishing, 2000); L. Barani, 'The role of the European Court of Justice as a political actor in the integration process: the case of sport regulation after the Bosman ruling' (2005), **1**, *Journal of Contemporary European Research*, 42; S. Van den Bogaert and A. Vermeersch, 'Sport and the European treaty: a tale of uneasy bedfellows' (2006), **31**, *European Law Review*, 821.

[10] Cases C-51/96 & C-191/97 *Deliège* v *Ligue de Judo* [2000] ECR I-2549.

an international high-level sports event, which necessarily involves certain selection rules or criteria being adopted'.[11] Accordingly, the rules did not in themselves constitute a restriction on the freedom to provide services prohibited by Article 49 EC.

Deliège is important for its acceptance that a rule cannot be placed outwith the Treaty simply through incantation of the magic words, 'purely sporting rule'. Rather, the economic impact must be taken into account, but even where there is detrimental effect felt by an individual sportsman that does not mean the rule is *incompatible* with EC law. The *Deliège* judgment is respectful of sporting autonomy, but according to reasoning which treats EC law and 'internal' sports law as overlapping.

The Commission has adopted a functionally comparable approach in its application of Article 81 EC to sport. In *Champions League* it accepted that agreeing fixtures in a league would not be a 'restriction' on competition, but rather a process essential to its effective organization, However, by contrast, an agreement to sell rights to broadcast matches in common is not essential to the league's functioning, because individual selling by clubs is perfectly possible (though doubtless less convenient and lucrative). So collective selling *is* a restriction on competition within the meaning of Article 81(1) EC and it damages the economic interests of, in particular, broadcasters denied a market populated by competing individual sellers. So an agreement to sell rights in common can stand only if exempted according to the orthodox criteria set out in Article 81(3) EC.[12] The Commission also took account of sport's peculiar economics in its *ENIC/ UEFA* decision,[13] in which it concluded that rules forbidding multiple ownership of football clubs suppressed demand but were indispensable to the maintenance of a credible competition marked by uncertainty as to the outcome of all matches. A competition's basic appeal would be shattered were consumers to suspect the clubs were not true rivals. So Article 81 did not forbid sports rules confining individuals to ownership and control of one club only. The principal message here is that sporting practices typically have an economic effect and that accordingly they cannot be sealed off from the expectations of EC law, but within the area of overlap between EC law and 'internal' sports law there is room for recognition of the particular needs of sport, which may admittedly differ from 'normal' industries.[14]

---

11   Para. 64 of the judgment.
12   Dec. 2003/778, *Champions League* [2003] OJ L291/25, paras 125–31. Exemption pursuant to Art. 81(3) *was* granted on the facts.
13   COMP 37.806 ENIC/UEFA, IP/02/942, 27 June 2002.
14   For economic analysis, see e.g., S. Dobson and J. Goddard, *The Economics of Football* (Cambridge University Press, 2001); S. Rosen and A. Sanderson, 'Labour markets in professional sports' (2001), **111**, *The Economic Journal*, F47; L. Buzzacchi,

MECA-MEDINA AND *MAJCEN*: THE STATE OF THE ART IN EC SPORTS LAW

The case law has now moved on to a firmer footing – or, at least, since even in Luxembourg one swallow does not make a summer, what may prove to be a firmer footing. In *Meca-Medina and Majcen* v *Commission*, a Decision of July 2006,[15] the Court offered a significantly adjusted analysis when compared with its earlier rulings. This ruling abandons the notion of the 'purely sporting rule' which has an economic effect yet automatically falls outwith the reach of the EC Treaty. It reveals that denial of overlap between rules of both a sporting nature and an economic nature is not sustainable. But in the area of overlap sport's special concerns should be carefully and sensitively fed into the analysis.

The straightforward fact pattern of the case illuminates the sensitive issues at stake when sport and the law collide. The applicants were professional swimmers. They had failed a drug test administered as part of the overall control exercised over the sport by FINA, swimming's governing body. Consequently, they had been deprived of their means of making a living by a ban from competition which, after an appeal, was set at two years in duration. So the economic detriment of the action taken against them was plain. And yet this was clearly not *only* a matter of economics. Sport is based on fair play – it is structured around rules which define the essence of the endeavour. Keeping out drug cheats has an undeniable economic context, but at the same time it is an existential choice: sport is only sport if there is a level playing field for competitors.

The swimmers complained to the Commission that the anti-doping arrangements that had led to their exclusion from the sport constituted a violation of the Treaty competition rules. The Commission decided to reject their complaint.[16] The swimmers applied to the Court of First Instance (CFI) for annulment of the Commission's decision to reject their complaint, but the CFI rejected their application.[17]

In *Meca-Medina and Majcen* the CFI did the law a great service by making unpersuasive use of the notion that a rule may be of purely sporting interest and therefore non-economic, with the result that it escapes the application of EC law. Reliance on this unconvincing cleavage between sport and the economy

---

S. Szymanski and T. Valletti, 'Equality of opportunity and equality of outcome: open leagues, closed leagues and competitive balance' (2003), **3**, *Journal of Industry, Competition and Trade*, 167.
[15]   Case C-519/04 P [2006] ECR I-6991.
[16]   COMP 38.158, 1 August 2002.
[17]   Case T-313/02 [2004] ECR II-3291.

provoked the European Court of Justice (ECJ) in July 2006 to correct the development of the law and to find (what I consider to be) the right path. The ECJ set aside the CFI's judgment, though it still concluded that the swimmers' application for annulment of the Commission decision had to fail. Of more profound importance than the outcome of the litigation at hand, the ECJ's ruling is significant for taking a much less generous approach to the scope of sporting autonomy to apply rules with economic effects than had been admitted by the CFI. The ECJ judgment is readily capable of being read as having extinguished the notion that EC law recognizes and therefore leaves untouched the 'purely sporting rule', at least where such a rule has economic consequence. *Meca-Medina and Majcen*, then, is a landmark judgment.

It is worth dwelling briefly on the approach taken by the CFI, even if it has now been set aside by the ECJ, because it illuminates the complexity of the overlap between EC law and 'internal' sports law.[18] In *Meca-Medina and Majcen* v *Commission*,[19] the CFI began by repeating the orthodox judicial view that sport is subject to Community law only in so far as it constitutes an economic activity within the meaning of Article 2 EC.[20] It then attempted to insist that anti-doping rules concern exclusively non-economic aspects of sport, designed to preserve 'noble competition'[21] and therefore outwith the scope of the EC Treaty. This led it into intellectually murky alleyways. At paragraph 41 the CFI referred to 'purely sporting rules, that is to say rules concerning questions of purely sporting interest and, as such, having nothing to do with economic activity' and juxtaposed this to a description of 'regulations, which relate to the particular nature and context of sporting events, are inherent in the organisation and proper conduct of sporting competition and cannot be regarded as constituting a restriction on the Community rules on the freedom of movement of workers and the freedom to provide services'. But this is to conflate two different points. Perhaps there is a (small) category of purely sporting rules unassociated with economic activity, but regulations inherent in the organization and proper conduct of sporting competition form a much larger category in which economic effect is commonly present. Similarly, at paragraph 44, the CFI observed that the 'the campaign against doping does not pursue any economic objective'. That may not be true, for the CFI itself refers at paragraph 57 to the economic value of a 'clean' sport to its organizers, but even if true, this is not of itself a reason for locating that campaign outside the Treaty. Anti-doping rules certainly have economic

---

18   For criticism of the CFI judgment, see S. Weatherill, 'Anti-doping rules and EC Law' (2005) *European Competition Law Review*, 416.
19   Case T-313/02 [2004] ECR II-3291.
20   Para. 37.
21   Para. 49.

effects on those found to have contravened them. Attempts to present such rules as 'sporting' and not 'economic' are unhelpful. They are both.

The notion that there is in principle a separation between sporting rules (which escape the scope of application of EC law) and rules of an economic nature (which do not) reflects the nature of the EC as an institution possessing a set of attributed competences, of which sport is not one.[22] This, in fact, is the core of the 'no overlap' thesis: there is sports governance and there is EC law, and there is no overlap between the two. But the implications of sporting activity leak beyond what the CFI labels 'noble competition' and are commonly economically highly significant; while EC law, though not explicitly aimed at sport by the Treaty, has a broad functional reach because so few activities exert no economic impact. The CFI's attempt in *Meca-Medina* to assert 'no overlap' was doubtless a source of delight to sports federations, for such an analysis maximizes the room for sporting autonomy, but it is constitutionally deeply unconvincing. Rules governing the composition of national sports teams or the conduct of anti-doping controls may plausibly define the nature of sporting competition, in the sense that the very existence of sporting endeavour is undermined without such rules. They are sporting rules. But they are not *purely* sporting rules. They visibly have economic repercussions (for players most of all). What is really at stake is not a group of sporting rules and a separate group of economic rules, but rather a group of sporting rules which carry economic implications and which therefore fall for assessment, but not necessarily condemnation, under EC trade law.

This was the approach preferred by the ECJ on appeal. It is, of course, one which embraces the overlap of legal orders, that of the EC and that arranged by sports federations. In *Meca-Medina and Majcen* v *Commission* the ECJ dismissed the swimmers' application for annulment of the Commission Decision rejecting their complaint, but it corrected the legal analysis put forward by the CFI.[23]

The ECJ began by adding *Meca-Medina* to the list of cases in which it has asserted that 'sport is subject to Community law in so far as it constitutes an economic activity within the meaning of Article 2 EC'. It added that the prohibitions contained in Articles 39 and 49 EC 'do not affect rules concerning questions which are of purely sporting interest and, as such, have nothing to do with economic activity', citing *Walrave and Koch*. It then referred to 'the difficulty of severing the economic aspects from the sporting aspects of a sport' (which of course derives from *Bosman*, though that ruling is not cited in

---

[22]   Article 5(1) EC, vigorously applied by the Court in Case C-376/98 *Germany* v *Parliament and Council* [2000] ECR I-8419 in finding the 'Tobacco Advertising' Directive invalid.

[23]   Case C-519/04 P cited above fn. 15.

connection with this phrase), confirming its view that the free movement provisions 'do not preclude rules or practices justified on non-economic grounds which relate to the particular nature and context of certain sporting events', adding in line with long-standing judicial practice that such a restriction on the scope of the provisions in question must remain limited to its proper objective.

The Court then stated that 'the mere fact that a rule is purely sporting in nature does not have the effect of removing from the scope of the Treaty the person engaging in the activity governed by that rule or the body which has laid it down'.[24] And if the sporting activity in question falls within the scope of the Treaty, the rules which govern that activity must satisfy the requirements of the Treaty 'which, in particular, seek to ensure freedom of movement for workers, freedom of establishment, freedom to provide services, or competition'.[25] It is most likely this part of the judgment which carries most long-term significance. It is a rejection of the notion that a 'purely sporting' rule is of itself apt to escape the scope of application of the Treaty and therefore does not need to comply with the expectations of EC trade law. The equivocation of *Walrave and Koch* is abandoned. This part of the judgment is instead, I believe, an embrace of the 'overlap' analysis (an admission that a practice may be of a sporting nature) and perhaps even 'purely sporting' in *intent*, but that it must be tested against the demands of EC trade law where it exerts economic *effects*.[26]

The CFI was adjudged to have made an error of law in assuming that purely sporting rules which have nothing to do with economic activity and which therefore do not fall within the scope of Articles 39 EC and 49 EC equally have nothing to do with the economic relationships of competition, with the result that they also do not fall within the scope of Articles 81 EC and 82 EC. Instead the specific requirements of Articles 81 and 82 should be considered. In the absence of such analysis, the contested judgment was therefore set aside. However, the ECJ did not remit the case to the CFI. In accordance with Article 61 of the Statute of the Court of Justice, it felt it appropriate to give judgment on the substance of the appellants' claims for annulment of the Commission decision rejecting their complaint. And it rejected their applica-

---

[24] Para. 27.
[25] Para. 28.
[26] Note that another implication of the ECJ's approach, in contrast to that of the CFI, is a strengthening of the argument that the EC has a competence to develop a legislative approach in the area of anti-doping: cf. A. Vermeersch, 'The European Union and the fight against doping in sport: on the field or on the sidelines?', *Entertainment and Sports Law Journal*, **4**(1), available via http://www2. warwick.ac.uk/fac/soc/law/elj/eslj/. It is, of course, open to question how useful the *exercise* of any such EC competence might be.

tion. It took the view that the general objective of the rules was to combat doping in order for competitive sport to be conducted on a fair basis; and the effect of penalties on athletes' freedom of action must be considered to be inherent in the anti-doping rules. Restrictions must be limited to what is necessary to ensure the proper conduct of competitive sport, and this relates to both defining the crime of doping and selecting penalties.[27] An excessive intervention into an athlete's freedom would generate unlawful adverse effects on competition,[28] but in the case the appellants had failed to establish that the Commission made a manifest error of assessment in finding the rules on quantities of permitted nandrolone to be justified. Nor, in the absence of pleading by the appellants, would it treat the penalties imposed as excessive. The Court is wary of questioning the expertise practised by sports federations, a caution which is typical of a court or tribunal in sports cases,[29] but it will not place such practices beyond the scope of judicial review as a matter of principle.[30] The Court considered that the rules did not constitute a restriction of competition incompatible with the Common Market, within the meaning of Article 81 EC, since they pursued a legitimate objective and were no more restrictive than was necessary to achieve it.[31]

So the swimmers lost. But it is crucial for the development of the law that they lost *not* because the rules were treated as 'purely sporting' in nature and therefore immune from EC law's overlap. Put another way, EC law affords sporting bodies a *conditional* autonomy. FINA's anti-doping law and practice met the conditions and so the ban on the swimmers was not upset.

FITTING *MECA-MEDINA* AND *MAJCEN* INTO THE FRAMEWORK OF EC TRADE LAW

In *Meca-Medina and Majcen* the ECJ was prepared in principle to put sporting practices to the test under Article 81, but it was also prepared to invest that test with recognition of the particular context in which sport is organized. So

---

[27] Para. 48.

[28] Para. 47.

[29] Cf. K. Foster, '*Lex Sportiva* and *Lex Ludica*: the Court of Arbitration for sport's jurisprudence', *Entertainment and Sports Law Journal*, **3**(2), available via http://www2.warwick.ac.uk/fac/soc/law/elj/eslj/.

[30] Of course in Europe there is a great diversity in the approaches chosen at national level: e.g. for refusal under English law to employ public law principles as a basis of review of decisions of sporting bodies, see *R* v *Disciplinary Committee of the Jockey Club ex parte Aga Khan* [1993] 1 WLR 909.

[31] Para. 45.

EC trade law overlaps with 'internal' sports law, but it absorbs, albeit not uncritically, the special expectations of sports governance.

In reaching this conclusion the ECJ was not creating a walled garden of EC sports competition law. Quite the contrary: it connected its analysis to existing precedents in the interpretation of Article 81 EC which have no material association with the sports sector. The ECJ stated:

> the compatibility of rules with the Community rules on competition cannot be assessed in the abstract (see, to this effect, Case C-250/92 *DLG* [1994] ECR I-5641, paragraph 31). Not every agreement between undertakings or every decision of an association of undertakings which restricts the freedom of action of the parties or of one of them necessarily falls within the prohibition laid down in Article 81(1) EC. For the purposes of application of that provision to a particular case, account must first of all be taken of the overall context in which the decision of the association of undertakings was taken or produces its effects and, more specifically, of its objectives. It has then to be considered whether the consequential effects restrictive of competition are inherent in the pursuit of those objectives (*Wouters and Others*, paragraph 97) and are proportionate to them.[32]

Anti-doping rules cannot simply be excluded from the scope of review pursuant to EC competition law by reference to their role in ensuring fair play. They must be examined in their proper context, including recognition of their economic effect. But placing the rules within the ambit of the Treaty does not mean they will be forbidden by it. The general objective of the rules was to combat doping in order for competitive sport to be conducted on a fair basis; and the effect of penalties on athletes' freedom of action must be considered to be inherent in the anti-doping rules. This *contextual* examination of the rules was crucial in the Court's conclusion that rules affected the athletes' freedom of action but that they did not constitute a restriction of competition incompatible with the Common Market within the meaning of Article 81(1) EC.

The linkage made in *Meca-Medina and Majcen* to the judgment in *Wouters*[33] is of potentially immense significance. *Wouters* too is an 'overlap judgment'. It had nothing whatsoever to do with sport. The Court was asked to consider the compatibility with Article 81 EC of a Dutch rule forbidding the creation of multidisciplinary partnerships involving barristers and accountants. The Court took the view that the national rule 'has an adverse effect on competition and may affect trade between Member States'.[34] A multidisciplinary partnership could offer a wider range of services, as well as benefiting

---

[32]   Para. 42.
[33]   Case C-309/99 *J.C.J. Wouters, J.W. Savelbergh, Price Waterhouse Belastingadviseurs BV* v *Algemene Raad van de Nederlandse Orde van Advocaten* [2002] ECR I-1577.
[34]   Para. 86 of the judgment.

from economies of scale generating cost reductions. The prohibition was therefore liable to limit production and technical development within the meaning of (what is now) Article 81(1)(b) EC.

Having found unambiguously that the 'rules restrict competition',[35] the Court proceeded to state that, for the purposes of application of Article 81, account must 'be taken of the overall context in which the decision of the association of undertakings was taken or produces its effects. More particularly, account must be taken of its objectives. . . . It has then to be considered whether the consequential effects restrictive of competition are inherent in the pursuit of those objectives'.[36]

Here, the purpose of the rules prohibiting partnerships between barristers and accountants was to guarantee the independence and loyalty to the client of members of the Bar as part of a broader concern to secure the sound administration of justice. Though there were, the Court repeated, 'effects restrictive of competition'[37] they did not go beyond what was necessary in order to ensure the proper functioning of the legal profession in the Netherlands. There was no breach of Article 81 EC.

The statement of principle that the notion of a restriction falling within Article 81(1) must be assessed in context is readily capable of broader application. In the case of sport, the reasoning in *Wouters* invites an argument that the overall context in which sports regulation occurs, built around pursuit of a broad objective of fair competition, produces effects which, though apparently restrictive of competition, are nonetheless inherent in the pursuit of those objectives and therefore permitted. This is the route chosen by the ECJ in *Meca-Medina and Majcen.*

In fact, in *Meca-Medina and Majcen* the Commission had explicitly quoted the judgment in *Wouters* in its Decision.[38] It concluded that there could be no true sport without anti-doping controls and that accordingly there was no breach of Article 81 EC.[39] By contrast, the CFI had sidelined *Wouters* for reasons that were logical once it had chosen to analyse the anti-doping rules as 'purely sporting'. The CFI considered that *Wouters* concerned 'market conduct', an 'essentially economic activity, that of lawyers'. Anti-doping cannot be likened to market conduct without distorting the nature of sport, which 'in its very essence . . . has nothing to do with any economic consideration'.[40] The

---

35 Para. 94.
36 Para. 97.
37 Para. 110.
38 Cited above fn. 16, p. 10.
39 Under a similar analysis, nor, in my view, would there be a breach of the free movement provisions.
40 Para. 65 (CFI).

Commission's reliance on *Wouters* was, however, not fatal to the validity of its Decision, largely because the Commission persuaded the CFI at the oral hearing that this was an analysis performed 'in the alternative' or more 'for the sake of completeness'.[41] The core of the Commission's approach was to find anti-doping rules 'purely sporting' in nature, a conclusion of which the CFI approved, as an aspect of its basic refusal to accept that EC trade law 'overlaps' with sporting practice. But in *Meca-Medina* this approach was not accepted by the ECJ in the part of the judgment that will carry most important long-term resonance. As mentioned, at paragraph 27 the ECJ states that 'the mere fact that a rule is purely sporting in nature does not have the effect of removing from the scope of the Treaty the person engaging in the activity governed by that rule or the body which has laid it down'. In its treatment of the substance of the application the ECJ does not even bother to mention the 'purely sporting' rule. A bold but sustainable interpretation of the ECJ decision in *Meca-Medina and Majcen* would hold that the so-called rule of 'purely sporting interest', originating in *Walrave and Koch*, has now been eliminated as a basis for immunizing sports rules which have an economic effect from review under EC law. All that can be intended by the 'purely sporting rule' is a reference to the small category of rules which govern sport but which are devoid of economic effect – such as the offside rule and fixing the height of goalposts. In the unlikely event that such rules were to provoke litigation, they would be found to lie outside the scope of the EC Treaty.

So *Wouters*, absorbed by *Meca-Medina*, offers itself as the basis for understanding the scope of sporting autonomy permitted by Article 81 EC. There is an overlap between EC law and 'internal' sports law but the peculiar demands of the latter may be used to nourish a submission that an apparent restriction is nevertheless an essential element in sports governance. This is roughly how *Meca-Medina* itself was decided by the ECJ. Competition lawyers will certainly wish to reflect on how far this reasoning stretches. In its judgment the ECJ moves seamlessly between case law which insists that an agreed restriction on commercial freedom is not to be treated as a restriction on competition within Article 81(1) EC provided it is necessary to ensure that the relevant arrangements function properly[42] and *Wouters* itself, where a restric-

---

41   Para. 62 (CFI).
42   For example, Case C-250/92 *Gottrup Klim* v *DLB* [1994] ECR I-5641, cited by the ECJ in para. 42 of *Meca-Medina and Majcen*. In Case T-328/03 *O2 (Germany)* v *Commission* [2006] ECR I-1231 the CFI treated that decision as a particular manifestation of a wider principle that insists that an agreement be considered in its true context: 'The examination required in the light of Article 81(1) EC consists essentially in taking account of the impact of the agreement on existing and potential competition . . . and the competition situation in the absence of the agreement . . . those two factors being intrinsically linked' (para. 71).

tion of competition is acknowledged but no violation of Article 81(1) EC is found provided those restrictive effects are inherent in the pursuit of legitimate objectives.[43] Both approaches have important implications for the structure of Article 81 EC: allowing practices to escape subjection to Article 81(1) EC curtails the importance of Article 81(3) EC, which affects the way arguments about the economics of competition are loaded into Article 81 EC cases, as well as affecting more practical matters such as the burden of proof. In principle, however, these lines of case law are capable of being treated as analytically distinct.[44] The fear generated by the second approach, but not the first, is that *Wouters* may cause the interpretation of Article 81(1) EC to become infected by all manner of obscure 'non-economic' values. The Court has not used *Meca-Medina* to provide clear guidance on that broader debate about the future of Article 81(1), which has important descriptive and normative dimensions that will not be entered into here, save only to note the deep anxiety of some competition lawyers lest their field be polluted by hostile values.[45] These 'overlap' cases are deeply sensitive.[46] Probably, however, *Meca-Medina* should *not* be read as favouring a wider application of *Wouters*. The Court has run together two analytically distinct lines of case law because in sport (but not necessarily more generally) they are functionally equivalent. The heart of the legal analysis asks whether the challenged rules, which exert a prejudicial economic effect on those excluded from participation by them, are necessary to achieve legitimate objectives. If so – but only if so – they do not infringe Article 81(1) EC. In sports cases it does not matter whether one's conclusion is that there is no restriction of competition or that there is a restriction of competition which is permitted. Whichever line of analysis is followed, the result should be the same: context is all. *Wouters* is fit for the purpose of examining how the law should treat sporting rules that define the nature of the activity but have an

---

[43] Para. 42 of the judgment, set out above (text attached to fn. 32), also para. 45.

[44] For an exploration of the nuances in the relevant case law, see R. Whish, *Competition Law* (London: Butterworths, 2003), pp. 115–28.

[45] See, e.g., with differing points of emphasis, O. Odudu, *The Boundaries of EC Competition Law: the Scope of Article 81* (OUP, 2006); R. Nazzini, 'Article 81 EC between time present and time past: a normative critique of restriction of competition in EU law' (2006), **43**, *C.M.L.Rev.*, 497; E. Loozen, 'Professional ethics and restraints of competition' (2006), **31**, *E.L.Rev.*, 28; A. Komninos, 'Non-competition concerns: resolution of conflicts in the integrated Article 81 EC', University of Oxford Centre for Competition Law and Policy Working Paper (L) 08/05, available via http://www.competition-law.ox.ac.uk/competition/portal.php; S. de Vries, *Tensions within the Internal Market: the Functioning of the Internal Market and the Development of Horizontal and Flanking Policies* (Gronigen: Europa Law Publishing, 2006), esp. pp. 189–98.

[46] Case C-67/96 *Albany International* [1999] ECR I-5751 is another important 'overlap' case, dealing with social/labour market policy and competition policy.

impact on (would-be) participants, as it was fit for the purpose of dealing with rules of the Dutch bar association in the case itself. But this does not mean it is helpful as a general tool in the interpretation of Article 81 EC beyond cases involving rules established by non-State actors to govern the conduct of a profession.

In fact, it seems that the rules of sporting federations need to be assessed in the same contextually sensitive way whichever Treaty provision they happen to be attacked under. The possibility that they fall under Articles 49, 81 and 82 EC again reveals their unusual, if not quite *sui generis*, quasi-regulatory nature. For sport, there should be a convergence between the economic law provisions of the Treaty. But this claim requires some explanatory support.

Meca-Medina does not authoritatively decide that EC trade law generally applies to sport under this 'contextually sensitive' reasoning. The case concerns only Article 81 EC. Indeed, the fact that the ECJ concluded that the CFI had made an error of law in assuming that purely sporting rules which have nothing to do with economic activity and which therefore do not fall within the scope of Articles 39 EC and 49 EC equally have nothing to do with the economic relationships of competition, with the result that they also do not fall within the scope of Articles 81 EC and 82 EC, may be read as a firm rejection of any 'convergence' thesis.

Not so, in my view. It is submitted that the reasoning found in *Meca-Medina* is apt for transplant to all the provisions of the Treaty that apply to sport. The ECJ in *Meca-Medina and Majcen* rebukes the CFI for failing to separate out the different detailed elements at stake in an analysis under Articles 39 and 49 EC, on the one hand, and Articles 81 and 82 EC, on the other, but I do not think the ECJ is doing anything more remarkable than drawing attention to the CFI's neglect of possible detailed differences between the provisions, which could encompass personal scope, need for market analysis, the role of 'internal situations', burden of proof and so on.[47] The ECJ is not making any deeper normative criticism of the convergence thesis. My own view is that it would be unsatisfactory for a practice that is considered necessary for the organization of sport under the free movement provisions then to be condemned under the competition rules, and it would be equally unsatisfactory for a practice that is treated necessary for the organization of sport under the competition rules to be found incompatible with the free movement provisions. There is and should be an ultimate functional comparability between the inquiries conducted under these economic law provisions in order to discover the scope of conditional autonomy properly allowed to sporting

---

[47]   So the ECJ, in paragraphs 32–3, is merely drawing attention to the inadequacy of paragraph 42 in the CFI's judgment.

bodies. If rules are shown to be necessary for the effective organization of sport, then they are not incompatible with EC trade law, whichever provision is invoked. And, as a corollary, where the restrictive effect trespasses beyond what is necessary to achieve the rule's proper objective, the basic Treaty prohibitions bite. So, by insisting on sensitive appraisal of sporting rules in their proper context, I argue here for 'convergence in outcome' between free movement law and the competition rules. And I share the view that there is a methodological comparability in the general trend in EC economic law to allow a 'softening' of basic Treaty provisions by reference to factors other than those expressly set out in the derogations contained in the Treaty (Articles 30, 46, 81(3) EC).[48] So competition law overlaps with concerns for the administration of justice and social policy just as free movement law overlaps with consumer protection law,[49] environmental law,[50] social security and welfare law,[51] taxation[52] and even the maintenance of public order and the safeguarding of internal security.[53] Trade law is a rich mixture of regulatory concerns and the dynamic project of economic integration compels the development of a much more elaborate structuring of priorities than the skeletal terms of the Treaty foresee.[54] In the case of sport, this rich mixture should lead to 'convergence in outcome' across the several relevant provisions of EC economic law, and I do not think *Meca-Medina* is in any way inconsistent with that approach. In fact, *Meca-Medina*'s acceptance that the anti-doping rules did not constitute a restriction of competition incompatible with Article 81 EC, since they pursued a legitimate objective, is functionally aligned with the Court's Article 39 judgment in *Bosman* which accepts as 'legitimate' the perceived sports-specific anxiety to maintain a

---

[48]   See R. Nazzini, 'Article 81 EC between time present and time past: a normative critique of restriction of competition in EU law' (2006), **43**, *C.M.L.Rev.*, 497. Also on convergence, see K. Mortelmans, 'Towards convergence in the application of the rules on free movement and on competition' (2001), **38**, *CMLRev.*, 613. Cf. S. Weatherill, ' "Fair play please!": recent developments in the application of EC law to sport' (2003), **40**, *CMLRev.*, 51, 80–86; R. O'Loughlin, 'EC competition rules and free movement rules: an examination of the parallels and their furtherance by the ECJ *Wouters* decision' [2003] *ECLR*, 62.

[49]   E.g. Case 120/78 *Rewe-Zentrale AG v Bundesmonopolverwaltung für Branntwein* [1979] ECR 649; Case 382/87 *Buet* [1989] ECR 1235.

[50]   Case C-379/98 *Preussen Elektra* [2001] ECR I-2099.

[51]   Cf., e.g., Case C-512/03 *J E J Blankaert* [2005] ECR I-7685; Case C-372/04 *ex parte Watts* [2006] ECR I-4325, para. 121.

[52]   Cf., e.g., Case C-446/03 *Marks and Spencer v Halsey* [2005] ECR I-10837.

[53]   Case C-265/95 *Commission v France* [1997] ECR I-6959.

[54]   I argue that this is a reason for scepticism that the EU Charter effects a qualititative change in EC trade law in 'The Internal Market', ch. 7 in S. Peers and A. Ward (eds), *The EU Charter of Fundamental Rights: Politics, Law and Policy* (Oxford: Hart Publishing, 2004). For an extended investigation, see De Vries, cited above at fn. 45.

balance between clubs by preserving a certain degree of equality and uncertainty as to results and to encourage the recruitment and training of young players[55] and the finding in *Deliège*, an Article 49 EC case, that selection rules limited the number of participants in a tournament, but were 'inherent' in the event's organization.[56] Such rules are not beyond the reach of the Treaty, but they are not incompatible with its requirements.

THE IMPACT OF *MECA-MEDINA AND MAJCEN*: SOME OLDER DECISIONS VIEWED WITH THE ADVANTAGE OF HINDSIGHT

Let us now revert to *Walrave and Koch*. The result is right, but the reasoning is flawed. Let us now abandon the claim that selection policies for national representative teams are rules of 'purely sporting interest'. Instead the key to the ruling is that economic effects of the rule are a necessary consequence of their contribution to the structure of sports governance. So nationality rules governing the composition of national representative teams do have an economic effect – by confining the opportunities enjoyed by players to choose which country to play for, by structuring international football in a way that appeals to spectators, sponsors and so on – but they serve to define the very endeavour of international competition, the character of which would be destroyed without such rules, whereas, by contrast, nationality-based discrimination in club football has economic effects, but the Court will *not* treat it as inherent in the organization of the game and therefore it is fatally exposed to the EC Treaty's prohibition of nationality-based discrimination contained in Article 12 EC as well as, in appropriate cases, other prohibitions too (such as Article 39 EC in *Bosman*).

The *Wouters* formula, absorbed by *Meca-Medina*, has therefore been used to allow the peculiar features of sport to inform the application of the relevant legal rules. It represents the triumph of the 'overlap' thesis. So, for example, this analytical framework can cope satisfyingly with the following:

- rules governing selection of individuals for teams participating in high-level international competition – which are restrictive but necessary;[57]
- rules framing transfer windows – which are restrictive but necessary to create the conditions for fair competition, especially in the later stages

---

55   Case C-415/93 cited above at fn. 3, para. 106.
56   Cases C-51/96 & C-191/97 cited above at fn. 10, paras 64, 69.
57   Cases C-51/96 & C-191/97 *Deliège* v *Ligue de Judo* [2000] ECR I-2549.

of a tournament, but only provided they do not vary according to the origin of the player;[58]

- rules limiting ticket sales for major events to particular nationals or residents – which are restrictive and unnecessary, so unlawful;[59]
- rules forbidding multiple ownership of football clubs.[60] Eliminating any suspicion of match-fixing is indispensable to genuine sporting competition, and therefore any consequent restriction on commercial opportunity to acquire clubs is not regarded as a restriction falling foul of Article 81(1) EC.

My argument is not at all that this line of reasoning makes it simple to discover what rules are necessary for the effective organization of sport. My argument is that the *Wouters* line of analysis ensures that the right questions are asked. It prevents intellectually wasteful arguments about what is 'sporting' and what is 'commercial', and instead embraces the overlap of the two spheres. Then, within that zone of overlap, there is room for serious discussion of what is necessary for and/or inherent in the structure of sports governance. So, for example, might 'salary caps' be treated as restrictions on commercial freedom that are nonetheless necessary in the delivery of a viable sporting competition and therefore not restrictions within the meaning of EC trade law? *Wouters*, absorbed in *Meca-Medina*, provides the appropriate legal framework for analysis.[61] Similarly, *Bosman* heralded the demise of the prevailing system for transfer of players between clubs, for the challenged rules were treated as restrictive and inapt to achieve their claimed objectives.[62] However, there remains scope for debate about the permitted shape of a modified transfer system and the analysis should follow that set forth in *Meca-Medina and Majcen*, that is, is a modified system no more restrictive than necessary to achieve the objectives recognized by the Court in *Bosman* as legitimate?[63]

---

[58] Case C-176/96 *Lehtonen et al.* v *FRSB* [2000] ECR I-2681.

[59] Dec. 2000/12 *1998 Football World Cup* [2000] OJ L5/55. For comment, see S. Weatherill, '0033149875354: Fining the Organisers of the 1998 Football World Cup' (2000), *European Competition Law Review*, 275.

[60] COMP 37.806 ENIC/ UEFA, IP/02/942, 27 June 2002.

[61] Cf. S. Hornsby, 'The harder the cap, the softer the law?' (2002), **10**, *Sport and the Law Journal*, 142; J. Taylor and M. Newton, 'Salary caps – the legal analysis' (2003), **11**, *Sport and the Law Journal*, 158; N. Bitel, 'Salary caps: lawful, workable and imminent' (2004), **12**, *Sport and the Law Journal*, 132.

[62] Case C-415/93 cited above, fn. 3.

[63] Case C-415/93 cited above, fn. 3, para. 106. On the revised version that has been subsequently introduced, see B. Dabscheck, 'The globe at their feet: FIFA's new employment rules' (2004), **7**, *Culture, Sport and Society*, 69; J.-C. Drolet, 'Extra time: are the new FIFA transfer rules doomed?' (2006) **1**(2), *International Sports Law Journal*, 66.

Even though the Court has taken a firm line on nationality discrimination (allowed in selection for national teams, but not at club level) this does not preclude arguments that it is wrong or, at least, that its approach is inapt for all sports. On the first argument, that the Court is wrong,[64] it was pressed on the Court in *Bosman* that the influx of footballing migrants that would follow the abolition of nationality-based quotas in club football would diminish the opportunities available to aspiring local players, and so drain the pool of players from which the national side is picked. But the Court calmly replied that footballers may find their home labour market less hospitable but that they could expect compensation in the shape of new prospects of employment in other Member States.[65] This is an orthodox statement of the transformative effect of market integration, but it misses the point. In football, integration of the labour market will not create more jobs. The number of clubs will remain stable. And it is improbable that, absent quotas, the same distribution of players by nationality will prevail. States that supply a lot of skilled labour will be able to take advantage of access to newly opened markets, while less productive States with clubs that can afford to import players will find they lose the share of local players they were previously able to protect. So the pool of players available to the national team will in some States dwindle in size, jeopardizing the strength of that State's national team. Perhaps that is simply a price international teams must pay in order to improve labour mobility in line with the demands of EC trade law. That, however, is not what the Court said in *Bosman*. It denied there is a price. But there is. On the second argument, that the Court's approach may fit football but is inapt for application to other sports, one may by way of illustration refer to cricket where, unlike football, professional activity outside the international arena exists only because of large subsidies from the international game. Accordingly, there are good arguments that some degree of discrimination operating at levels of the game below the national team in favour of those qualified for selection for the national team, designed to deepen the pool of available strong players, is necessary for the sport's very existence.[66]

---

64   It is now largely forgotten that Advocate General Trabucchi in *Donà* v *Mantero*, cited above at fn. 2, had been prepared to be much more receptive to the maintenance of discrimination even in club football. See also J.-P. Dubey, *La libre circulation des sportifs en Europe* (Berne: Staempfli Editions/Brussels: Bruylant, 2000), esp. ch. 5, making arguments in the same area as, though not identical to, those in the text.

65   Para. 134 of the judgment in Case C-415/93, cited above, at fn. 3.

66   Cf. S. Boyes, 'Caught behind or following-on: cricket, the European Union and the "*Bosman* Effect" ', *Entertainment and Sports Law Journal*, 3(1), available via http://www2.warwick.ac.uk/fac/soc/law/elj/eslj/.

I do not here take a stand on these intriguing controversies. Rather, I dip into them in order to confirm that *Wouters*, absorbed in *Meca-Medina*, does not offer an uncontroversial formula for adjudicating disputes about how far EC law demands sport to change. Rather, it offers a statement of the *conditional* autonomy of sports federations under Article 81 EC, but, crucially, it pushes the correct questions about the extent to which sport is freed from the orthodox assumptions of EC law to the fore. In short, are these rules *necessary*? Moreover, as suggested above, this approach is capable of application in a functionally comparable manner to provide routes under other relevant provisions of EC trade law to ensure scope for continued application of proper sporting practices. Such practices might survive inspection against the requirements of the Treaty but not because they are devoid of economic effect. Such rules are not, as a category, outwith the scope of the Treaty, but, provided they are shown to be necessary elements in sports governance, the conclusion is that they do not fall foul of the network of provisions regulating trade under the Treaty.

THE *OULMERS* CASE: PUTTING *MECA-MEDINA* TO THE TEST

Under FIFA's rules governing the release of players for international representative matches, clubs must release players – their employees – for a defined period of time and for a defined group of matches. The rules make no provision for the clubs to receive payment. The clubs, not the national association or the international federations, are explicitly stated to be responsible for the purchase of insurance to cover the risk that the player will be injured when playing for his country. Even if the player is not injured, he will arrive back at his club tired. There is no question of compensation for the club. This system seems imbalanced. Is it lawful?

Litigation is under way. In Belgium, Charleroi found that a highly promising young player, Oulmers, returned seriously injured in November 2004 from international duty with his home country, Morocco. Charleroi's fortunes on the field slumped without their young star, while they continued to have to pay his wages. They were entitled to no compensation. They brought a case before the Belgian courts, claiming damages from FIFA, alleging a violation of Article 82 EC. The case was the subject of an intervention supportive of Charleroi's case by the G-14 group of 18 (!) major clubs, who pay the highest wages and consequently have the largest incentive to procure adjustment of the current rules. FIFA, for its part, enjoyed the support of interventions from over 50 continental and national associations. In May 2006, the *Tribunal de Commerce* in Charleroi agreed to make an Article 234 preliminary reference to

Luxembourg.[67] It brushed aside a number of arguments advanced by football's governing bodies, some involving technical points of procedure, others of a more fundamental nature, some rooted in Belgian law, others arising under EC law. The *Tribunal* concluded that, as a matter of Belgian public policy, it would not defer to the jurisdictional exclusivity claimed by FIFA for the Court of Arbitration in Sport – doubtless an important finding on a point likely commonly to arise in such litigation. Of particular current relevance, the *Tribunal* was asked to treat the rules as purely sporting in nature. It considered the matter only briefly, and took the view that the complexity of the case law, combined with the transnational importance of the issue under examination, made this an appropriate case for referral to Luxembourg in search of an authoritative uniform interpretation of EC law.

That the Court in Charleroi refused to set aside the commercial implications of the rule, and proceeded to make a reference to the ECJ despite the 'sporting' context, is doubtless of tactical value to the clubs. However, in line with the case advanced in this chapter, this is not to make any assumption that the economic context overrides the sporting. The point is that both value systems are involved. The test will be to assess whether the player release rules survive being put to the test under EC law. If they do not, the damages claim will proceed, raising in its turn some fiendishly difficult questions of causation and quantification of loss in the context of an activity as unpredictable as football.

And *Wouters* will surely supply the relevant framework for analysis in Luxembourg, given its ready acceptance by the ECJ in *Meca-Medina*. Account must be taken of 'the overall context in which the decision of the association of undertakings was taken or produces its effects. More particularly, account must be taken of its objectives . . . It has then to be considered whether the consequential effects restrictive of competition are inherent in the pursuit of those objectives'. That needs to be adjusted to take account of the role of Article 82 EC, but it is the consistent assumption of this chapter that the same basic analysis does and should apply: that is, the essence of the inquiry asks whether the objectives pursued by the practice can be met by measures which exert a less prejudicial impact on affected parties. If so, the practice is unlawful: in Article 82 terms, it would not be proportionate, nor could it be held to be objectively justified.

EC law contains nothing that calls into question the legitimacy of international football, and there is nothing that would rule out *a priori* action taken by football governing bodies to protect and promote international football.

---

[67]   The ruling is available via the *Tribunal*'s website: http://www.tcch.be/. The case is Pending Case C-243/06, referred to the European Court by the Tribunal de Commerce de Charleroi in May 2006. For background, see S. Weatherill, 'Is the pyramid compatible with EC law?' (2005) **3**(4), *International Sports Law Journal*, 3.

Nevertheless, such measures would be classic examples of measures taken for sporting reasons which also have economic effects for those clubs which get their players back in a state of disrepair. If clubs were free to choose whether to release players, international football would be reduced to a competition dependent on the whims of clubs. So mandatory player release seems indispensable if international football is to survive. But is *this* system of mandatory player release necessary to achieve that end?

International football is extraordinarily lucrative, yet the clubs, who provide the players, their often highly-paid employees, as indispensable resources to adorn the major tournaments, receive no direct financial benefit. Any advantage they receive arrives only indirectly, via proceeds transferred to the national association of which they are a member. Football's 'pyramid' structure of governance rules out any direct formal contact between clubs and international governing bodies, instead routing the representation of club interests through national associations. One may also note that there is an element of competition at stake. International football tournaments are to some extent in the same market as club competitions for potential interest from broadcasters and sponsors. So clubs are required to provide a free resource, the players, to an undertaking that is at least in part seeking to make profits from exactly the same sources on which the clubs would wish to draw. In this way sports federations' activities as regulators spill over into the commercial sphere, creating conflicts of interest. One would not find anything like obligatory and uncompensated supply of resources to a competitor in a normal industry. Sport truly is special.

The crispest objection to the system is that mandatory player release is necessary, but not in a form that leaves clubs uncompensated. The arrangements can be treated as compatible with EC law only provided clubs are allowed to defray at least part, if not all, of the cost of paying their players while they are absent on international duty by being allowed access to the pot of gold accumulated by the organization of international football tournaments.

I find this convincing. Admittedly, exposure to a wider audience watching international representative football raises the value of the player to the club, so clubs conceivably acquire an indirect benefit from international football. But that is no reason for arguing for a system of mandatory uncompensated release of the extreme type that currently prevails. It is merely a basis for considering whether players' wages need not be paid in full out of the proceeds of international football. Similarly, although it is true that international bodies, unlike the clubs, have responsibilities to nurture the game throughout the world by sharing money raised from international tournaments, it is submitted that this too seems a plausible reason for running a system in which clubs cannot raid the entirety of the income generated by international football, not a good reason for denying the clubs *any* share in the money.

An apparently more promising argument would assert that some national associations are too poor to compensate clubs. This would mean that such associations would simply not pick highly-paid players. Countries would field teams that would not reflect their true strength, and the pattern of international competitions would be distorted. However, one could respond that international governing bodies could cope with this by establishing a revenue pool into which a slice of profits from international competitions could be paid before distribution to individual countries, and from which clubs could be compensated. Rich countries would subsidize poor countries from profits made through international football – at present clubs subsidize all countries despite taking no profits from international football. Is this feasible? Are there impediments to making such arrangements? That would require close analysis of the way that the industry works, and could work. The point is that it is precisely this inquiry that would and should follow from the adoption of the *Wouters* formula, absorbed in *Meca-Medina*, as the basis for the legal investigation. That the (mandatory, uncompensated) player release rules are of sporting interest in no way immunizes them from review. The route to securing shelter from condemnation under EC law is to demonstrate that their prejudicial economic effect is essential in order to preserve the activity of international football. It sees to me hard to make the case that the current extreme model is necessary in this sense.

Moreover, there is a procedural dimension to the submission that the current arrangements violate Article 82 EC. There is support in EC law for the case that sporting bodies' *conditional* autonomy in setting rules to govern the game depends on something more democratic than the 'pyramid'. Soft law material pertaining to sport issued at EU level has been a common feature of the last few years and, as the Court has made clear in *Deliège* and in *Lehtonen*,[68] this material is apt for citation in exploring the nature and scope of the relevant EC rules. The Declaration attached to the Nice Treaty includes consideration of the *Role of sports federations*. It refers inter alia to the need 'for a democratic and transparent method of operation' and 'a form of organisation providing a guarantee of sporting cohesion and participatory democracy'. Insistence on the virtues of participation chimes with the broader agenda mapped by the Commission in its 2001 White Paper on European Governance.[69] It is perfectly possible to argue that football's neglect of these broad recommendations of transparent and participatory governance serves as a powerful reason for arguing that practices imposed on clubs fall foul of EC

---

[68]   Cases C-51/96 & 191/97, cited above at fn. 57, paras 41–2 of the judgment; Case C-176/96, cited above at fn. 58, paras 32–3 of the judgment.

[69]   COM (2001) 428.

law.[70] It is not *necessary* for the federations to exclude direct input by clubs. A committee representing a wider range of affected interests could readily be set up to determine the balance of rights and obligations in this matter. By formalizing dialogue between transnational governing bodies and clubs-as-employers this, of course, would challenge the pure lines of the organizational 'pyramid'. It is an argument that has purchase in other contexts, such as the aspirations of the clubs to acquire a more direct role in the management of club tournaments such as UEFA's Champions League and to exert heavier influence over the management of the fixture calendar where, again, the governing bodies are enmeshed in a conflict of interest given their financial interest in the success of the competitions which yield them most direct benefit. It is no secret that the *Oulmers* litigation is an element in a broader political strategy pursued by richer clubs eager for a louder voice in the game's governance.

I take the view that the current rules governing mandatory uncompensated player release go too far, both in substance and in the exclusionary way they are agreed and administered. Large profits are made through international football, and it is abusive for federations to enforce rules which allow them to take the benefit while imposing the burden of supplying players on the clubs. I suspect that, just as in *Bosman* the Court did not rule out the possibility that a transfer system could be justified but would not accept the particular transfer system under attack in the case, so too in *Oulmers* the Court will conclude that a mandatory player release system is justifiable but that this one is not. One could readily imagine an adjusted and potentially lawful system involving an obligation to release players imposed on clubs with corresponding obligations imposed on the governing bodies to provide compensation (inter alia to take account of the element of market competition for broadcasting and sponsorship money which is also at stake in this matter of regulation). One could also envisage a much more radical, though doubtless politically less likely, adjustment of the structure of the game involving the stripping of profit-making functions out of the hands of sports federations, confining them strictly to a regulatory role shorn of any potential conflict of interest. The point of this chapter is that the ECJ in *Meca-Medina and Majcen* has prepared the ground for *Oulmers* to be decided with due recognition for both the sporting and the economic context of the player release rules, and has set aside the unhelpful separation between the spheres clumsily attempted by the CFI. Assuming I am correct to suppose that the current system is incompatible with

---

[70] The Treaty establishing a Constitution for Europe would have provided fertile supporting material in Article III-282(1)(g): Union action shall be aimed at 'developing the European dimension in sport, by promoting fairness and openness in sporting competitions and cooperation between bodies responsible for sports', but that document is now destined only for a humble home in footnotes.

Article 82 EC, that then allows relevant actors within the game to re-shape a new model. EC law does not dictate the precise dimensions of that replacement model, though, by precluding practices that do not meet the demands of the Treaty, it plainly steers choices in particular directions.

CONCLUSION

More than ten years ago I argued that the Court in *Bosman* was wrong to use the language of 'justification' in connection with sporting practices that escape condemnation under Community law.[71] In part my concern was that the precise juridical source and nature of that justification was troublingly elusive. Instead, I took the view that the correct way to understand a ruling such as *Walrave and Koch* was that the relevant discrimination (in selection for national teams) escaped the scope of application of the Treaty, not because it is 'justified'; that is to say, I argued for a solution rooted in the constitutional point that the EC possess only an attributed, not a general, competence. The Court has now done something different again, but it has chosen a solution which meets my concerns. It brings the challenged practice in principle within the reach of the Treaty's prohibitions, only to slide it back out again if shown to be necessary to achieve legitimate sporting objectives and/or inherent in the organization of sport. This is not justification in the orthodox sense covered by Articles 30 and 81(3) EC, but nor is it to place the practices outwith the Treaty. Rather, it is, it seems, to accept that some sporting practices fall within the scope of the Treaty but are not condemned by it. The Court may be criticized for its constitutional audacity, but what is at stake is a reading of EC trade law which connects the scope of the trade law prohibitions with the widening if rather fragmented and ambiguous scope of EC competence more generally. *Wouters* is the key: Article 81 EC is interpreted in the light of concern for values that are developed outwith the framework of competition law but which overlap with it, in a manner which is functionally comparable to the 'softening' of free movement law pioneered in *Cassis de Dijon*.[72]

Meca-Medina applies this model to sport and, for sport, it is a solution that works. The Court has taken a broad view of the scope of Community trade law, but, having brought sporting rules within the scope of the Treaty, it shows itself readily prepared to draw on the importance of matters not explicitly

---

[71]   In 'European Football Law', pp. 339–82, published in the *Collected Courses* of the 7th Session of the Academy of European Law, European University Institute, Florence (1999).

[72]   Case 120/78 *Rewe-Zentrale AG* v *Bundesmonopolverwaltung für Branntwein* [1979] ECR 649.

described as 'justifications' in the Treaty in order to permit the continued application of challenged practices which are shown to be necessary to achieve legitimate sporting objectives and/or are inherent in the organization of sport. That, then, becomes the core of the argument when EC law overlaps with sports governance: can a sport show why prejudicial economic effects (for some sportsmen) must be tolerated? This is a statement of the *conditional autonomy* of sports federations under EC law – an overlap between EC law and 'internal' sports law is recognized but within that area of overlap sporting bodies have room to show how and why the rules are necessary to accommodate their particular concerns (fair play, credible competition, national representative teams, and so on) just as good environmental practice plays a part in adjudicating free movement cases[73] and social policy concerns affect the checking of collective labour agreements under Article 81 EC.[74] The Court has shaped EC law so that it allows assessment of the strength of the competing interests at stake when sport intersects with the economic project mapped out by the EC Treaty. And the result of *Meca-Medina* itself demonstrates that the sporting expertise informing (*in casu*) anti-doping inquiries will not lightly be set aside by judges.

---

[73] Case C-379/98 *Preussen Elektra* [2001] ECR I-2099.
[74] Case C-67/96, cited above at fn. 46.

4. Competition and free movement issues in the regulation of Formula One motor racing

Adam Cygan

INTRODUCTION

The fundamental question considered throughout this book is whether sporting activity has, or should have, a special status in relation to its legal regulation. In the oft quoted *Bosman* judgment[1] the Court stated:[2]

> In view of the considerable social importance of sporting activities and in particular football in the Community, the aims of maintaining a balance between clubs by preserving a certain degree of equality and uncertainty as to results and of encouraging the recruitment and training of young players must be accepted as legitimate.

As both Szyszczak and Bogusz argue elsewhere in this volume sport fulfils an important sociocultural function which must be maintained. Yet sport, as a discipline which requires an institutional and regulatory structure, has altered radically from the Corinthian days of amateur sport, or even the postwar era, when professional sportsmen basked in the glory of on-field success rather than being motivated by financial gain. Today, while sport as a generic concept may be considered as a cultural pursuit with a distinct social function, it is not possible to place all sports within this definition. Though the social function that sport may play in the community is arguably present in the case of football, it is difficult to see how such an analysis can be extended to sports such as motor racing, where access to financial resources at *all* levels of the sport is a prerequisite for participation. In this sense motor racing generally, and Formula One in particular, is different from football and many other popular participatory sports. Though an amateur market may exist in football, which seeks to achieve the aims set out by the Court, there is no real equivalent in motor sports. Perhaps the difference can be summed up through the observa-

---

[1]   Case C-415/93 *URBSFA* v *Jean-Marc Bosman* [1995] ECR I-4921.
[2]   Ibid., at paragraph 106.

tion that in motor sport there is no equivalent level of amateur participation which exists in football where the 'jumpers for goalposts' metaphor characterizes the accessible nature of the sport.

It may therefore be appropriate to ask a different question to the one posed by Szyszczak. The question to answer may not be whether sport is special, but rather whether professional sport, performed at the highest level, has become primarily a commercial activity. That is not to suggest that on-field success is no longer important – it clearly is. But in the modern world of professional sport, on-field success is the catalyst to increased revenue and commercial opportunities which in many cases outstrip the income generated through on-field activities. It is for this reason that regulators, at all levels of governance, have become more interested in sport and increasingly so from a competition perspective. In the twenty-first century sport is big business and consequently has become subject to legal rules which traditionally were applied to undertakings manufacturing goods or providing services in commercial markets.

Formula One motor racing is the best example of such a sport/business crossover[3] where on-field, or more appropriately on-track success, provides proportionately limited revenues. Formula One motor racing has a combined global audience of around 1.9 billion people who followed the sport's annual 17 or 18 race programme. This will mean that, over the course of a season, over 100 sponsorship logos will flash before their eyes. Sponsorship alone brought in over €664m to F1's 11 teams in 2006[4] and the major multinational car manufacturers that own six of these teams invested well over a billion euros.[5] Yet the rewards for on-track success are by comparison miniscule. In 2006, a typical team received approximately €20m in prize money from the sport's commercial rights. This sum varies slightly according to the team's positions in the standings at the end of each season but, overall, it equates to 47 per cent of the previous year's television revenues. The teams currently receive no other share of the sport's revenues, though this situation will change when their current race contract expires in 2008. From 2008, a new, more commercially lucrative arrangement will provide a greater share of television

---

[3]   A typical manufacturer-backed F1 team has costs of around €170m, of which the biggest burden is the wage costs of a workforce of around 400 as well as the multi-million euro salaries of their drivers. In total, a team's wage bill comes to around €55m and this expense is matched by the sum they spend on testing and operations at F1 races. This expenditure is comparable to that of many successful medium sized enterprises.

[4]   Source: CNBC European Business; available at: http://www.european business.eu.com/features/2006/apr/formula.html.

[5]   The six car manufacturers – Ferrari, BMW, Mercedes, Renault, Honda and Toyota – are each spending between €150m and €300m on F1, providing around 80 V-8 engines and technical support to their teams.

and commercial revenues for the teams while simultaneously reducing the costs involved.

Any commercial venture operating on this scale is likely to attract the interest of regulators and, since the late 1990s, Formula One has been subject to several legislative developments and regulatory inquiries. In some instances, for example through the EU-wide ban on tobacco advertising, Formula One has been indirectly affected as an enduring beneficiary of tobacco sponsorship and from the start of the 2007 season no team will be sponsored by a tobacco company. By contrast, the 1999 Commission investigation into the abuse of a dominant position by Formula One's governing body, the FIA,[6] went to the heart of the way motor sport and its commercial exploitation is organized on an international scale. This inquiry raised specific competition law and policy issues which have, to varying degrees, been faced by other commercial entities which operate across the EU and generate the level of income seen in Formula One. When placed within this regulatory environment, Formula One, and arguably many professional sports which generate comparative revenues, has crossed the boundary from being considered as *just* a sport, to arguably an activity which is commercial first and sport second.

REGULATION OF SPORT BY THE EU: IS FORMULA ONE UNIQUE?

In the absence of specific Treaty provisions concerning the regulation of sport, it has been left to the general principles of Community law to provide the framework within which sport operates.[7] When applying these general principles of free movement and equality the Court has primarily been concerned with the impact upon the economic rights of individuals and paid less attention to the commercial activities of sporting federations. In *Walrave and Koch*,[8] the Court took a conservative approach as to the extent to which Community law would apply and suggested that this would be the case only when the rights under Articles 39 or 49 EC are infringed. The Court stated: 'the practice of sport is subject to Community law only in so far as it constitutes an economic activity within the meaning of Article 2 of the Treaty'.[9]

---

6   The Fédération Internationale de l'Automobile (FIA).
7   The EU is seeking to define a clearer position in relation to sporting activity and its regulation. See COM (99) 644 *Helsinki Report on Sport*. For an evaluation of this strategy see S. Weatherill, 'The Helsinki Report on Sport', (2000), **25**, *ELRev.*, 282.
8   Case 36/74 *Walrave and Koch* v *Union Cycliste Internationale et al.* [1974] ECR 1405.
9   Ibid., paragraph 4.

The requirement that the activity be economic in nature within the meaning of Article 2 EC applies in general to Articles 39, 43 and 49 EC.[10] The Court further stated in *Walrave*[11] that the Treaty provisions on the free movement of workers and services apply when such economic activity has 'the character of gainful employment or remunerated service'. Since *Walrave*, the Court has examined, most notably in *Bosman*, whether the practice of sport constitutes an economic activity, and has then proceeded to ascertain whether it is caught by either Articles 39 or 49 EC. However, the test laid down by the Court in *Walrave* was conceived to apply to the free movement provisions and would not appear to extend to Articles 81 and 82 EC. This is of note as the test in *Walrave* extends only to individual sports men and women and would seem to exclude sporting administrative bodies from its scope.[12] It could be argued that, when exercising their regulatory powers, sporting federations which operate in an anti-competitive manner *may* impede an athlete's right under Articles 39 and 49 EC.[13] In the case of Formula One racing and specifically the regulatory role of its governing body, the FIA, this regulatory function would seem to fit within the scope of Articles 39 and 49 EC and also be caught by EC Competition provisions.[14] If, as this chapter contends, Formula One is

---

[10] The economic nature of the activity was at issue in the non-sports case of Case 196/87 *Udo Steyman* v *Staassecretaris van Justitie* [1988] ECR 6159 which concerned the extent of application of Article 39 EC.

[11] *Walrave and Koch*, at paragraph 5.

[12] See S. Weatherill, 'Anti-doping rules and EC law' (2005), **26**(7), *ECLR*, 416 at 419, who is highly critical of the judgment in T-313/02 *David Meca-Medina and Igor Majcen* v *Commission* judgment of 30 September 2004. Weatherill argues that the CFI is wrong in this case to suggest that anti-doping measures are outside the scope of EC law and are 'purely sporting issues' and suggests that the application of such rules by a sporting authority may, in certain circumstances, affect both free movement and competition provisions. See also P. Colomo, 'The application of EC Treaty rules to sport: the approach of the European Court of First Instance in the Meca Medina and Piau cases', *ESLJ*, **3**(2), available at http://www2.warwick.ac.uk/fac/soc/law/elj/eslj/issues/volume3/number2/colomo/.

[13] One of the objections raised by the Commission during its inquiry into the FIA is that individual drivers could participate in FIA events only if they received a licence from the FIA. This is a prime example of regulatory powers being used to restrict rights under Articles 39 and 49 EC. In 1994, David Coulthard was in a contractual dispute with incumbent team Williams about a move to Mclaren the following year. Coulthard had a valid contract with Williams for the 1995 season but had also signed a contract with Mclaren. FIA threatened to withdraw his racing licence unless he honoured the agreement with Williams for 1995. Arguably, such a power goes beyond the criticism levelled at UEFA and national football associations in *Bosman*.

[14] On the relationship between sport and competition law generally, see C. Stix-Hackl and A. Egger, 'Sports and competition law: a never ending story' (2002), **23**(2), *ECLR*, 81.

more business than sport, the requirement of economic activity for Community law to bite would appear to satisfy both the definition of economic activity in *Walrave* and also that which is applied to the competition rules.

Professional sporting activity, the purpose of which is to maximize profits for its governing body, is in character no different from any other form of commercial venture and would fall within the concept of an economic activity. For the purposes of Articles 81 and 82 EC this will *prima facie* mean that individual sporting bodies, such as the FIA, which have sole responsibility for all regulatory and financial decisions concerning the sport, will be subject to the Community competition rules. In the case of *Höfner and Elser* v *Macroton*,[15] the Court defined an undertaking very broadly: 'the concept of an undertaking, in the context of competition law, covers any entity engaged in an economic activity, regardless of the legal status of the entity or the way it is funded'.

The concept of 'economic activity' under Articles 39 and 49 EC refers to the practice of sport by the athlete alleging the infringement of EC law. By contrast, the question of whether the athlete's activity is of an economic nature bears no consequences for the application of Articles 81 and 82 EC. Indeed, the economic nature of the activity is only important to the extent that it relates to the association of undertakings and/or the undertakings taking part in an agreement.

The assessment of the Court and the Commission when applying the competition rules in Articles 81 and 82 EC is different. While Articles 81 and 82 EC require, as much as Articles 39 and 49 EC, the exercise of an economic activity, this requirement is fulfilled if a given body can be qualified as an undertaking. This leads to the question of whether the *Walrave* test may be reconciled with the application of the competition provisions. In *Bosman*, Advocate General Lenz argued they could be and this Opinion was the first step towards a recent convergence between the principles which underpin Article 39 EC and those which form the basis of the EC competition rules.[16] The Advocate General argued that the rules at stake were most likely a decision of an association of undertakings, having an effect on trade between Member States. He stated: '. . . it is also perfectly clear that the effect of the rules at issue in this case is a restriction of competition within the meaning of

---

15   Case C-41/90 *Höfner and Elser* v *Macroton GmbH* [1991] ECR I-1979.
16   See, for example, Case C-309/99 *J.C.J. Wouters, J.W. Savelbergh, Price Waterhouse Belastingadviseurs BV* v *Algemene Raad van de Nederlandse Orde van Advocaten* [2002] ECR I-1577. See also S. Weatherill, ' "Fair play please": recent developments in the application of EC law to sport' (2003), **40**, *CMLRev.*, 51.

Article 81(1)'.[17] Consequently, the Advocate General's Opinion did not follow a decisive element of the *Walrave* test,[18] as the Advocate General sidestepped the question of whether the rules at issue were of 'purely sporting interest' and therefore fell outside the scope of Article 81 EC. In situations such as where FIA licenses drivers to race in its events it would seem that this is not just a 'sporting issue' but one which raises questions regarding both the dominance of the FIA as a regulator and also its powers to restrict individual drivers from selling their professional services.

In *Höfner* the policy of the Court was to cast as wide as possible the reach of Articles 81 and 82 EC. The reference to entities 'regardless of their legal status' would, unintentionally, appear to open the door to allow for the application of EC competition rules, inter alia, to single regulatory sporting bodies such as the FIA or UEFA who regulate, at a European level, their constituent national federations. This is of interest because such regulatory bodies would not traditionally have been considered as comparable to, for example, a multinational company with subsidiaries or branches in the Member States. The conventional view, expressed in *Walrave*, was that the primary purpose of sports governing bodies was to ensure the organization of and maintain good discipline within the sport over which they exercised responsibility.[19] External legal regulation rarely intrudes into what are considered as private activities concerning discipline within the sport. The interpretation of the Court in *Walrave* would appear to reinforce this minimalist approach to regulation of

---

[17]   At paragraph 262.

[18]   At paragraph 8.

[19]   The CFI judgment in Case T-313/02 *David Meca-Medina and Igor Majcen* v *Commission* judgment of 30 September 2004 distinguished, using a *Keck*-type analysis, what sporting activity came within the scope of Community law. In its judgment, the Court of First Instance held that purely sporting legislation had nothing to do with the economic assumptions of competition law and did not fall within the scope of Articles 81 EC and 82 EC. These cases concerned the issue of whether enforcement of anti-doping rules breached Articles 81 and 82 EC. The CFI held that, as the rules on anti-doping were 'intimately linked to sport as such', they fell outside the scope of EC competition rules. See also Weatherill, at note 12, above. On appeal to the ECJ, Meca-Medina and Majcen challenged the CFI judgment on the basis that it had erred in law and not held that the anti-doping rules came within the scope of the free movement and competition rules. Though the ECJ acknowledged that the anti-doping rules may be excessive and could interfere with an individual's free movement rights, it felt that the penalty in this case was not disproportionate and was necessary to ensure that sport functioned properly. The ECJ upheld the judgment of the CFI that the Commission's decision not to commence legal proceedings against the International Swimming Federation was consistent with Articles 81 and 82 EC. See C-519/04 P *David Meca-Medina and Igor Majcen* v *Commission of the European Communities* judgment of 18 July 2006.

sport as being restricted to occasions when it has an impact upon the exercise of Treaty rights by individuals. These issues are addressed in more detail by Szyszczak and Weatherill elsewhere in this volume.

Judgments such as that in *Höfner* may be credited with broadening the concept of 'the undertaking' and consequently bringing the principles of competition law to the regulation of sporting authorities. If *Höfner* is considered together with the Advocate General's Opinion in *Bosman*,[20] it is apparent that, through the Court's application of rules relating to the regulation of the internal market, sport, its regulation and how it interacts with the citizen is firmly within the scope of Community law, including competition law. This approach offers greater scope for Community law regulation than that perceived by the Court in *Walrave*. Furthermore, it is Community law, rather than the laws of Member States, which through its supranational characteristics can effectively regulate sporting activity that is organized on a pan-European level. Community regulation covers not only the entitlement of sportsmen and women to exercise their rights under Articles 39 and 49 EC, but, as evidenced through the FIA inquiry, also applies the competition rules to regulatory bodies.[21] As for the latter, the primary application has been to ensure fair access to sporting events for satellite and terrestrial broadcasters and that governing bodies do not abuse their dominant position to prevent new competitions from being established which compete with its own events. Significantly, this has permitted Community competition law to challenge the decision-making of single regulatory bodies such as the FIA or UEFA.

THE COMMISSION'S FIA INQUIRY OF 1999

Prompted by a number of complaints[22] from broadcasters about the way inter-

---

[20]   Though in *Bosman* the Court was only concerned with the application of Article 39 EC, the definition provided by the Court in relation to sport as an economic activity is much broader than that in *Walrave*.

[21]   See *Wouters*, at note 16 above, Weatherill at note 12 above, pp. 419–21. Weatherill argues that *Wouters* offers a better analysis for single sporting federations and one which is based on considering the overall impact of the measure. For Weatherill, the starting point should be to acknowledge that the rules of a sporting federation *will* have an economic impact but that this itself will not justify the application of Community law. EC rules both on free movement and competition will only bite after an overall assessment of the rules, including their objectives and whether the consequences of those rules go beyond what is necessary to achieve those objectives.

[22]   In May 1997, the Commission received the first formal complaint about the way the FIA acquired broadcasting rights to international motor sport events. The complainant was AETV, a German television production company specializing in the

national motor sports are organized and commercially exploited, the Commission commenced competition proceedings against the FIA. The Commission argued that, *prima facie*, it considered the FIA to be abusing its dominant position and restricting competition. In addition, the Commission broadened the investigation to include two companies controlled by Bernie Ecclestone: Formula One Administration Ltd (FOA), which sells the television rights to the Formula One championship, and International Sportsworld Communicators (ISC), which markets the broadcasting rights to a number of major international motor sport events.

The Commission identified four competition problems which suggested that the FIA was abusing its dominant position.

The FIA used its Power to Block Series which Compete with its own Events

The FIA is the sole regulatory body of international motor racing in Europe and consequently occupies a monopoly position. Anyone wishing to take part in an international motor sports event would require authorization from the FIA and would have to obtain a FIA licence. This requirement extended to track owners, vehicle manufacturers, organizers of motor sport events and drivers alike. The situation could be most appropriately described as one where the FIA controlled all the factors of production necessary to produce motor sport. Licence holders were tied in to the FIA and were only permitted to enter or organize events authorized by the FIA. Any licence holder found to ignore this prohibition can be stripped of the licence. Losing the FIA licence would prevent the licensee from participating in almost all international motor sport events held in Europe.

In addition to restricting competition from a rival series the requirement of individual drivers to obtain a FIA licence had the potential to restrict their rights under Articles 39 and 49 EC. One consequence of this is that participants were extremely reluctant to enter events which had not been authorized by the FIA. This was particularly problematic as, through its commercial activities, the FIA was involved in the organization and promotion of a number of events itself. This meant that the FIA controlled the access of the inputs, such as drivers or circuits, which are necessary for organizers or promoters who wish to stage a championship which could compete with one of FIA's own events.

---

marketing of international motor sport championships such as the European truck racing championship. AETV argued that the FIA had used its power to seize total control of the broadcasting of international motor sports for its benefit and the benefit of Ecclestone through the use of the broadcasting resolutions. As a result, AETV had lost the right to market the broadcasting rights of this championship in favour of ISC.

The FIA has used this Power to Force a Competing Series out of the Market

Having concluded a preliminary investigation, the Commission stated that it had found evidence which suggested that, in at least one case, the FIA abused this dominant power to force a competing promoter, the GTR Organisation, out of the market. The FIA then replaced the GTR series with a similar FIA championship (the FIA GT championship).

The FIA used its Power abusively to Acquire all the Television Rights to International Motor Sports Events

As a spectator sport, television coverage is vital to the success of a motor sport event. This is because organizers and promoters rely heavily on sponsorship to finance their events. The Commission's investigation suggested that the level of sponsorship generated depends to a large extent on the television coverage a promoter or organizer can guarantee.

In 1995, the FIA introduced new rules under which it claimed the television rights to all the motor sport events it authorized. It then transferred these rights to International Sportsworld Communicators Ltd (ISC), a company that was controlled by one of FIA's vice-presidents, Bernie Ecclestone. The introduction of these rules also meant that a promoter wishing to establish an international series was forced to assign the television rights for that series, whether it wished to or not, to a competing promoter, namely the FIA. Although the FIA changed these rules at the end of 1998 to limit their scope of application, the Commission argued that it continued to abuse its power by acquiring the television rights, in this way, to championships incorporating the FIA name in their title. These rules on television rights are not directly applicable to the Formula One championship, which is governed by an agreement between the FIA, FOA and the teams which participate in the Formula One championship, known as the 'Concorde Agreement'.

The Concorde Agreement as originally notified to the Commission was agreed on 5 September 1996 and was for a period of five years from 1 January 1997. On 27 August 1998, the parties notified the 1998 Concorde Agreement which replaced the earlier agreement and runs from 1 January 1998 until 31 December 2007. The agreement was between FIA, all of the Formula One teams and FOA, the latter being designated as the commercial rights holder. The agreement sets out terms for the organization and running of the FIA Formula One World Championship and the voting structure for its control, by reference to other agreements, contracts, FIA rules and regulations.

In the Concorde Agreement, the teams recognized FIA's exclusive intellectual property in the FIA Formula One Championship, including in particular

the trade marks, the right to the title thereof and responsibility for its organization.[23] The teams undertook to participate each year for the duration of the
agreement[24] and not to participate in any other race, competition, exhibition or
championship for open wheel single seat cars other than Formula One, or a
race for cars complying with an existing FIA-approved race series.

Clause 4.1(b) of the Concorde Agreement defined FIA rights as all rights
that are, or become, lawfully vested in and held by or on behalf of FIA, including all rights granted by the teams. For the teams this meant that they would
grant to FIA, on an exclusive basis, the rights in, and ancillary to, their performance, the performance of all cars, machines, equipment and persons
connected to the teams (including the drivers) as well as the rights in the
formula one events.[25] According to clause 4.10, the teams had no rights to the
championship elements, that is, to any film footage of the relevant events and
any official timing information,[26] intellectual property rights, trade names or
logos owned by or on behalf of and/or vested in FIA and/or FOA. However,
the teams retained certain rights, such as the right to produce and market their
own merchandise as well as computer games.[27]

Additionally, there were also separate agreements between FOA and the
promoters of individual grand prix events. For the Commission the primary
concern was one of market access and viable competition in the lucrative
motor sport market. Though the institutional set-up of Formula One was
acknowledged by the Commission to be different to that of football, the effect
of the measures was to permit the FIA to use its regulatory power to force
participating teams to transfer to FIA any rights they may have in the broadcasting of the Formula One championship. The FIA then transferred these
rights to FOA. The promoters' rights are taken directly by FOA, which has
been given the power by the FIA to determine who can and cannot be a
promoter of a grand prix.

FOA and the FIA protect the Formula One Championship from Competition by Tying up Everything that is needed to Stage a Rival Championship

This final objection raised by the Commission was based on concerns about

---

[23]   Clause 1.1 of the Concorde Agreement.
[24]   Ibid., clauses 5.2 and 5.3.
[25]   Ibid., clause 4.2(a) and (b).
[26]   The intellectual property issues surrounding access to data from sporting
events is discussed by Estelle Derclaye elsewhere in this volume.
[27]   Ibid., clause 4(d). This multi-media market has proved very lucrative for the
teams and will, for the more successful teams, surpass the income they receive annually from the media rights.

the content and structure of broadcast agreements, some of which the FIA was party to, between FOA and the various broadcasters, promoters and the teams which are involved in the Formula One championship. The Commission was of the opinion that the terms of these agreements increased the difficulties, which were already substantial, for those who wish to stage and televise a competitor to the Formula One championship. Specifically the Commission identified three key issues:

- the promoters' contracts prevented circuits used for Formula One races from being used for races which could compete with Formula One;
- the 'Concorde Agreement' prevented Formula One teams from racing in any other series comparable to Formula One for a very long period of time;
- the agreements with broadcasters placed a massive financial penalty, ranging between 33 per cent to 50 per cent of the price paid, on them if they televised anything deemed by FOA to be a competitive threat to Formula One.

The Commission argued that, as the FIA abusively acquired the broadcasting rights, contrary to Article 82 EC, to international motor sports events, it could not validly assign these rights to FOA and ISC. Consequently, FOA and ISC were not in a position to conclude legally enforceable contracts with broadcasters, giving them all the rights which FIA claimed to have.

The nature of the Commission inquiry into the FIA, though concerned with the application of EC competition rules, shares some similarities in principle with the Court's reasoning in the judgments of *Höfner*, *Bosman* and *Meca-Medina and Igor Majcen*. Following *Höfner* and *Bosman*, it is evident that the Commission viewed the activities of the FIA as being intrinsically economic and within the scope of EC competition law. This nexus with economic activity is the defining feature which justified the investigation and which distinguishes it from the approach taken by the Court of First Instance and Court of Justice in *Meca-Medina and Igor Majcen*. In these cases the Commission in its submission stated that the anti-doping rules at issue may limit the athlete's freedom of action but are 'intimately linked to the proper conduct of sporting competition' and consequently do not infringe Articles 81 and 82 EC. In the words of former Competition Commissioner Mario Monti:[28]

---

[28]   Speech by Mario Monti, European Commissioner for Competition, 'Competition and Sport: the Rules of the Game', conference on 'Governance in Sport', European Olympic Committee, FIA, Herbert Smith, Brussels, 26 February 2001.

the Commission is not, in general, concerned with genuine 'sporting rules'. Rules, without which a sport could not exist (that is, rules inherent to a sport, or necessary for its organisation, or for the organisation of competitions) should not, in principle, be subject to the application of EC competition rules. Sporting rules applied in an objective, transparent and non-discriminatory manner do not constitute restrictions of competition.

Yet this statement by Mario Monti, which would appear consistent with the Court of First Instance in *Meca-Medina and Igor Majcen*, does not necessarily sit squarely with the Commission investigation of infringement by the FIA and related parties of EC competition rules. This inquiry originally began life in 1994 as a Commission investigation into the safety of motor sports,[29] coming under the control of the FIA and metamorphosed following the initial competition complaint in 1997. The question of safety within a sport would, in relation to the broader competition issue, appears, in principle, to be similar to the question of how a sports governing body operates an anti-doping policy and falls outside the remit of Community law. Weatherill argues[30] that, though the rules of a sporting federation may have an economic impact, this will not immediately justify the application of Community law. He suggests, in criticism of the judgment in *Meca-Medina and Igor Majcen*, that the EC rules on both free movement and competition will only take effect in circumstances following an overall assessment of the rules, including their objectives and whether the consequence of those rules goes beyond what is necessary to achieve those objectives.

While it may be argued that the Commission was duty bound to investigate a complaint of abuse, it is difficult to understand how this may have formed part of an already established inquiry into safety within motor sport. An inquiry into safety should, arguably, fall foul of Mario Monti's self-imposed boundary of Commission activity. What is interesting to note is that the Commission's investigation of the FIA regulations and commercial agreements relating to the FIA Formula One Championship came about following *voluntary* notifications in 1994 (coincidentally, the same time as the Commission's investigation into safety) and also in 1997 (following the complaint to the Commission) requesting clearance from EC competition rules. While a conspiracy against the FIA is unlikely, the question of what *is* within the scope of EC regulation is a legitimate one and appears to be unclear from this series of events. Though this may be a moot point in the circumstances of the FIA inquiry, given the establishment of prima facie abuse by

---

[29]   This investigation commenced following the deaths of Ayrton Senna and Roland Ratzenberger at the Imola Grand Prix in 2004.

[30]   At note 12, above.

FIA, the broader question remains open of the extent to which Community competence may extend to cover activities of sporting bodies which are non-economic and whether such a clear division *is* possible. While the Court, in judgments such as *Meca-Medina and Igor Majcen* and *Deliège*,[31] has sought to provide judicial clarity as to the scope of application of the Treaty rules, the FIA case demonstrates at least a past willingness by the Commission to extend its regulatory tentacles and examine the activities of sports regulatory bodies more generally.

THE COMMISSION'S FINDINGS

The primary objection raised by the Commission was on the basis that FIA had abused its power by putting unnecessary restrictions on promoters, circuit owners, vehicle manufacturers and drivers. Additionally, the Commission contended that certain provisions in the commercial agreements with television broadcasters were anti-competitive. The FIA case is interesting because it highlights the dilemma that exists when regulating the activities of sporting authorities. The Commission, in its findings,[32] acknowledged that single sporting federations such as the FIA must have the ability to regulate the organization of its sport, its sporting rules and its competitions. This includes such sporting bodies being able to exploit the commercial characteristics of the sport through marketing, franchising and selling of media rights. On the question of exploitation of sporting brands and the protection of related intellectual property rights,[33] the Court in *Arsenal* v *Reed*[34] has recognized the importance of this.

However, in terms of competition rules, the Commission's inquiry would appear to address the problem from a different perspective and one which is based upon market access. In its ruling the Commission noted 'the spectacular transformation of sports such as football and motor racing into "big busi-

---

[31]   Joined Cases C-51/96 and C-191/97 *Christelle Deliège* v *Ligue francophone de judo et disciplines associées ASBL, Ligue belge de judo ASBL, Union européenne de judo and François Pacquée* [2000] ECR I-2549.

[32]   2001/C 169/03. Notice published pursuant to Article 19(3) of Council Regulation No 17 concerning Cases COMP/35.163; Notification of FIA Regulations, COMP/36.638; Notification by FIA/FOA of agreements relating to the FIA Formula One World Championship, COMP/36.776; GTR/FIA & others.

[33]   For example, the name 'Formula One', variations of it and non-English language versions, are subject to a trademark registered at the OHMI.

[34]   Case C-206/01 *Arsenal Football Club* v *Reed* [2002] ECR I-273. The question of commercial exploitation of intellectual property rights and their marketing is considered by Bogusz elsewhere in this volume.

ness" '. One consequence of sports such as motor racing acquiring an increased commercial character, which eclipses the sporting element, is that it has inevitably led to third-party challenges of certain rules and commercial agreements under the competition rules. As the financial rewards increase, so does the scope for litigation.

The Commission's Statement of Objections issued on 29 June 1999 made the preliminary assessment that FIA had a 'conflict of interest' in that it was using its regulatory powers to block the organization of races which competed with the events promoted or organized by FIA (that is, those events from which FIA derived a commercial benefit). Moreover, for a certain period of time, FIA may have been abusing a dominant position under Article 82 of the EC Treaty by claiming the TV rights to motor sport series it authorized. An analogous situation was created in Formula One by the imposition of certain clauses in the Concorde Agreement. Finally, certain notified contracts appeared to contravene Article 81 and/or Article 82 EC in that they increased the barriers to entry for a potential entrant. Specifically, the promoters' contracts prevented circuits used for Formula One from being used for races which could compete with Formula One for a period of ten years. The Concorde Agreement prevented the teams from racing in any other series comparable to Formula One and the agreements with broadcasters placed a financial penalty on them if they showed motor sports that competed with F1 series. Certain agreements between FOA and broadcasters appeared to restrict competition within the meaning of Article 81 EC by granting broadcasters exclusivity in their territories for excessive periods of time.

Following discussions with the then Competition Commissioner Mario Monti, the FIA agreed to modify its rules to bring them into line with EU law, though the FIA continued to disagree with the substance of the Commission's objections. The modifications proposed by FIA stated that it will:

- establish a complete separation of the commercial and regulatory functions in relation to the FIA Formula One World Championship and the FIA World Rally Championship where new agreements are proposed which place the commercial exploitation of these championships at arm's length;
- improve transparency of decision-making and appeals procedures, and create greater accountability;
- guarantee access to motor sport to any person meeting the relevant safety and fairness criteria;
- guarantee access to the international sporting calendar and ensure that no restriction is placed on access to external independent appeals;
- modify the duration of free-to-air broadcasting contracts in relation to the FIA Formula One World Championship with a maximum duration of three years (reduced from five years).

The agreement between the FIA and FOA for the sale of any rights that the FIA may have in Formula One has been concluded for a period of 100 years. On the expiry of this period, the rights will revert to the FIA. The effective separation of the FIA's commercial and regulatory roles will during this time be ensured by the fact that FIA's interests will be represented by an independent third party. The role of this third party is to safeguard this reversionary interest, and the third party will not be involved in the commercial exploitation of Formula One.

Essentially, FIA was arguing that Formula One racing, and motor sport generally, was different in terms of its organization to other sports, which necessitated the terms of the Concorde Agreement. Though the Commission was not fully convinced of this argument, the solution reached between the parties does suggest that the Commission has acknowledged that motor sport raises different organizational and therefore competition issues in comparison to football. In relation to commercial exploitation of media rights, the Commission was adamant that this could not continue to be handled by the FIA, but would seem to be content with the rights continuing to be sold on a collective basis, a position it has not accepted in the selling of Champions League and Premier League football rights. Given the nature of motor racing, it is logical that one broadcaster per Member State can show all the events. A splitting of rights between two or more broadcasters as occurs in, for example, the Champions League would not work. Motor sport viewers are interested in the development of the championship throughout the season, rather than dipping into coverage to watch a specific match including a team they may support. Whereas a football supporter will have loyalty to a particular club and choose to watch primarily their games, a motor sport viewer is engaged by the chronological development of the championship and will watch all the races.

THE EXPLOITATION OF AUDIOVISUAL RIGHTS

Formula One differs from football as there is no inherent interest among the participants to see the television coverage transferred, either exclusively or jointly, to pay-per-view television or to subscription channels. By comparison the revenue currently generated within football is based upon the selling of television rights to subscription broadcasters. Formula One is an exception to the generally held view that sport programmes are the driving force behind the development of pay-TV services. In the case of Formula One motor racing, this is financed by sponsorship and through the financial backing of several leading car manufacturers. It will be recalled that the share of Commercial rights under the current Concorde Agreement running until 2007 is around

€20m per team and amounting to only 47 per cent of total commercial revenues raised through the sale of related rights.

For the teams which are so heavily reliant on sponsorship for income and the companies who invest hundreds of millions of euros annually in the search for on-track success, there is no inherent demand for coverage to be transferred exclusively, or in the main, to what remain minority sports channels. In motor racing, and Formula One particularly, the primary concern is to maximize exposure for the sponsor. Interestingly, Formula One's foray into pay-per-view through Ecclestone's dedicated digital television channel that broadcast races and offered additional individual options to the armchair viewer, failed after just one year because of the lack of interest amongst armchair race fans. Formula One motor racing is second only to the Football World Cup in terms of annual viewing figures and reinforces an argument often put forward that terrestrial television offers better value for money to sponsors and participants when seeking to generate interest in the sport.

Generally, the Commission remains committed to creating an active market in the sale of media rights and has consistently opposed exclusivity and collective selling. In the case of rights to the UEFA Champions League, these have been sold to a mixture of satellite and terrestrial broadcasters. The recent solution in the arrangements for the FA Premier League rights from 2007–2010 demonstrates that multiple rights holders are favoured by the Commission.[35] The Commission is particularly concerned about the impact on the structure of the TV market, which carries with it the risk of development of oligopolistic market structures.

When considering the FIA/Commission compromise, there is no doubt that Ecclestone's companies benefited from the agreement and this leads to the question of whether this sale, to a closely associated party, was within the spirit if not the letter of Article 81(1) EC.[36] The answer to this would appear to lie within a Commission understanding of how it views its own remit and also the objections which it raised to the way motor sport was being regulated. Interestingly, in the FIA inquiry the Commission adopted a 'hands off' approach to this question, which is rather surprising given that the original inquiry into safety within the sport would not immediately appear to fall within its remit either. Implicit in this agreement with FIA is that it is the role of the Commission, not to determine who owns what part of the motor sport

---

[35] The Commission formally approved this on 22 March 2006.

[36] In order to achieve a more complete separation between sporting and commercial matters and in order to increase transparency, FIA proposed that Ecclestone would relinquish his seat on the FIA Senate and his role as FIA Vice-President for Promotional Affairs. FIA proposed to make Ecclestone an honorary Vice-President of FIA, which was accepted.

business, but rather to ensure that the regulatory and commercial arrangements comply with the competition rules. Economic activity is therefore confined to operational questions rather than questions of ownership. The combination of FIA divesting its commercial interests in Formula One, and FIA strengthening its rules to ensure that all potential motor sports organizers and participants are treated equally, satisfied the Commission in principle to address the competition objections raised.

In the FIA case, the Commission's concern was that FIA used its regulatory power to determine the owner and the manager of valuable broadcasting rights. This created a strong monopoly in relation to the sale of these rights. In the end, FIA accepted, albeit reluctantly, the Commission's view that such commercial issues were within the scope of Article 81(1) EC and should be dealt with by negotiating with all interested parties. Despite this investigation, the outcome of which with hindsight may suggest the initial complaint was taken out of proportion, the impact for the armchair viewer has been negligible. For the participants, that is particularly the teams, the rather poor financial income they receive from commercial rights sales under the Concorde Agreement was not challenged by the Commission inquiry and remains intact until December 2007. It is this aspect of the Agreement that causes most grievance for the teams, rather than the issue of collective selling of television rights. In the overwhelming majority of EU Member States, Formula One remains available on free-to-air television and with a sole broadcaster, as was the case prior to the commencement of the inquiry. The solution reached between the Commission and FIA would suggest that while collective selling of television rights will *prima facie* breach Article 81(1) EC, they will in certain circumstances be exempt under Article 81(3) EC. This case would suggest that, as long as certain safeguards are in place, an exemption under Article 81(3) EC will be permitted.

The solution reached in the FIA case does not prevent the selling of collective television rights for motor sport events; it merely requires that strict conditions relating to the length of the contract and any collateral restrictions are kept to a minimum. Given the nature of motor racing, the solution reached, which appears to be a case of regulated competition, would seem to fall within the Article 81(3) EC exemption that it promotes technical progress (for the teams through guaranteed, albeit low, revenue from television rights sales), while allowing consumers (that is, the viewer) to share the resulting benefits of free-to-air access.

One benefit of the FIA inquiry would appear to be the opening up of the motor sports market to allow for greater competition to Formula One and other motor sport events. The Commission stated that FIA could not object to new competitions being established other than on grounds of safety. This is interesting because implicit in this condition is the idea that FIA, as a single federation governing motor sport, would retain this licensing role. The question this raises is, what are genuine 'sporting rules'? We have already seen that the Court is of the Opinion that rules, without which a sport could not exist (that is, rules inherent to a sport, or necessary for its organization, or for the organization of competitions) should not, in principle, be subject to the application of EC competition rules. Sporting rules applied in an objective, transparent and non-discriminatory manner do not constitute restrictions of competition. This was the position of the Court in the *Deliège* judgment. Here, the Court confirmed that selection rules applied by a federation to authorize the participation of professional or semi-professional athletes in an international sports competition inevitably limit the number of participants. Such a limitation does not interfere with Treaty rights, if it derives from an inherent need in the organization of the event in question. This would appear to extend to safe participation in the sport by an athlete.

However, this aspect of the FIA decision does leave the door open to future challenges where a refusal by FIA to license a motor sport series on grounds of safety may de facto be a decision motivated by the aim to prevent the establishment of a competitor series. If this is the case then the analysis of the role of sporting federations offered by Weatherill is a better interpretation than the narrow view taken by the Court. Though the Commission dispute with FIA has been resolved, the attempt by several leading Formula One teams, together with their car manufacturer backers, had the potential to challenge this part of the Commission ruling. Unhappy with their share of revenue from the sale of television rights under the Concorde Agreement, which runs until 2007, they threatened to establish a rival series unless their demands, for increased revenue after the expiry of the Concorde Agreement in 2007, were not met. Despite seeking FIA approval, FIA stated that it would not license such a competitor series which would be in breach of the Commission finding, unless made exclusively on grounds of safety. The rival series did not appear to raise any specific safety issue which would justify a refusal to license, but leads to a broader question of the extent to which the FIA should be able to protect the commercial viability of its premier motor racing series from commercial competitors. The rival series consisting of most of the top teams would in practice result in the commercial death of Formula One.

In March 2006, the matter was resolved when Ecclestone relinquished the commercial rights to Formula One by selling them to a private equity company, CVC Capital Partners, who also hold the commercial rights to the Moto GP Motor Cycle Championship. What is interesting about this sale of the commercial rights is that it forms part of a wider package of FIA-inspired reforms, to regulatory, commercial and safety matters within Formula One, which will occur after the expiry of the current Concorde Agreement in 2007. FIA has considered these as being part of a strategic step to reduce the costs of Formula One, and to avoid a rival series being established, but does this conflict with the Commission's requirement of commercial and regulatory separation?

This sale, which was investigated and subsequently cleared by the Commission, was subject to certain requirements. The Commission's market investigation showed that the proposed acquisition by CVC of Ecclestone's interests could significantly reduce competition as regards the selling of the media rights to Moto GP events in Italy and Spain, the countries within the EU where these events are most popular. In addition, concerns were raised that, in Member States where Moto GP is less popular than Formula One, CVC might bundle the media rights for both events. The Commission's clearance was conditional upon the divestiture by CVC of its Spanish subsidiary Dorna, which is the promoter of the Moto GP Motorcycle Championship. In light of these commitments by CVC, the Commission concluded that the transaction would not significantly impede effective competition in the televising of motor sport events.

The Commission was satisfied that the principles of the 2001 agreement with FIA are upheld by this sale. But the comprehensive nature of the settlement in Formula One, leading to the signing of a new Concorde Agreement between FIA and the teams for 2008 which covers commercial rights, safety and regulation, still ensures de facto control for the FIA over *all* aspects of the sport. For the Commission, the primary issues would appear, from the clearance of the transfer to CVC Partners, to revolve around key competition issues in the selling of commercial rights. Regulation and safety, which are more closely concerned with the participants and therefore the rights under Articles 39 and 49 EC, have not been considered. Perhaps the Commission, influenced by the recent judgments of the Court, is imposing its own remit in relation to regulation of sports, as Mario Monti suggested it should in 2002,[37] but this remains to be seen.

SINGLE FEDERATION GOVERNING BODIES

One final issue which the FIA case raised, and which has already been touched upon, relates to the question of powers of single federation bodies which regulate a particular sport. Clearly, the role and organization of such a body will concern how a sport is regulated and what aspect of its activities comes within the scope of Community law. Traditionally, a single federation exists to regulate the affairs of a sport. In addition, sporting federations such as FIA are

---

[37]   See note 28, above.

active in the market for the organization of sporting events, either by laying down rules for their members or by organizing events directly themselves. While the existence of a single federation overseeing both the regulatory and organizational aspects of a sport is common in Europe, other scenarios exist or can be envisaged.[38]

What the FIA case demonstrates is that, where regulation and organization being vested in a single body leads to significant commercial conflicts of interest, the Commission will look carefully at whether another scenario should be required. Such a solution would appear to follow the principles laid down in the *Wouters* judgment and in particular that, when the Commission applies Article 81 EC, it must take an overall analysis before deciding whether the competition rules have been infringed. Weatherill prefers this approach to that suggested by the Court in *Meca-Medina and Igor Majcen* as it takes a more holistic approach to resolving any competition issues

Following this interpretation, it is difficult to see how Formula One could continue to operate as a commercially successful sport without the FIA maintaining its pre-eminent regulatory position in the sport. In the FIA case it agreed to divest itself of its commercial interests in Formula One, suggesting that FIA's future interest in Formula One will be limited to that of a sport's regulator. This is why the Commission believes that an agreement under which FIA disposes of its commercial rights for 100 years is acceptable. A shorter period, for example ten years, would continue the conflict of interest to which the Commission objects. Yet, given the nature of Formula One and the centricity of the Concorde Agreement to its operation, which is negotiated by FIA with the teams and other interested parties, it is a moot point whether this separation does indeed exist. This position would seem to reinforce Weatherill's holistic approach to the regulation of sporting federations.

It is no coincidence that, in March 2006, new safety regulations, improved provisions for revenue distribution between the teams and the sale of the commercial rights for 2008 onwards were all concluded at a time when FIA was seeking to avoid a competitor series being established. These arrangements will compose the new Concorde Agreement which the teams have signed in September 2006 to participate in Formula One beyond this date. It is fair to say that these aspects of the sport are very closely interrelated and do undoubtedly have an impact upon each other. Any review of one cannot be carried out in isolation from the other areas which come under FIA control.

---

[38]   As in the FIA case with the separation of the regulatory and commercial activities of the sporting federation.

CONCLUDING REMARKS

The FIA case demonstrates, as does the Court's judgment in *Bosman*, that EC law will operate in a manner to ensure that private organizations such as sporting authorities who occupy a monopoly position do not impede market access. In many respects the FIA case is a good example of the way sporting federations may resolve disputes with the Commission without resorting to litigation. Yet the FIA case is also interesting because it demonstrates that, when it comes to the regulation of sport in the EU, there is no 'one-size-fits-all' methodology which has to date been adopted. Whether this arises from inherent differences in sports, how they are organized and how they are made access-ible to the public may be one possible explanation. Perhaps a more appropriate answer is that sport is not necessarily as special as some commentators may argue as it ticks many, if not all, of the boxes of what amounts to an economic activity. The thrust of the argument throughout this chapter is that all sports are different, and some, such as Formula One motor racing, have attributes that are closer to a commercial enterprise which is profit-motivated, rather than being primarily concerned with winning or losing. Consequently, when being subjected to EC competition provisions, sporting regulatory bodies such as the FIA require certainty of rules and procedure. In practice this means that they ought to be regulated on the same basis as any other commercial enterprise and decisions made against them should not be clouded by unhelpful discussions of what amounts to sporting regulation or economic activity. Formula One motor racing, above any other sport, demonstrates how interdependent the two have become.

PART 2

The regulation of 'labour' markets

5. Disciplinary regulation of sport: a different strand of public law?

Tim Kerr

INTRODUCTION

I would answer the question posed in the title with a simple 'no'. Disciplinary regulation of sport is not a strand of public law. It is a *sui generis* branch of the law relating to sport, which is international in character and partakes of both public and private law principles. The fast-growing body of international sports law jurisprudence does not, for the most part, concern itself with whether the legal rules governing disciplinary issues occupy the private or the public sphere. Put simply, disciplinary regulation in sport is neither private law nor public law but, ultimately, sports law.

SPORT, SOCIETY, ECONOMY AND GOVERNMENT

In English law, 'public' is closely allied to 'governmental'. The susceptibility of a decision to judicial review depends on whether the decision challenged is directly or indirectly part of our system of state regulation. The thesis that sport straddles the public and private sectors is now probably untenable. In the sporting field, governments (at least in the liberal western democracies) in the main do not intervene because they have quite enough to do, and do not need to intervene except where sport impinges on classic areas of state responsibility: public order, public safety and, in some countries but not Britain, doping control.

The role of government is mainly facilitative: drumming up finance for new stadia, lobbying to secure the Olympic Games, promoting dialogue between bodies in dispute, linking availability of funding to adoption of the World Anti-Doping Code (WADC) and, it is hoped, but not always, preventing local playing fields from being buried under concrete.

No one seriously advocates wholesale statutory regulation of sport, either nationally or internationally. Sport's international constitutional instruments are not treaties between sovereign states but agreements between international bodies, many of which are private limited companies. But that does not mean sport is an entirely private affair; in the present epoch it would be going too far to assert that all public activity is synonymous with state activity.

If you ask the average fan about whether sport is a public matter you will probably get a schizophrenic answer: on the one hand, sport belongs to the people so it is public in the sense that it is 'popular', that is, of the people. On the other hand I doubt whether the average punter wants government interfering in sport. We heartily approve of private interests pumping money into sport, but we do not like it when they ration it for profit unless the product is plentiful and cheaply available, and unless the profits are ploughed back into the game and not into shareholders' pockets.

SPORTS LAW AND LAW GENERALLY

What place does the law governing the practice of sport occupy in our jurisprudence? In 1999, I and others advanced the thesis that 'the time has come for the term "sports law" to be accepted as a valid description of a system of law governing the practice of sports'.[1] We noted that there are 'vertical' (activity-led, for example health, education) and 'horizontal' (rule-led, for example trusts, contract) branches of the law, and that other activity-led branches of the law had achieved recognition as discrete fields of law in England, albeit mainly through direct legislative intervention.

We rejected the then widespread view that 'there is no such thing as sports law',[2] and propounded a tentative definition: 'a loose but increasingly cohesive body of rules governing the practice of sport and the resolution of disputes in sport'.[3] We noted that, unlike other great activity-led branches of the law, sports law was gaining momentum under its own steam, not by dint of state intervention, and was doing so at an international level, simply because of the need to evolve a coherent method of dispute resolution in an increasingly global activity.

Later the same year the Court of Arbitration for Sport (CAS) had to decide a challenge to the validity of a UEFA rule preventing two or more commonly owned clubs from taking part in the same competition, a challenge which (after interim relief had been granted) ultimately failed, mainly on the ground that the rule did not violate Swiss or EU competition law, nor the principle of

---

[1]   M. Beloff, T. Kerr and M. Demetriou, *Sports Law* (Oxford: Hart Publishing, 1999), p. 1.

[2]   Woodhouse, quoted in *Sport and the Law Journal*, 5(2), (1997), p. 12.

[3]   *Sports Law*, at p. 6.

proportionality.[4] The challenge was also founded on the 'general principle of law that a quasi-public body exercising regulatory powers must not abuse its powers'.[5]

The CAS Panel held[6] that:

> all sporting institutions, and in particular all international federations, must abide by general principles of law. Due to the transnational nature of sporting competitions, the effects of the conduct and deeds of international federations are felt in a sporting community throughout various countries. Therefore, the substantive and procedural rules to be respected by international federations cannot be reduced only to its own statutes and regulations and to the laws of the country where the federation is incorporated or of the country where its headquarters are. Sports law has developed and consolidated along the years, particularly through the arbitral settlement of disputes, a set of unwritten legal principles – a sort of *lex mercatoria* for sports or, so to speak, a *lex ludica* – to which national and international sports federations must conform, regardless of the presence of such principles within their own statutes and regulations or within any applicable national law, provided that they do not conflict with any national 'public policy' ('ordre public') provision applicable to a given case. Certainly, general principles of law drawn from a comparative or common denominator reading of various domestic legal systems and, in particular, the prohibition of arbitrary or unreasonable rules and measures can be deemed to be part of such *lex ludica*.

The case law of the CAS since then has developed rapidly and its decisions have begun to harden into a cohesive body of principles governing the national and international practice of sport, the resolution of disputes in sport and, in particular, disciplinary proceedings in sport. This is not the place to give a full account of that body of law, but its prominent features reveal the following major influences:

1. the principle of fair play and sportsmanship, inspired by the Olympic Charter; that is, the principle that sporting competitions must be conducted fairly and won or lost on merit, and that sports associations must conduct themselves fairly;
2. the major contribution of Swiss domestic law – a legal system whose jealous protection of private and commercial interests has helped to attract many international sports governing bodies – in particular, the Swiss law of associations which accords great (though not absolute) autonomy to the association; and

---

[4]   *AEK Athens and Slavia Prague* v *UEFA*, CAS 98/200, judgment dated 20 August 1999.

[5]   Ibid., at para. 187.

[6]   Ibid., at para. 188.

3. in the field of disciplinary regulation, the proposition that anti-doping rules must be supported and upheld rigorously and vigorously, even at the expense of harshness in the way they operate in individual cases. This means, in particular, strict liability for doping offences, no need to prove any actual effect on performance, and automatic disqualification of the player's result in, at least, the competition at which the player tests positive for a banned substance.

A further major step towards harmonization was taken with the advent in 2003 of the World Anti-Doping Code (the WADC or the Code) promulgated by the World Anti-Doping Agency (WADA), itself established in 1999. The provisions of the Code are now routinely applied by domestic sports tribunals across the globe, and on appeal to the CAS, and across most sports, but for the moment with the notable exception of the most important sport of all, association football.

By 2003, a consensus was beginning to emerge that there is such a thing as sports law, at any rate to the extent that 'in at least some areas, for example where international institutions such as the Court of Arbitration for Sport review the decisions of sports governing bodies, a separate and distinct body of law inspired by general principles of law common to all states is in the process of development'.[7] By 2005, a leading commentator could assert with confidence that sport was no longer a recreation but a business; that 'lawyers have a duty, not a choice, to seek to bring order and justice to the table' and that 'In that valuable exercise, the development of a *lex sportiva* will play a vital part'.[8]

So I remain a proponent of the thesis advanced in our book of 1999: that sports law is best viewed not as ordinary law applying to parties who happen to be involved in the world of sport, but as a developing body of principles applicable to the resolution of disputes in sport. Sport is *special* in its relation to the law because the *lex sportiva* is developing internationally with little impetus from governments (Malaysia and *dirigiste* France being exceptions), fuelled by a potent mixture of competitive instinct, commercial interest, insatiable public demand and, even in this day and age, Corinthian idealism.

We are witnessing the early infancy of a nascent international legal system governing relations between participants, organizers, spectators, broadcasters and others with a stake in the game. But it is still in its infancy. On 21 April 2006 the CAS issued a non-binding advisory opinion at the request of FIFA and the WADA. Each, independently of the other, asked a series of written

---

    [7]   Lewis and Taylor (with other contributors), *Sport: Law and Practice* (London: Butterworths, 2003), Preface at pages vii–viii.
    [8]   Beloff, *Is There a Lex Sportiva?* (2005), *ISLR*, **3**(5), 49, at 60.

questions for the opinion of the CAS concerning the compatibility of FIFA's anti-doping rules with those set out in the WADC, and concerning FIFA's obligation, if any, to sign up to the Code.[9]

The case arose out of FIFA's concern as to whether certain provisions of the Code concerning the imposition of sanctions for anti-doping rule violations are in conformity with Swiss law, in particular the automatic two year ban for a first doping offence in the absence of a defence of 'no fault or negligence' or 'no significant fault or negligence'.[10] FIFA argued that, under the Swiss law of associations it could not adopt provisions of the WADC which were contrary to Swiss law. The Panel of three Swiss lawyers noted that the question was governed by Swiss law and primarily by the Swiss law of associations, but also by '*general principles of law* which are not limited to a specific area of law'.[11] The Panel noted that one such general principle is that of proportionality:

> a principle which has its roots in constitutional and administrative law. On the other hand, the Panel is not prepared to take refuge in such uncertain concepts as that of a '*lex sportiva*', as has been advocated by various authors. The exact content and the boundaries of the concept of a lex sportiva are still far too vague and uncertain to enable it to be used to determine the specific rights and obligations of sports associations towards athletes.[12]

The above is accepted, but *non sequitur* that the concept does not exist or is not developing. It might have developed further in that very case had FIFA not been domiciled in Switzerland and accordingly subject to Swiss law and in particular a right to apply for a review by the Swiss Supreme Court.

DISCIPLINARY REGULATION OF SPORT: WHAT IS IT?

With that introduction, it is convenient next to consider what we mean when we speak of disciplinary regulation of sport. Broadly speaking, the term embraces three specific situations: (i) the regulation of play on the field; (ii) the regulation of conduct off the field; and, more specifically (iii) the enforcement of anti-doping rules.

---

[9]   *CAS Advisory Opinion*, CAS 2005/C/976 and 986, FIFA and WADA.
[10]   Articles 10.2 and 10.5 of the WADC.
[11]   *CAS Advisory Opinion, supra*, at para. 124; emphasis in original.
[12]   Ibid., para. 124. The CAS held that, with one relatively minor exception, the Code conforms to Swiss law. It cited CAS international jurisprudence as well as purely Swiss law doctrine in dealing with the scope of the principle of proportionality: see at paras 138–9.

A simple example of (i) would be, in football, the sending off of a player for violent conduct, and the subsequent three-match ban issued to the player. An example of (ii) would be the payment of secret financial incentives to players or managers in breach of the rules requiring transparency in respect of remuneration. The paradigm in the case of (iii) is the requirement to submit to in-competition and out-of-competition drug testing, the absolute prohibition against ingestion of banned substances or their presence in the body, the automatic disqualification of the result of any competition in which the player tests positive, and the imposition, normally, of a period of ineligibility to participate in the sport concerned.

DISCIPLINARY REGULATION OF SPORT IN ENGLAND: PUBLIC LAW?

In English law it has long been recognized that the contractual status of rules adopted by an association should not prevent the courts from imposing procedural requirements of fairness and requiring the association to interpret its rules properly.[13] 'The rules are in reality more than a contract. They are a legislative code . . .'.[14] That reality has not persuaded the English courts to open the gates of public law to the decisions of domestic associations including sports governing bodies. The swift and convenient judicial review procedure enabling judicial scrutiny of public law decisions within short time limits remains firmly closed to participants in sport, and is likely to remain so unless the House of Lords decides otherwise.[15] The non-amenability to judicial review of sports bodies' decision has attracted and continues to attract criticism,[16] but it would be difficult in practice to secure reconsideration of the issue by the House of Lords.

In the field of sport the English courts are more reluctant to interfere than in other fields, such as that of trade unions in the 1960s and 1970s. The practical threshold for an intending claimant seeking relief against a sports associ-

---

13   *Lee v Showmen's Guild of Great Britain* [1952] 2 QB 329, CA; *Breen v AEU* [1971] 2 QB 175, CA, both containing celebrated judgments of Lord Denning, the latter a dissenting one but no less seminal for that.

14   *Breen, supra,* per Lord Denning MR (dissenting) at p. 190F.

15   *R. v Disciplinary Committee of the Jockey Club ex p. Aga Khan* [1993] 1 WLR 909, CA; *R. (Mullins) v Appeal Board of the Jockey Club* [1005] EWHC 2197 (Admin) (Stanley Burnton J, 17.10.5).

16   For example, most recently, Beloff, editorial in (2006), **1**(3), *ISLR*, prompted by the *Mullins* case, echoing earlier criticisms drawing a contrast with the different position in some overseas jurisdictions.

ation is a high one. The judicial starting point is that sports governance is best left to sport in the absence of a compelling case for interference. This is well travelled ground for English sports lawyers and need not be rehearsed in detail here.[17]

The practical consequence is that practitioners tend to advise potential claimants that they risk failure to persuade the court to grant discretionary relief in the form of an injunction or declaration even where the merits are relatively strong. Those remedies are by far the most important (damages are rarely sought or awarded), are always discretionary and often refused on practical grounds such as delay. Conversely, governing bodies are often advised that the chances of successful resistance to a claim are good even where its conduct is obviously susceptible to criticism.

Decisions relating to the regulation of play are almost always a no-go area for the English courts, other than on procedural grounds such as where the hearing is unfair. This judicial self-restraint loosely corresponds to the 'sporting exception' whereby the relevant articles of the Treaty of Rome do not apply to sport except in so far as it is treated as an economic activity. A rare interim injunction granted to a rugby player preventing the Welsh Rugby Union from suspending him for 30 days for alleged violent conduct has been subject to criticism in some quarters. In England, Scotland and Wales, only a handful of such cases have succeeded in the past 50 years or so.[18]

Where sports bodies engage in disciplinary regulation of conduct off the field of play, including the commission of alleged doping offences, the courts are more likely to intervene, but there is still a marked reluctance because of the undesirability of lawyers colonizing the territory to the detriment of smooth self-government of sport by sport. The absence of deterrence against high-handed and arguably unlawful conduct by governing bodies is considered to be a price worth paying to keep lawyers and the courts out of sport where possible.[19] The work of the Sports Dispute Resolution Panel is also helping by providing a much needed voluntary and relatively informal system of dispute resolution outside the framework of the courts – a sort of national level equivalent of the CAS but at an earlier stage of development.

---

[17]   *McInnes* v *Onslow-Fane* [1978] 1 WLR 1520 per Megarry VC at 1535; *Cowley* v *Heatley*, the *Times*, 24.7.86 per Browne-Wilkinson VC; *Gasser* v *Stinson*, Scott J, transcript 15.6.88.

[18]   *Jones* v *WRU*, Ebsworth J, the *Times*, 6.3.97. The other cases are helpfully listed in Lewis and Taylor, *supra*, note 7, at A3.11, footnote 2, p. 92.

[19]   A selection of English and overseas common law cases is helpfully gathered at A3.12 in Lewis & Taylor, *supra*, note 7, pp. 93–4. Many other cases (e.g. involving Tottenham, Chelsea and Middlesbrough Football Clubs in this author's professional experience) are determined in the domestic arena without recourse to the courts, usually behind closed doors but with some subsequent publicity.

Recent English jurisprudence has reaffirmed the absence of any difference in the standard of review in a contract-based claim from that applied where there is no contract between the parties. For a time it was sometimes thought that an English court could not grant a free-standing declaration of right or injunction in a case where a player or club sought relief against an allegedly unlawful decision affecting the claimant's private rights, but where the claimant lacked any contractual relationship with the defendant. However, the contrary is well established and it is now tolerably clear that the standard of review is (subject to any express terms of any contract) the same as that which would be applied in judicial review proceedings if the proceedings were governed by public law.[20]

DISCIPLINARY REGULATION OF SPORT IN THE CAS: PUBLIC LAW?

Disciplinary regulation of sport on the international plane is the subject of CAS case law which is now quite developed. In general, it would not be accurate or helpful to describe the jurisprudence as a strand of public law. The concept of a divide between public and private law differs from country to country and is not the same in Swiss law – the domestic legal system exerting the greatest influence over CAS decisions, for obvious reasons – as in English law.[21] That said, the principle of proportionality, a civil law and EU law concept only partially and recently imported into our domestic jurisprudence, 'has its roots in constitutional and administrative law' and 'pervades Swiss jurisprudence'.[22]

The CAS recognizes and applies the 'sporting exception' developed in the well-known case law of the European Court of Justice, whereby decisions, including disciplinary decisions which are by their nature sporting only and

---

[20]   See *Newport AFC* v *the FA of Wales* [1995] 2 All ER 87, and transcript 12.4.95 (Blackburne J) granting a declaration at p. 55; *Stevenage FC* v *the Football League Ltd.*, transcript 23.7.96 (Carnwath J); (1997) 9 Admin LR 109, CA; *Modahl* v *BAF*, 28.7.97, unrep., CA; *Bradley* v *the Jockey Club*, Richards J [2004] EWHC 2164, and [2005] EWCA Civ 1056; *Mullins* v *Macfarlane*, transcript of judgment of 5.5.6, per Stanley Burnton J at paras 37–9, stating his provisional and assumed view that the jurisdiction to interfere is not confined to cases where the domestic tribunal has acted in restraint or trade, in breach of the claimant's so-called 'right to work', or unfairly in a procedural sense.

[21]   This author disclaims any professional expertise in Swiss law and is indebted to Swiss lawyer colleagues for their invaluable assistance given when in need of it.

[22]   *CAS Advisory Opinion*, 21.4.6, *supra*, note 11, at para. 124; though Lord Denning would no doubt argue that we have had a home grown proportionality principle for decades: *R.* v *Barnley Metropolitan BC ex p. Hook* [1976] 1 WLR 1052, CA (a urine sample case).

not economic, are not subject to the relevant articles of the Treaty of Rome and, normally, not justiciable. However, the CAS has commented on the difficulty of defining the limits of the exception[23] and may be inclined to interpret it narrowly in order not to shrink its jurisdiction, as appears from the discussion of the football-related authorities[24] (in the context of a UEFA rule limiting CAS jurisdiction to 'pecuniary' disputes and excluding jurisdiction in cases of a decision 'of a sporting nature') in *The FA of Wales v UEFA*,[25] in which the CAS noted the similarity with the Swiss law doctrine of the non-enforceability of the 'rules of play'.

A CAS panel has decided that the 'rules of the game' are the 'rules which are intended to ensure the correct course of the game and competition respectively', and that 'save in exceptional circumstances [cannot] lead to any judicial review'.[26] It is noteworthy that even in this protected sphere, the approach is one of judicial self-restraint rather than absence of jurisdiction. In a number of ad hoc cases decided at the Athens Olympics the panels declined to interfere where challenges to sporting decisions were brought, for example in a case of a rower allegedly trespassing into the lane of another rower.

Disciplinary decisions concerning conduct off the field of play may be challenged more readily. Of these, the most common relate to alleged doping offences and the sanctions imposed in respect of them.[27] It can be argued that the harmonization of anti-doping rules achieved by the WADA by means of the Code represents a significant step towards the creation of a global disciplinary regime applicable across sports and across jurisdictions; an international and in a rather vague sense 'public' law of sport.

It would be premature to conclude that the regime is already established; the very recent *CAS Advisory Opinion* case with its preference for reliance on Swiss domestic law rather than international sports law, indicates that it is not. However, the limits of permissible judicial decision making in anti-doping cases determined under the Code are currently being subjected to scrutiny before independent domestic sports anti-doping tribunals across the world and on appeal from them to the CAS.

---

[23] See *AEK Athens and Slavia Prague v UEFA*, CAS 1998/200, paras 111–16.

[24] *Real Madrid v UEFA*, CAS Digest II, 490–9, at 492 (one match ban on use of stadium held to be sporting only); *Anderlecht v UEFA*, Digest II, 469–478 (one season ban for corrupt practice held to affect club's pecuniary interests); *PSV Eindhoven v UEFA*, CAS 2002/A/423.

[25] CAS 2004/A/593; [2004] ISLR 62, paras 28–35.

[26] *WCM-GP Ltd. v FIM*, CAS 2003/A/461; see also the other cases mentioned in Beloff, *supra*, note 8, *Is There a Lex Sportiva*? ISLR, (2005), **3**(5), at 52–3.

[27] For a scholarly and comprehensive survey of the CAS anti-doping jurisprudence, see McLaren, *CAS Doping Jurisprudence: What Can We Learn?* at (2006), ISLR, 4–23.

A major and critical issue which has yet to be clearly decided at CAS level is whether mandatory fixed or minimum-term periods of ineligibility set at deterrent levels (such as eight years for a second offence where there is 'no significant fault or negligence'[28]) without regard to the individual circumstances of the offence, are lawful; and if they are not, whether the objective of uniformity and harmonization intended to be achieved through the Code will be undermined or destroyed.

CONCLUSION

Disciplinary regulation in sport is not public law, nor private law. It is, ultimately, part of sports law and, like sports law itself, partakes of both private and public law.

---

[28]   *ITF* v *Mariano Puerta*, ITF Anti-Doping Tribunal, 21.12.5, available on the ITF's website; cf. on appeal CAS/A/2006/1025, 12.7.6 reducing the period of suspension on the basis of a supposed 'lacuna' in the rules attracting the application of a freestanding proportionality principle; cf. *Knauss* v *FIS*, CAS/2005/A/847; *Squizzato* v *FINA*, CAS/2005/A/830.

6. The regulation of sport in the European Union: courts and markets

Luca Barani

INTRODUCTION

Building on the survey of sport-related issues at the European level made in other parts of the book, this chapter focuses on the policy alternatives and legal dilemmas of sport regulation. More specifically, it will analyse the regulation of professional football in the context of the European Union (EU), and principally how the European Court of Justice (ECJ) has approached it. The development of sport regulation is tackled from a political perspective, without neglecting its economic and legal aspects.

This chapter aims at deepening the understanding of the relationship between public institutions and private parties in the regulation of sport. It is possible to describe such an interaction as a situation characterized by imperfect alternatives provided by legislators, courts and administrative agencies attempting to regulate. Simultaneously, private agents try to foresee (and often to influence) the type of intervention that will prevail and to shape their interaction according to the constraints and the opportunities present in the economic and institutional environment. Significant contributions to this kind of inquiry come from law and economics literature, which analyses regulation on the basis of transaction costs[1] and recently extends this approach to public bureaucracies.[2]

The perspective of such a Comparative Institutional Approach (CIA) is used to disentangle the complex dynamics of interaction between public and private parties. Starting from the idea that two dimensions move along a continuum of cooperation and competition, the focal point of the analysis refers to the choice of venue where the rule making is taking place. It is possible, therefore, to

---

[1] N. Komesar, *Imperfect Alternatives: Choosing Institutions in Law, Economics, and Public Policy* (Chicago: University of Chicago Press, 1994).

[2] O.E. Williamson, 'Public and private bureaucracies: a transaction cost economics perspectives' (1999), **15**(1), *Journal of Law Economics & Organization*, 306–42.

develop a comparative analysis of institutional equilibria that explore the connections between the allocation of regulating power and the characteristics as well as capabilities of public and private institutions. The dominance of centralized solutions or the adoption of decentralized regulatory regimes are certainly influenced by institutional design and historical legacy, but they can also be interpreted as the outcome of a bargaining process which allocates the regulatory competence on the basis of costs/benefits of choices and thus inclines institutions toward opportunistic performance.

Building on this literature and approach, the chapter analyses the unstable regulatory equilibrium within the EU in three main stages. First, the current situation is presented concerning sport at the national and EU level, highlighting its fragmented nature and exposure to market forces, which is particularly the case of collective sports like football. Incidentally, the rise of the EU as a regulatory level for sporting activities that have an economic dimension has been concomitant to the phenomenon of increased commercialization of sport, but it is riddled with contradictions and internal tensions. Second, in order to explain in detail how the EU judiciary and legislature have dealt with the challenge of sport regulation, a specific theoretical framework will be introduced which is built on CIA. Third, this approach will be applied to the institutional EU landscape, in order to explain the threefold development of sport regulation: first, the emergence of ECJ as the sport regulator of first resort is considered; second, the clash of demands and counterdemands of related policy coalitions around the EU regulatory venues is analysed; and, finally, the current developments within the EU concerning sport regulation are reviewed.

CURRENT STATE OF PLAY IN SPORT REGULATION WITHIN THE EU

Although it is possible to make some generalizations about the current state of sport regulation in Europe, the concept of a 'European Model of sport', proposed by the Commission in its communications and policy papers,[3] is highly unreliable as a starting point.[4] In reality, throughout Europe, the rules and procedures governing sport are left at the discretion of sport bodies and

---

[3]   See http://ec.europa.eu/sport/index_en.html for all EU official documents cited in the chapter: in particular, the *Helsinki Report on the European Model of Sport* (1999).

[4]   S. Szymanski, 'Is there a European model of sport?' in Rodney Fort and John Fizel (eds), *International Sport Economic Comparisons* (Westport: Prager, 2004), pp. 14–45.

are heavily biased against market competition and individual economic freedoms.[5] Moreover, the most pertinent level of analysis remains at the state level.[6]

National Structures

In order to classify different national models of sport regulation in the EU,[7] they will be positioned along two axes: governmental and non-governmental. These cleavages provide a useful matrix to classify different national sport models according to different configurations of state policy making and the logics of private sport organization. State supervision can be interventionist or restrained. The organization of sport practices can lean towards either competitive or participative sports.[8]

As Table 6.1 illustrates, the current system of sport regulation at the national level in the EU is rather fragmented and displays characteristics of a variety of reference models. However, despite stark differences among national sport models, they all have one common feature: articulation of the relationship between sport laws emanating from the state and sport by-laws defined by sport bodies.[9]

In Western Europe, the common regulatory condition consists in the existence of a more or less developed sphere of autonomy, which is left to sport bodies for their own self-regulation.[10] As far as the articulation between national laws and sport by-laws is concerned, this relationship can be defined as 'assisted sport self-regulation', autonomous to different degrees. In such a

---

[5]   S. Weatherill, ' "Fair play please!" Recent developments in the application of EC law to sport' (2003), **40**, *Common Market Law Review*, 51–93.

[6]   C. Miège, *Les Institutions Sportives* (Paris: Presses Universitaires de France, 1993).

[7]   K. Petry, D. Stainbach and W. Tokarski, 'Sport systems in the countries of the European Union: similarities and differences' (2004), **1**(1), *European Journal for Sport and Society*, 15–21.

[8]   Concerning the governmental level, broadly speaking, relatively few governments have ministries dedicated to sport alone (France) while a number of them include sport in a wider portfolio (Belgium, Czech Republic, Hungary, Ireland, Lithuania, Poland, Slovenia and the UK). (See *Revue française d'administration publique*, 2001.) Regarding the organization of sport practices, different sport national models seem to be sensitive to the level of participation of population (van Bottenburg, Rijen, van Sterkenburg, *Sport Participation in the European Union*, Amsterdam: Mulier Institute, 2005).

[9]   A.-N. Chaker, *Etudes des legislations nationales relatives au sport en Europe* (Strasbourg: Editions du Conseil de l'Europe, 1999).

[10]   The former European Communist countries provide an instructive counterpoint of practices (*The Times*, 2004).

Table 6.1   Sport regulation, national level, EU

State supervision Sport organization	Interventionist	Restrained
Participative–amateur	Germany Sweden	United Kingdom
Competitive–professional	France Spain	Italy

way, sport governing bodies are submitted to external scrutiny by public authorities in exchange for the recognition of relative sport autonomy, supposedly justified by the public interest. Consequently, the internal 'legal order' of sport is recognized, but the outcomes of its self-regulation are subjected to external control. National instances can define the practical scope of decision making allowed to sport, but only as far as it concerns the compatibility of sport self-regulation with the national law. In other words, states are providing for a permissive framework, within which sport structures have more or less considerable autonomy to make any relevant choice. As a consequence, sports' governing bodies have been able to manage and regulate their internal affairs almost independently, thanks to their expertise in the subject and, moreover, their ability to have their decisions implemented and enforced.

The justification for such a situation is based on the theoretical existence of control of sport activities by public bodies, which act as an external check. In practice, however, principles and rules governing collective sports are defined primarily by the top layers of sports' governing bodies at the national and global levels. First, national sport federations are left to themselves to define rules concerning their organization. Second, rules at the national level are usually aligned with rules of a specific branch of sport defined at the regional and/or global levels.[11]

As a result, regulation of sporting activities, which can have economic relevance, has been traditionally left in the hands of private actors and associations. This autonomy was guaranteed by public authorities, which were nominally supervising the activities of private bodies. For instance, this self-regulation resulted in a heavily regulated labour market in collective sports, like football and basketball, which favoured clubs and employers against players and employees. Moreover, the contractual guarantees of the latter were compressed, nominally for reasons inherent to sport organizations. Nowhere

---

[11]   C. Miège, *Les Institutions Sportives* (Paris: Presses Universitaires de France, 1993).

has this trend been more obvious than in professional collective sports.[12] The often monopolistic organization of professional sports is reflected in anti-competitive practices regarding professional athletes and the public, in the form of pricing strategies and cartel arrangements. Arguably, for the time being, sport governing bodies are reluctant to introduce free competition into professional sports. They prefer to run professional sports increasingly according to monopolistic business logic, which allows them to retain maximum control over the whole process.[13]

Underlying economic pressures, however, are mounting against this regulatory system. Increasingly, European sport governing bodies have to accept progression of professional practices within bona fide *amateur* organizations. Moreover, existing sporting practices are being reshaped in the direction of commercial exigencies. This change has been particularly reinforced by the linking of sport events with mass media, which has given sporting champions the celebrity status of show business icons.[14] Televised sport disciplines, in particular, have been gradually redefined as entertainment products subject to a marketing logic (see Bogusz, elsewhere in this volume). Consequently, traditional regulatory arrangements are increasingly in conflict with the continuing transformation of sport financing, characterized by rising commercialization of sport activities and increased weight of television sponsorship in its funding.[15]

Despite mounting economic pressures, however, the regulatory framework has remained locked in the previous status quo.[16] It has remained aimed at preserving barriers and protectionist measures, mainly at the national level, to limit inflows of foreign players in professional teams.[17] In addition to that, individual athletes are profiting only marginally from the increase in profits circulating in the system[18] because commercialization is restricted to the top professional layers.[19]

---

[12]   S. Rosen and A. Sanderson, 'Labor markets in professional sports' (2001), **111**(469), *Economic Journal*, 47–68.

[13]   L. Kahn, 'The sports business as a labor market laboratory' (2000), **14**, *The Journal of Economic Perspectives*, 75–94.

[14]   S. Sobry, 'The income of top level athletes relating to televised sports entertainment' (2001), **30**(5), *Journal of Socio-Economics*, 431–6.

[15]   J.-F. Bourg and P. Staudohar, 'The evolving European model of professional sports finance' (2000), **1**(3), *Journal of Sports Economics*, 257–76.

[16]   D. Prilmaut, 'Quelle régulation pour les sports collectifs professionnels' (2001), **97**, *Revue française d'administration publique*, 1–5.

[17]   S. Weatherill, 'Discrimination on the grounds of nationality in sport' (1989), **9**, *Yearbook of European Law*, 55–92.

[18]   F. Carmichael, D. Forrest and R. Simmons, 'The labour market in association football: who gets transferred and for how much?' (1999), **51**(2), *Bulletin of Economic Research*, 125–50.

[19]   *Economist*, 'Golden Goals', 29 May 1997, 32.

Market Forces and the Transformation of Football

Professional football is changing at a faster pace than any other branch of sport, owing to its extreme commercialization.[20] Gradual adaptation of football regulatory arrangements to pressures generated by economic change is one of the characteristics of this evolution. This has slowly led to a gradual transformation within the sports' regulatory system. In the UK, for instance, football players and their representative groups were successful enough to claim certain substantive rights and procedural guarantees concerning their employment as early as the 1970s.[21] Their achievements in the UK, however, had little impact on the overall regulatory system in Europe, partly because of feeble incentives to collective action among professional sportspersons. Moreover, national authorities continued to be reverent towards the concept of sport autonomy, either by referring to the contractual freedom of private parties or by reinforcing the specificity of sport arrangements.

This resistance to change was steadily eroded during the 1980s and 1990s. From the perspective of individual athletes, the salary and recruitment of top players since the early 1980s were subject to high inflationary pressures, largely due to pressures imbedded in a labour market characterized by the economy of talent and rarity thereof (see Disney, elsewhere in this volume). In fact, football can be better understood by comparing it to similar sectors, like cinema or art, where the majority of demand concentrates on a minority of people, whose celebrity status commands a more-than-average salary. These dynamics point to a non-linear distribution of wealth and the division of a labour market into different segments.[22]

As a consequence of increasing commercialization since the 1990s, professional football clubs have in fact been acting as employers operating purely according to business logic. A range of disputes involving top players' contracts customarily erupted between professional teams, mostly during post-season periods. Moreover, a stream of cases has routinely been generated by attempts to reconcile the transnationalized sport labour market with national legal barriers, especially in the areas of naturalization and assimilation.[23]

---

[20] *Financial Times*, Wednesday 24 May 2006, *Business of Sport*, Special Report.

[21] G. Walters, 'The Professional Footballers' Association: a case study of Trade Union growth', *Occasional Papers* (Football Governance Research Centre, 2004).

[22] C. Lucifora, and R. Simmons, 'Superstar effects in sport: evidence from Italian soccer' (2003), **4**(1), *Journal of Sports Economics*, 35–55.

[23] In 2001, a passport scandal emerged, threatening to tarnish football's image and undermine the credibility of some of the world's top national championships. England, Spain, Italy and France have all been affected at the beginning of the 2000s. Such was the incentive for players to obtain the necessary papers to qualify as an EU national, and to avoid the need for a work permit altogether, that some were reportedly willing to falsify their documents.

The emergence of these tensions in professional football prompted action on the part of national sport authorities, coordinated at the regional level by UEFA. The existing status quo, however, was only marginally reformed, owing to the self-interest of national sport authorities to maintain the anti-competitive rules in place and so allow only limited room for manoeuvre of market forces within professional sport. As a consequence, the fragmented landscape of national sport models and pan-European anti-competitive rules, defined by private bodies, led to a dysfunctional European market. Simply put, the interaction between market forces and national structures in collective sports was not able to redress the in-built imbalances of the sport labour market.

Sport Regulation at the EU Level

The emergence of the European level as a relevant venue for economic regulation presented a challenge to the established order in the sport system and imposed its own rules on sport practices (see White, elsewhere in this volume). European courts and agencies gradually but steadily became involved in questions of sport regulation. Individual athletes challenged restrictive sport labour rules on the basis of freedom of movement guaranteed in the EU, whereas clubs attacked the anti-competitive league discipline enforced by sport governing bodies, to enhance their profits and negotiating power.

As a consequence, power struggles within the sport system were externalized by recourse to European law and policy venues as tools of leverage. The initial uncompromising stance made by the Commission and the ECJ to apply Community law to sporting by-laws created incentives to disturb the sport regulatory equilibrium by resorting to external regulators. It was soon realized, however, that resort to the European level is not a guarantee of a straightforward outcome, as different regulatory solutions emerged.

Initially, the ECJ and the Commission were pressing for the application of the Treaty dispositions. In 1995, the ECJ issued the *Bosman* ruling, which upheld the principle of the free movement of workers within the meaning of Article 39 of the EC Treaty. This provision should be applied to professional football players inside the EU and the European Economic Area (EEA). The judgment stated that, when a contract with a footballer who is a national of one Member State (MS) expires, the club may not prevent the player from signing a new contract with another club in another MS or agreeing to the payment of transfer fees. It should be noted that the *Bosman* ruling did not address the issue of the application of competition rules to transfers.

In 2000, the issue of professional footballers' transfers was raised again. Following several complaints, the Commission, as guardian of the Treaties, expressed a number of reservations with regard to the FIFA transfer system by issuing a statement of objections concerning competition rules and the free movement of workers. The Commission and the 'world of football', that is, international organizations such as FIFA, UEFA and professional footballers' representatives, held protracted discussions with the aim of finding a solution that would be compatible with both Community law and the specific nature of football. A satisfactory solution was finally found on 5 March 2001, when the Commission identified a number of principles concerning transfer rules, which were adopted by FIFA on 5 July 2001.

In a parallel way, governments and the European Parliament (EP) were pushing in a different direction by advocating the placement of sport outside the remit of the Community law, because of its sociocultural functions. The 1997 Amsterdam Declaration noted the importance of amateur sport practices and consultation with sporting bodies about European initiatives having a major impact on sporting activities. The 1998 Vienna Conclusions reinforced the commitment of the EU to safeguarding existing sport structures and maintaining the social function of sport within the Community framework. This led directly to the 1999 Helsinki Report on the European Model of Sport and its Survival. Finally, the 2000 Nice Declaration dwelt on the recognition of the specificity of sport in respect of its multidimensionality. In fact, the Commission identified sport as performing five functions: educational, public health, social, cultural and recreational. The educational function was prioritized, firstly, by the declaration of 2004 as the Year of Education through Sport and, secondly, by the insertion of a reference to sport and its European dimension in Article III-182 of the Constitutional Treaty, which concerned education.[24]

The role of the ECJ and the Commission in the regulation of sport at the European level continues to be decisive. Their importance is highlighted by the ruling on doping rules and their economic relevance provided by the Court of First Instance on a specific decision of the Commission in *Meca-Medina*.[25] This point was stressed by a 2002 memo by the Commission on matters of competition.[26]

On the whole, the ECJ is the most important arena for the regulation of sport practices, as its past jurisprudence (see White, elsewhere in this volume)

---

[24]   This stance reconnects with the 1986 Adonnino Report, which identified sport as a vehicle for raising awareness of the impact of European integration on daily life. See W. Tokarski, D. Steinbach, K. Petry and B. Jesse, *Two Players One Goal? Sport in the European Union* (Aachen: Meyer and Meyer 2004).

[25]   Case T-313/02 *David Meca-Medina and Igor Majcen* v *Commission* [2004] ECR II-3291.

[26]   MEMO/02/127, *The application of the EU's competition rules to sports*, available at http://ec.europa.eu/sport/sport-and/comp/competition_en.html.

and the pending *Oulmers* case[27] well demonstrate. The latter refers to a recent lawsuit brought by the Charleroi club, which was joined by the group of major European football clubs (G14), against FIFA in order to obtain compensation for injuries suffered by one of its players during an international match organized under FIFA rules, which do not recognize indemnities for the employer.

To sum up, economic structures and legal tenets of the sport system are increasingly under strain. This has led to progressive transformation of the sport regulatory environment, both internally and externally. At the European level, the judicial process, rather than the Commission, was a central factor in dismantling the established practices of sport organizations in the EU. The EU legislative process mainly limited himself to declarations intended to preserve the social and cultural dimensions of sport non-professional activities. In the next section, we discuss theoretical perspectives on regulatory analysis before embarking on the enquiry as to why the deregulation of sport activities in the EU took the judicial path.

THEORETICAL PERSPECTIVES ON COURTS AND REGULATION

The objective of this section is to assess the available opportunities for judicial intervention in sport regulation at the European level, by way of comparing this intervention with other alternatives, either at the national or at the European level.

The issue of desirability and feasibility of judicial regulatory interventionism is one of the main preoccupations of those studying the judicialization of politics.[28] Two different macro perspectives are usually put forward in this literature to explain the capacity of courts to have an impact on regulatory policy: the constrained and the dynamic approaches.

The constrained approach focuses on the barriers that prevent courts from being effective regulatory agents. It underlines three types of barriers. First, the contested nature of rights, the stickiness of legal culture, and the cautious attitude of the judiciary personnel make it very difficult to persuade courts to move in the direction of novel interpretations and decisions. Second, courts are reluctant to use their independence to find innovative solutions that defy

---

27 Case C-243/06 OJ C-212/11 (pending).
28 A comprehensive summary of impact studies of judicial activities is almost impossible, given the wealth of the literature in question. However, for a good overview, see T. Riddell, 'The impact of legal mobilization and judicial decisions: the case of official minority-language education policy in Canada for Francophones outside Quebec' (2004), **38**, *Law and Society Review*, 583.

mainstream consensus either owing to their deference to other political bodies or because of the fear of possible retaliation. Third, even in the presence of judicial victories obtained by litigants, courts lack the tools to enforce their own decisions. Thus implementation of judicial decisions has to rely on other regulatory agencies and can be jeopardized by diffused opposition among the target groups.[29]

The dynamic approach, on the contrary, assumes that the judiciary has the capacity to act and have an impact, even in the presence of strong opposition from other bodies within the political system. A key tenet of this approach is the assumption that access to and influence upon the courts is not premised on the same resources that are necessary to exert influence upon bureaucracies and legislatures. In fact, influence upon courts can be exerted through different means of advocacy: initiating a test case, supporting and intervening in related cases, diffusing its views in legal reviews and favourable coverage by information media. From such a perspective, an individual or a group, even with little economic and political leverage, can achieve policy change through litigation in courts that leads to securing jurisprudence with long-lasting effects. In such a way, these actors not only promote directly policy change, but also strengthen their position *vis-à-vis* other players and thus can acquire stronger positions in other regulatory arenas.

In his book, *The Hollow Hope: Can Courts Bring About Social Change?*, Rosenberg focuses on the impact achieved by the decisions of the Supreme Court of the United States in the area of social regulation and provides a summary of his findings concerning both the possibilities and the limits of judicial intervention in social regulation.[30] In Rosenberg's view, the dynamic approach is overoptimistic, as court-led policy making is rather inefficient, at least in terms of direct results. Though major victories in courts can be achieved, their long-range impact is more symbolic than real. Practically, courts can achieve significant results only under certain conditions. In the first place, the change which is advocated in a specific policy area needs to rely on favourable legal precedents. Second, other political bodies should support the move from the courts. Third, no or little opposition should be present in the policy community affected by the decision or in charge of its implementation. In case there is real opposition to changes, the implementation of judicial decisions is dependent on mechanisms of compliance that are outside the reach of courts. These means of compliance can consist of either positive incentives or negative costs that relate to judicial decisions. As a consequence, judicial deci-

---

29   B.C. Canon and C.A. Johnson, *Judicial Policies: Implementation and Impact* (Washington, DC: QC Press, 1999).

30   G. Rosenberg, *The Hollow Hope: Can Courts Bring About Social Change?* (Chicago: University of Chicago Press, 1991).

sions can be effective either if they flow in the direction of market dynamics or if they can be instrumentalized by administrators and officials who are willing to act upon and to use judicial decisions to promote their own agenda. However, according to Rosenberg, these conditions are rarely met and consequently the judicial route is an ineffective one, diverting resources from other alternatives without delivering results.

From this standpoint, the successful implementation of the decision in the *Bosman* ruling was due, not to some intrinsic quality of the ECJ judgment, but rather to the double pressure generated from market mechanisms and Commission enforcement machinery against football bodies.[31] In the long term, however, the single-minded tactic of promoting judicial interventions in sport matters under the cover of the Community law has backfired against the early beneficiaries of the *Bosman* ruling. The consequences of such a strategy were to prove overwhelmingly negative when compared with initial objectives. In fact, this ruling framed the defence of the rights of professional players under the banner of economic freedoms and market competition that are enshrined in the Treaties. Different plaintiffs went to great lengths to present their cases and sporting activities, more generally, in a purely economic light. This strategy was deemed to be ineffective because of the broader counterattack from the defenders of the status quo in sport regulation, who resorted, under the banner of multidimensionality of sport, to a different range of ideas to stop the would-be reformers.[32]

To sum up, a range of environmental conditions profoundly shape the impact of judicial decisions. The formal judicial legal pronouncement is submitted to in-built constraints and depends on external factors to deliver results. The underlying argument is that social regulation through litigation can produce results only if a whole set of particular circumstances are present, which is seldom the case. As a result, the principled ambitions of judicial policy making are often frustrated on a practical level. Rosenberg emphasizes that, given the judicial and extrajudicial effects of social regulation by courts, the dynamic model of judicial intervention has very limited application. He argues that, in order to obtain substantial results, it is more interesting to address alternative regulatory avenues rather than courts.

Such a stark conclusion about the limited regulatory role of courts can be tempered by the approach laid down by Neil Komesar, who decisively contributed to the so-called comparative analysis of problem-solving institu-

---

[31]   M. Haan, R. Koning and A. van Witteloostuijn, 'Market forces in European soccer' (2004), *CCSO Working Papers*, 11; available at http://www.eco.rug.nl/ccso/homenext.html.

[32]   D.G. Dimitrakopoulos, 'More than a market? The regulation of sport in the European Union' (2006), **41**(4), *Government & Opposition*, 561–80.

tions. In fact, he proposes a framework to analyse the effectiveness of the resort to courts by comparing it to other possible alternatives.[33] The most important insight underlying this methodology concerns the critique of the mono-institutional bias common in most of academic analysis related to regulatory institutions. Rosenberg, for instance, argues that courts cannot adequately address certain regulatory problems and that responsibility for problem solving should be shifted to another institution, but he does not analyse in depth the possible shortcomings of other alternatives.

The problem with this way of dealing with institutions, according to Komesar, is that, by focusing only on the shortcomings of one institution, the analysis fails to consider whether the alternative institutional arrangement that is being offered could in fact provide a more appealing solution. If all institutions have their strengths and weaknesses, the specific shortcomings of the judicial process do not guarantee that another institution, like the legislative process, provides a necessarily better alternative. Similarly, calls for more rigorous judicial oversight to rectify perceived problems in the market or the legislative process usually do not consider adequately specific limitations facing courts. The result is an unrealistic presentation of the judiciary as a perfect solution for inadequacies in markets and representative politics.[34]

Komesar insists that, in order to avoid these problems, analysis of institutions should be comparative in essence. According to him, institutions should be seen as fungible solutions to social regulatory problems with their own particular strengths and weaknesses. Proposals for taking a specific path of regulation should not simply focus on imperfections in existing institutions, but also consider whether another institutional framework can provide a preferable solution. Komesar stresses that institutional analysis is more likely to be successful and relevant when it is confined to comparing feasible alternatives, rather than relying on an 'implicit assumption . . . that a perfect or idealized institution is waiting in the wings'.[35]

In his subsequent book,[36] which was built on the same methodological assumptions, Komesar defines institutions as 'large-scale social decision-making processes' that are designed to reduce and regulate social problems.[37]

---

[33] N. Komesar, *Imperfect Alternatives: Choosing Institutions in Law, Economics, and Public Policy* (Chicago: University of Chicago Press, 1994).
[34] L. Kalman, *The Strange Career of Legal Liberalism* (New Haven: Yale University Press, 1996).
[35] See footnote 33, p. 24.
[36] N. Komesar, *Law's Limits: The Rule of Law and the Supply and Demand of Rights* (New York: Cambridge University Press, 2001).
[37] Ibid., p. 31.

The author's central contention rests on the assumption that all man-made institutions deteriorate in their ability to provide appealing solutions to regulatory problems as the number of people involved grows or the complexity of issues to be decided increases. As a result, in trying to find a solution for social conflicts 'at high numbers and complexity, we are more likely to be choosing the best of bad or unattractive alternatives'.[38]

Naturally, this raises the question of the circumstances under which a particular institution is likely to be chosen as the best of the 'imperfect' alternatives. Komesar handles this tricky question by assuming a proper competitive framework, in which it is possible for actors to make a choice among different regulatory avenues. This choice is analysed according to a 'participation-centred approach', which focuses on the comparative analysis of costs and benefits of transactions within a particular institution that consequently provides a basis for choice between institutions.

The participation-centred analysis attempts to identify factors that best account for variations in using different institutions. Its central tenet holds that regulatory change will not happen without interested parties, who push for it. Willingness to participate in a given institution determines the performance of that institution. Participation, however, will not occur in any forum unless its benefits outweigh its costs in terms of gathering information and organizing action. Benefits from direct participation relate to the stake of the party in the outcome. Some characteristics of participative costs and benefits are the same across all institutions. In general, the more diffusely a benefit is spread, the lower is the stake in the outcome. Moreover, costs of participation increase when an issue is complex or highly technical, as it takes time and energy to collect and use information. In addition, the design of an institution creates its own costs that affect participation. Komesar advocates a detailed case-by-case examination in order to understand how the distribution of benefits and costs of action can affect the path different groups choose to get what they want:

> the propensity for large group action varies with such factors as the absolute per capita stakes of the majority, the non-uniformity of the distribution (which also affects the possibility of entrepreneurship), the size of the majority, the complexity of the issue, and the cost of information.[39]

Komesar's approach focuses on the actions of those policy actors, who generate legal change through their activities in each institution, whether as litigants, voters or lobbyists. A possible criticism of this approach is that effective choice

---

[38] Ibid., p. 24.
[39] Ibid., p. 88.

between alternative regulatory avenues presupposes a proper competitive framework and a rational approach to the selection among the options. Real-life policy actors can use all of the avenues available to them, subsequently or simultaneously, according to a more or less rational approach in relation to their resources and purposes. Alternatively, individuals and groups can use different avenues against each other, according to their respective relative advantage to them. While adjudication and legislation are analysed by Komesar as alternatives, in reality they are often interdependent and complementary.

Sport regulation is a good case study to apply a Comparative Institutional Approach (CIA), as it shows the latent tensions between alternative arenas of policy making within the EU: national and European levels, legislative and judicial processes. In fact, many of the twists and turns of sport regulation in the EU during the 1990s can be better understood by considering dilemmas underlying the choice of venue, under conditions of imperfect alternatives and their complex interaction.

First of all, this case study illustrates the imperfect options that are usually offered to policy actors. In fact, challengers of the established status quo within the sport regulatory system resorted to Community law and European bodies, owing to the shortage of other viable alternatives either within sport structures or at the national level. Therefore, this case confirms Komesar's assumption about the competitive conditions, in which individuals and groups choose to participate in policy making through different institutions in order to achieve their preferred outcomes.

Secondly, intervention by a certain institution to solve a regulatory problem does not preclude the subsequent use of alternative venues by other groups, sometimes even simultaneously, to solve the same problem. Resort to a regulatory institution can be seen either in isolation, which presupposes that one particular forum is chosen as the predominant target, or as part of a sequential dynamics, where an action by a specific institution elicits a counterreaction by another institution. In the latter case, as far as the case of sport regulation is concerned, both legislative and judicial processes can be put at work, but pushing in different directions.

Thirdly, sport regulation brings an additional element of complexity to the straightforward picture sketched by Komesar by way of hinting at the importance of different institutional levels in each policy area. In the particular case of sport regulation, the stickiness of sport bodies and national instances stimulated action at the European level. Once the European authorities intervened, however, national structures re-entered the game and have influenced the development of sport regulation in Europe.

In the next section, Komesar's theoretical framework is applied to provide a detailed analysis of the aforementioned developments.

OVERVIEW OF SPORT REGULATION AT THE EU LEVEL

Following CIA insights, EU institutional characteristics have to be considered in order to assess the relative merits of their regulatory performance. According to Komesar, differences in distribution of benefits and costs of participation as well as institutional design lead to differential paths of institutional performance. Consequently, participation is the result of a trade-off between top-down design and bottom-up participation. As far as the regulation of sport in the EU sport is concerned, there were two possible ways to introduce a new regulatory equilibrium, in place of established rules and practices. The alternatives are either regulation by adjudication by the ECJ or administrative regulation by the Commission. Following the CIA, features of this regulatory dilemma need to be analysed in detail, starting from the institutional design point of view, as this offers costs and benefits to participants in such a regulatory framework.

Analysis of EU Regulatory Background

From the angle of institutional design, sport regulation at the EU level has some peculiarities, especially in the areas of labour restrictions and anti-competitive practices. On the one hand, restrictive and discriminatory sport practices are subject to both Art. 39 EC and Arts 81–82 EC. Therefore, application of Community law to sport can require a different set of rules to be taken into account and result in divergence, which could create a problem of coherence at the very heart of the Treaty.[40] On the other hand, the means of enforcement of these sets of rules are different. In fact, sport practices are susceptible to parallel enforcement, either by the Commission, in its capacity as the 'guardian of the Treaties', or by private parties before national courts, by way of relying upon the direct horizontal effect of Arts 39, 81 and 82 EC.

Concerning the first problem, the overlap and discrepancies between Art. 39 EC and Arts 81–82 EC, make the issue of sport regulation complex. In fact, in the case of professional sport, legal treatment of discrimination on national grounds and obstructions to the freedom of movement for workers appear more lenient under competition law than under Art. 39 and its related secondary legislation. Regarding free movement, practices of discrimination and obstruction are prohibited without exception in professional sport, as was declared in the *Donà* case. Conversely, under competition law, sport practices

---

[40]   J.B. Cruz, *Between Competition and Free Movement* (Oxford: Hart Publishing 2002), pp. 86–8.

have the possibility to be granted an exemption under Art. 81(3), following discretional evaluation by the Commission.

Regarding the second problem, legal complexities, which emerge from the EC Treaty itself, have been compounded by the different means of enforcement available to address the potential tension between these provisions. In fact, concerning enforcement, there is a remarkable difference between interpretation of Art. 39 and Arts 81–82 EC from the point of view of the ECJ, exercising its preliminary-ruling jurisdiction under Art. 234 EC, and that of the Commission, acting in its administrative capacity as 'guardian of the Treaties' (Art. 226 EC).

On the Commission's side, there are no direct means by which it would be possible to enforce Art. 39 EC against private parties because it is a provision addressed to the Member States. An indirect way is to use infringement proceedings against governments, based on Art. 226 EC, which requires them to act against breaches of the Treaties. By adopting this approach, the Commission would indirectly address private sport organizations. In such a scenario, a Member State could be made liable for such unlawful activities carried out within its territory by private parties, with its more or less tacit assent. Such an eventuality is theoretically possible, but it is cumbersome and time-consuming. Moreover, the end results would be highly unpredictable, given the customary autonomy enjoyed by sport organizations at the national level.

Because of this institutional design, the potential for acting is different alongside the different routes provided at the European level. In fact, from the point of view of the claimants, recourse to the Commission against the sport organizations is more attractive in relation to competition law, which confers on the Directorate-General (DG) Competition of the Commission powers of investigation and discretional decision making to dispose of these cases. If the DG takes the view that football bodies are acting in breach of competition rules, the Commission has the power to issue a decision requiring termination of the anti-competitive practices and, in addition to this, it may decide to impose a fine. However, under existing rules, the use of these powers of investigation and enforcement under competition law is not transparent for private parties, who have a vested interest in these proceedings. Once the Commission is informed of possible infringements of Arts 81 and/or 82 EC, by 'natural or legal persons who claim a legitimate interest', the complainant is not entitled to a final decision. This means that, if the Commission decides not to pursue the infringement, for reasons of political considerations or resource shortcomings, the complainant has no other means of redress, except to pursue the matter before a national court. In such an eventuality, private parties may invoke all directly effective provisions of the Treaty in order to challenge the sport regulatory practices which they consider infringe the Community law. In fact, Arts 81–82 EC are directly effective, both vertically and horizontally.

In respect of the ways of competition law, whereas the DG Competition can have a much more expedient use of such *'complaints'*, the ECJ, because of its role in preliminary references, is called to answer all claims about *justiciables'* rights and is less inclined to neglect questions promoted by a national court. Even though the preliminary ruling procedure is subject to the national court's filter, it provides access to the ECJ for individuals seeking to challenge Community law infringements. For instance, from the point of view of a football *justiciable*, the Commission is the more effective avenue to deal with the labour restrictive practices, whereas the most relevant way is through Competition law. However, this point is true to the extent to which the Commission is willing to process these claims. The contrary route to the ECJ is easier to take but more expensive in terms of time and energy. Moreover, the pressure exerted over the ECJ by individuals or groups is more effective if carried out consistently in line with its jurisprudential principles and doctrine.

In spite of the general EU institutional design, however, it is necessary to consider the bottom-up dynamic of participation. As a general rule, for professional athletes, recourse to external regulation by agency or court is extremely costly. Given the short span of a professional career, the perspective of entering into a lengthy dispute over sport by-laws is highly unlikely and furthermore discouraged by eventual sporting sanctions. Consequently, only a small number of cases come before the Commission and Court, while only very few sportspersons have elicited some answers from the European level. The ECJ and Commission had to use these available occasions to develop a doctrine and take a position on sport practices and their compatibility with the European regulatory order.

Nonetheless, in the earlier stages of EU sport regulation, the breakthrough provoked by the *Bosman* ruling created a favourable conjuncture of opportunities, in which individuals and groups were able to overcome the aforementioned costs of participation. On the one hand, the claimants and litigants could count on sympathetic ears at the Commission and the ECJ, especially the Competition Commissioner Van Miert and Judge Mancini. On the other hand, it is necessary to mention the role played by supporting factors concerning the strategic use of Community law. Especially interesting is the case of the principal legal counsel of *Bosman*, Mr Misson. Himself a lawyer specializing in free movement of workers under Community law, and a former employee at the Commission, he used his expertise and connections to promote similar cases to that of Mr Bosman. His aim was to push for further EC jurisprudential and administrative development in sport, in order to advance the interests of sportspeople within the context of workers' rights. The two cases referred to the ECJ in 1996 were conducted with his assistance[41] and several of the complaints to the Competition DG in 1997 were made through his legal firm, on behalf of a professional players' union, FIFpro, which supported Bosman during his litigation. In other words, the *Bosman* ruling lowered considerably the threshold of information and participation costs and opened the gates for more challenges.

A participation-centred approach, applied to the case of sport regulation emanating from the EU level, provides an interesting reading of the latest developments. Individuals and generally weak groups took the judicial path, bypassing other forms of advocacy, whereas clubs and powerful associations tried to harness the Commission and its regulatory powers in their favour. Ultimately, however, both trajectories were destined to achieve only partial results owing to institutional strategies and counter-reaction of sport bodies, which successfully lobbied governments and the European Parliament in their defence.

Participation in the EU Regulatory Framework

In the light of the CIA, policy actors pursue their goals in a variety of complementary institutional venues, prioritizing their participation according to expected returns. In a real situation of conflicting regulatory perspectives and interests, however, institutions can be used either to obtain the desired outcome or to counter non-desirable gains from the opposing side in other institutional settings. Faced with a legal offensive, the sport establishment orchestrated a political counterattack, which used a different route from that of their opponents. As the regulatory status quo presented diffused costs and concentrated benefits inside the sport system, the sport governing bodies quickly mobilized in favour of a strong counter-attack.

Given the popularity of sport among Europeans and the facility with which it is being instrumentalized as a vehicle for political ambitions, the most logical path to follow for sports bodies was to approach the European Council and the European Parliament. Positive feedback could have been expected in these policy venues. On the one hand, sports bodies used the ties that bind national politicians to the sport status quo. On the other hand, a campaign was mounted to turn the European Parliament into a platform to air friendly statements in favour of established sport regulatory positions.[42]

---

[41]   A crucial factor in these preliminary rulings was the willingness of the Belgian legal context, contrary to other national cases (including judges, lawyers and defendants), to defer to the ECJ questions concerning sport issues.

[42]   Given the second-order nature of European elections, an important number of former athletes are present among the ranks of the European Parliament, lending a sympathetic ear to sport requests.

Sports bodies operated in a way that would allow them to avoid the intervention of supranational bodies and to escape their control by means of political compromises, for instance declaratory, but not legally binding, statements. Examples of these include the Amsterdam declaration on sport, informal political agreements, and the transfer agreement between Commission and FIFA. An alternative is back-door negotiation in judicial disputes with opposite parties in order to sideline legal proceedings. Nonetheless, short of a change of the dispositions inscribed at the heart of the Treaties, non-competitive practices by sporting authorities were not likely to find an escape from the established patterns of EU economic governance as carried over by European bodies.

In fact, the majoritarian approach is not a straightforward strategy at the European level, given the in-built anti-majoritarian bias in its design.[43] Sports bodies reliant on the support of friendly governments and members of the European Parliament had to face the structural disadvantage of advancing their cause through a dysfunctional path of advocacy at the EU level. The path of sport regulation through the EU legislative process is unfeasible, given the fragmentation of EU decision-making machinery, subject to multiple veto points and influences. These difficulties are increased by specific problems related to a legislative handling of sport regulation in the context of EU competencies. Currently, there exists no legal basis for an EU sport policy, which implies a considerable disadvantage for sports bodies relying on national government to preserve their privileges. The main reason for this asymmetry is the uneven balance between positive and negative integration, which is rooted in the EU institutional structure.

The functional process of integration was originally conceived as a combination of positive and negative action, having a logical complementarity.[44] However, this design overlooked the institutional structure assuring the nexus between negative and positive integration. On the one hand, negative integration was enshrined in the Community Treaty and implemented by supranational agents, like the Commission and the ECJ. On the other hand, positive integration was to be advanced through secondary legislation, depending on a cumbersome decision-making process, submitted to multiple veto players and complex negotiations, under the control of an intergovernmental Council.[45]

---

[43] G. Majone, 'Regulatory legitimacy', in G. Majone (ed.) *Regulating Europe* (London: Routledge, 1996), 285–87.

[44] J. Pinder, 'Positive and negative integration: some problem of economic integration in the EEC' (1968), **24**, *World Today*, 88–110.

[45] F. Scharpf, 'Balancing positive and negative integration: the regulatory options for Europe', *Robert Schuman Centre Policy Paper*, **97**(4), European University Institute, Florence (1997).

Moreover, the negative integration agenda defined in the Treaty concerning the four freedoms and competition is coupled with devices, such as the competition complaints procedure or the judicial preliminary reference, which maintain the integrative machinery under pressure with input from private parties. As a consequence of the deregulation programme advanced under the umbrella of the Single Market initiative, the established practices of sporting bodies, and especially football, were disrupted by the intervention of the EU supranational bodies, under Treaty aegis, to implement the Treaty dispositions.[46]

It is important to remember that EU sport regulation provided by the Commission and the Court took place in the context of a clash between two rival policy coalitions, expressing themselves through different institutional channels. On the one hand, there was a group more favourable to accommodation of sporting rules and practices, without their substantial transformation, in the framework of European integration. On the other hand, another group advocated a more confrontational approach, inducing sport actors to modify their private arrangements in the light of the '*acquis communautaire*'. The interaction between sport self-regulation and EU law has consequently been marked by both cooperative and confrontational aspects, depending on which approach the EU bodies adopted in their strategy toward sport. Generally speaking, the ECJ was more prone to the conflictual approach than the Commission, imposing full respect for Community law on sporting authorities. However, the result has been a compromise between these different strategies concerning the issue of EU sport regulation, which were determined by conflictual policy visions. The current EU position is trying to reconcile both sides, accommodating the social and cultural aspects of sport within the EU legal *acquis*. The resulting outcome is a dialogue between different regulatory positions taking place in different venues.[47]

This improbable compromise, produced by institutional manoeuvring among different coalitions of interests, is not uncommon in the EU owing to its complex structure. The most recent manifestation of such a tendency was the drafting of the Constitutional Treaty, where sport movements and certain governments managed to organize themselves in order to insert a reference to sport in the Treaties, establishing the first legal basis for an EU sport policy. The insertion of sport as a competence in the Treaties was the result of a difficult manoeuvre within the European Convention[48] under French

---

46   S. Weatherill, *Law and Integration in the European Union* (Oxford: Clarendon Press, 1995).

47   R. Parrish, 'The politics of sport regulation in the European Union' (1999), **10**(2), *Journal of European Public Policy*, 246–62.

48   Concerning the introduction of a reference to sport in the Treaties, a cleavage

leadership.[49] This reference to sport fell under Title III (Union competences), Article 16 (areas of supporting, coordinating or complementary action) and Chapter V (areas where the union may take coordinating, complementary or supporting action), Article III-182(4). However, this unsuccessful attempt to inscribe a sport competence in the Treaties, because of the ratification problems, is leading governments and sport bodies to try to rewrite the rules of the game at the EU level.

Rewriting the Rules of the Game

As explained in the preceding section, the legislative process and national governments within the EU have been generally responsive to the demands of the sporting establishment. Initially, their efforts were designed to block or reverse the application of the Community law to the sporting field. Subsequently, their energies were directed towards inscription of a sport competence at the EU level. After the failure of the Constitutional Treaty for reasons unrelated to the sport regulation saga, sports governing bodies have engineered a third initiative in combination with friendly governments.

In 2005, the UK presidency of the EU initiated a review of the challenges that different branches of European sports, and especially football, face nowadays.[50] This so-called Arnaut report was drafted with support from UEFA and FIFA and its main argument was that the series of legal challenges to sporting rules had weakened the system and created a climate of instability. The stated goal of the report was to indicate how best to implement the principles stated in the Nice declaration, which aimed at preserving the traditional sports' structures and their socioeconomic specificity from the pressures of individual athletes and clubs trying to apply the Community law. The reasons for this declaration were principally the conservative approach dictated by governments and their hostility towards any increase of EU competences outside its

---

appeared between the proponents of such a move, mainly Southern Member States (France, Spain, Portugal, Italy, Belgium and Greece) and Nordic Member States (Sweden, Denmark, Finland and United Kingdom), which were opposed. The determinant vote was cast by Germany.

[49]   See the document from the European Convention: *The place of sport in the future Treaty – contribution 183* (10 January 2003). In fact, the proposed text for an article on sport emerged from an extensive consultation between the International Olympic Committee (IOC), the European Olympic Committees (EOC), the Association of Summer Olympic International Federations (ASOIF), the Association of the International Olympic Winter Sports Federations (AIOWF) and football bodies FIFA and UEFA, and was prepared by the French delegation to the convention at the request of the Ministry of Sport.

[50]   Independent European Sport review (Arnaut, 2006) at http://www.independentfootballreview.com/index.html.

core business of market building. According to this report, sporting federations should have central responsibilities in the regulation of sport activities.[51]

The report concluded that 'sports in general and football in particular are not in good health. Only the direct involvement of political leaders, working together with the football authorities, can put it back on the road to recovery'.[52] As far as the EU is concerned, the report suggested that supranational bodies should create a formal structure of partnership and cooperation with UEFA, granting it official recognition as the regional body in charge of football decision-making. It was argued that the Commission, in particular, should provide clear guidance on the type of 'sport rules' compatible with Community law and allow UEFA room to manoeuvre within which sport actors would maintain their autonomy and make relevant choices about the competitive balance in European football.

These conclusions are in line with traditional arguments made by sports' governing bodies that sport self-regulation is an autonomous system, which has to be protected from interference by external entities in order to be able to function correctly. The football governing bodies have lobbied particularly hard in order to prevent the Commission and the ECJ from applying, in their own sphere of competence, Community law to football. Accordingly, the ECJ and the Commission misunderstood the special features of sporting activities, as their decisions are both preventing the sporting movement from performing its social and educational functions and accelerating the disruption of the sport system. The positive endorsement of sports' governance as a self-sufficient system adapted to the specific features of sport, which was offered by the Arnaut report, appears to be more or less a confirmation of this attitude towards the Common Market.

The argument about the specificity of sport, however, lacks substance, for a number of reasons. Firstly, the existence of EU regulation of sport economic matters is of vital importance to the professional sport industry, in spite of the resistance of sports' governing bodies. As more successful professional segments of certain popular sports become increasingly commercialized and disconnected from their sociocultural roots, they need a legal framework adapted to their economic functioning. Once certain sport structures have developed in this direction, it is very difficult to revert to the previous situation. In general, if the professional sport sector functions according to business logic, it is appropriate to regulate it in such a manner as to avoid dysfunctional

---

[51]   The only concession to the supervisory role of the European Union should be, according to the report, the creation of a European Sports Agency to oversee all sports institutions and bodies within the EU.

[52]   J.L. Arnaut, *Independent European Sport Review* (2006), UK Presidency of the EU.

outcomes. The influence of the Community law and EU regulation in sport economic matters can be depicted as remedies for market failures.[53]

Secondly, sport mechanisms of self-regulation are, to this day, not particularly known to be democratic or to ensure proper accountability. In fact, so far, sport structures have failed to implement principles of transparency and openness in their activities,[54] as well as principles of good governance in their internal disciplinary proceedings.[55] Paradoxically, the EU acknowledgment of the regulative function of sport bodies is not likely to accelerate implementation of the 'rule of law' and 'good governance', at least in the way they are conceived at the EU level.[56]

In spite of these reasons for rebuttal, the political attractiveness of the Arnaut report rests in the proposition of a hands-off scheme for sport regulation at the European level, which would fit with the present situation in most of the Member States. This would result in a pact among governments to offer a better protection to sports' governing bodies from EU scrutiny in return for promises of enhanced governance. If this report were to be implemented, it would project at the European level most of the characteristics of the crumbling model of sport regulation currently in place at the national level.[57] This sport model, based on the political supervision of sporting autonomy by public

---

[53]   A. Caiger and S. Gardiner, *Professional sport in the European Union: regulation and re-regulation* (The Hague: Asser Press, 2000).

[54]   Reporter Andrew Jennings alleged in a recent book that senior FIFA officials received bribes from the marketing company that used to negotiate FIFA's lucrative World Cup sponsorship deals. FIFA denied the allegations and tried to ban the sale of the book in Switzerland. This account of corruption and non-transparent practices within FIFA was banned in Switzerland. See A. Jennings, *Foul* (London: Harper Collins, 2006).

[55]   Doubts about reliable sport governance arose recently, on the occasion of the Football World Cup. The German Football Federation, the hosts of the World Cup, was mortified in 2005 by a scandal involving a leading referee and some players who received money from a network of Croatian gamblers in order to fix certain matches. In 2006, the former coach and ex-president of Olympique Marseille, winner of the UEFA Champions League, were convicted of involvement in embezzling club funds from the transfer of 15 players during the period 1997–99. Even more recently, Italian football was hit by revelations that many referees were part of a scheme to favour leading clubs. Similar scandals erupt frequently among FIFA 207 members. Self-regulation clearly did not prevent these recurring episodes of corruption, which are undermining the credibility of football.

[56]   For a view on the self-understanding of these issues among sport governing bodies, see the website and proceedings of the 2001 conference on governance and sport at http://www.governance-in-sport.com/index.html.

[57]   K. Foster, 'Can sport be regulated by Europe: an analysis of alternative models', in A. Caiger and S. Gardiner, *Professional sport in the European Union: regulation and re-regulation* (The Hague: Asser Press 2000), pp. 43–64.

authorities, is increasingly under strain, because of the progressive transformation of regulatory practices towards sport in Europe.

CONCLUSIONS

This chapter proposes an analysis of the current landscape of sport regulation within the EU, particularly taking into consideration three elements: national structures, market forces and EU regulatory action. These elements are locked in a relationship of mutual influence that is characterized by an ever-changing equilibrium. The chapter has discussed the background, the dynamics and the prospective lines of development of this unstable equilibrium. A theoretical framework, based on CIA, was introduced to highlight the latent tensions between alternative arenas of policy making within the EU. It has also analysed why and how, at the EU level, the choice between administrative and judicial alternatives of regulation was decided in favour of the ECJ as the main arbiter of the question.

From a general point of view, sport is a good case study to analyse the politics of regulation at the European level. On the one hand, this capacity is due to the specific status that sport, in the current state of the European integration process, has in the context of Community competencies. Not included in the legal reach of the European Treaties, sporting issues are nonetheless handled indirectly by the ECJ as well as by the Commission, under Community law related to competition and free movement of workers. On the other hand, the legal and technocratic drive to regulate sport under the core provisions of the Treaties is counteracted by the resistance of sports bodies and Member State opposition, whose reservations are usually most forcefully expressed in European Councils and Inter-Governmental Conferences. Such a confusing legal situation has created a competitive regulatory atmosphere.[58]

As a consequence, the development of sport regulation illustrates well the imperfect nature of policy alternatives and dilemmas related to the choice of the most appropriate venue to address them. In practice, once this choice is made, not always in optimal conditions, it has significant consequences beyond the case at issue. In fact, any proposed solution to a regulatory problem owes its features to the institutional setting in which the problem was raised and discussed. The EU as a setting is predominantly technocratic, prone to market solutions rather than majoritarian ways of solving social issues.

---

[58]   *Financial Times*, 'Ministers call new EU rules on sport offside', 8 May 2007.

Therefore, in the current state of the European integration process, the principle of subsidiarity applies loosely to sport regulation within the EU, where Member States and sporting organizations are entitled to develop their own specific sport policies, but are expected to comply with the obligations imposed by the EU legal framework as far as the economic dimension is concerned. This means that even fully-fledged EU regulation of sport would have, at best, a secondary and subordinate role in respect of national responsibilities.[59]

---

[59] See preparatory material for EU white paper on sport, http://ec.europa.eu/sport/index_en.html.

7. Remuneration of sports stars: implications for regulation

Richard Disney

In 1929, Babe Ruth, the greatest American baseball player, earned $70,000 . . . An indignant reporter asked Ruth to justify how he could be worth substantially more than what the President of the United States earned. Ruth is reported to have said: 'I had a better year'. (Quoted by Rosen and Sanderson, 2001)

Do I get value for money? What do you think? I personally don't get value for money from the players. If you see a Premiership player on, say, £5000 a week, do I get 20 times more pleasure than [from] a player in the Championship earning £250 a week? Of course I don't. Paying players £100,000–£150,000 is just insane. I earned all my money the old-fashioned way and you would have to send me back to school for me to understand why they get paid so much for doing so little.

We are the ones stupid enough to pay them, but they are overpaid for what they contribute. (Milan Mandaric, Portsmouth FC Chairman, quoted by the *Daily Mail*, 24 March 2006)

Pat Burrell is in a profession where failure is routine. The best players in the game only get a hit one out of every three times at bat. But when Burrell inked a six year, $50 million contract with the Philadelphia Phillies during the offseason, the left-hander's room for failure decreased exponentially.

'We play a game for a living, but this is a business,' the Phillies leftfielder says. 'There's a reason for the big contracts.'

As the boos rained down on Donovan McNabb a week ago Sunday, heckling the same player they cheered during player introductions in Week 1, Burrell flinched. Burrell knows the $115 [million] contract McNabb signed last September not only is an endorsement of McNabb's abilities and a security blanket for his future, it is an albatross.

'They make all that stuff so public', Burrell says, 'Everyone knows what you are making so they decide if you're worth it.' (Dana Pennett O'Neil, *Philadelphia Daily News*, posted 24 September 2003 on website: http://www.psychologyofsports.com)

INTRODUCTION

This chapter analyses remuneration in sports labour markets, ranging from semi-professional sportsmen and women through to superstars. It describes how the competitive model of sports remuneration, which suggests that pay is largely determined by preferences, abilities and the 'personal scale of operations' of sports stars, has implications for the allocative efficiency of the sports labour market in the presence of alternative regulatory structures and distributions of property rights, and for the incidence of 'punishments' levied on players, clubs or leagues. The implications of market power and collusion for pay and regulatory outcomes are explained. Finally, the chapter examines the issue of 'competitive balance' and how the organization of sports leagues and tournaments affects remuneration of sportsmen and women.

REMUNERATION OF SPORTS STARS: IMPLICATIONS FOR REGULATION

The Background: Superstars, Tournaments and Professional Leagues

There has long been an interest among economists in the labour market for sportsmen and sportswomen. The early literature that emerged in the United States stemmed from influential papers such as Rottenberg[1] and Rosen,[2] which sought to explain the high level of pay of sports 'stars', especially in baseball, and how this level was related to the organization of sport. Interestingly, this now-extensive literature has developed models of remuneration (pay) that have been applied not only to professional sport leagues but also to explain remuneration in other labour markets which share the same characteristics, such as the pay of CEOs of large corporations and rewards to City traders. These underlying characteristics are, broadly, a limited pool of exceptional talent and a large 'personal scale of operations':[3] that is where the volume of transactions affected by the star player's activities is very large (the volume of spectators, and the number of player-specific sporting items bought and sold, such as named shirts, equipment, products endorsements and so on) despite a low mark-up on each transaction. In such circumstances, in tournaments where there can only be one winner drawn from the ranks of only a few potential winners, remuneration levels for individual sports stars are potentially huge.

---

[1]   S. Rottenberg, 'The baseball players' labor market' (1956), **64**, *Journal of Political Economy*, 242–58.

[2]   S. Rosen, 'The economics of superstars' (1981), **71**, *American Economic Review*, 845–98; 'Prizes and incentives in elimination tournaments' (1986), **76**, *American Economic Review*, 701–15.

[3]   T. Mayer, 'The distribution of ability and earnings' (1960), **42**, *Review of Economics and Statistics*, 189–95.

Whilst such an explanation for individual remuneration levels can easily be applied to sports that reward individual achievement, such as golf and tennis (and to a lesser extent, athletics), many sports are essentially team sports in which performance is in part team-oriented and not simply a product of individual talents. Moreover, professional sport in the US is largely organized into 'closed' leagues with various explicit measures designed to ensure 'competitive balance' among teams (such as 'draft picks' inversely related to past team performance and salary bill caps). Here, arguably, the marketed product is not the performance of an individual sportsperson, or even an individual team, but is provided by the league as a whole. Individual remuneration can still be related to individual productivity because of the US sport's love affair with statistics (yardage gained, completed passes, home runs, runs batted in, fielding errors and so on) and because salary contracts are generally made public. However, in looking at contractual negotiations between leagues and, on the one hand, their employees and, on the other hand, outside bodies such as broadcasting companies, the argument has often been made that the activities of these professional sports leagues should be treated as 'joint ventures',[4] and that the product should be treated as the provision of a competitive tournament rather than success in a tournament per se.

The view that the 'product' is the competition itself rather than the outcome, and that this outcome can be enhanced by explicit collusion, has not found favour with all regulators, nor indeed with all economists.[5] It seems at first sight paradoxical that competition must be internally regulated by professional leagues in order to generate competition (in this context, a 'competitive balance' between teams) and that this may permit various non-competitive practices such as restrictions on new entrants, joint bargaining with purchasers of the product and various restrictions on duration, remuneration and other terms of employment contracts.

Traditionally, European sporting governing bodies are looser umbrella organizations that cover a hierarchy of leagues with promotion and relegation, such as the Football Association in England. Even before the *Bosman* ruling,[6] and other similar rulings, discussed in Erika Szyszczak's chapter, it has been harder for the organizers of such leagues (and of internal groups of clubs such

---

    [4]   As in M. Flynn and R. Gilbert, 'The analysis of professional sports leagues as joint ventures' (2001), **111**, *Economic Journal*, F27–F46.
    [5]   See, for example, R. Noll (ed.), *Government and the Sports Business* (Washington, D.C.: The Brookings Institution, 1974); 'The economics of promotion and relegation in sports leagues: the case of English football' (2002), **3**, *Journal of Sports Economics*, 169–203; 'The organization of sports leagues' (2003), **19**, *Oxford Review of Economic Policy*, 530–51.
    [6]   Case C-415/93 [1995] ECR I-4921.

as the Premiership or the G14 group) to form 'closed leagues' along US lines. Such an outcome, for example, a European 'superleague' in football, might occur in the future[7] if existing 'competitive balance' in domestic leagues is eroded by the concentration of talent and success among a small sub-set of clubs, but long-run trends are notoriously hard to predict.

These are among the key issues that underpin the economic analysis of remuneration in sports. The remainder of this chapter is structured as follows. In the next section, a basic structure of pay levels in sports, which I term the 'remuneration pyramid', is outlined. Pay levels are determined by preferences and productivity, but with a sub-set of 'superstars' who obtain incomes well beyond those suggested merely by considerations of individual or team production. Section 3 considers the point that an essentially competitive model of pay may be inapplicable in an economic activity characterized by market imperfections: both in selling of the sport itself and in the purchase and payment of players (monopsony). It considers the implications of this for total sports revenue, and the implications of the Coase theorem for both total revenues and the allocation of revenues among participants (players, owners, agents and so on). It also examines the implications of our remuneration model for 'crime and punishment', most notably the incidence of financial and non-financial penalties levied on clubs and players. Section 4 considers the issue of 'competitive balance', how to achieve it, and the implications of competitive balance for the remuneration of professional sportsmen and sportswomen. A brief concluding section follows.

SPORTS REMUNERATION

Most people are involved in sport because they enjoy it. Like musicians, sportsmen and sportswomen do not set off on a sporting career with the idea of making money, with the exception of a few well-publicized parents of tennis players. Forgone earnings early in life, and uncertainty both over talent and the prospect of injury or loss of form bringing an early end to a sporting career, limit pecuniary objectives at the outset. Given the uncertainties of a sporting career, however, it is also unsurprising that sportsmen and women are anxious to maximize the returns from whatever success, luck, or their talent, bring them. Pay to sportsmen and women can be thought of as defined by a 'remuneration pyramid' of the stylized type depicted in Figure 7.1.

---

[7]   See T. Hoehn and S. Szymanski, 'The Americanisation of European football' (1999), **14**, *Economic Policy*, 203–40.

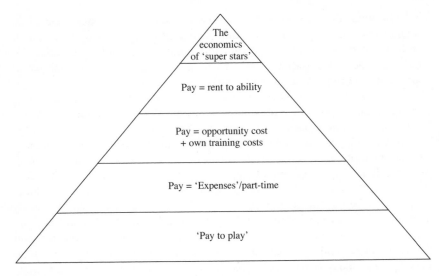

Figure 7.1   A remuneration pyramid in sport

Much of the interest of economists in sports remuneration concerns the apex of the pyramid, but, at the base, large numbers of people engage in sport with no remuneration at all. In part this stems from a lack of any exceptional talent, but also from the fact that their activity generates no revenue from which any type of remuneration can be exacted.

At the next level of the remuneration pyramid are the sports, such as the lower leagues of football and, until recently, rugby union, where there is some talent and where there is some revenue from sporting events, largely derived from gate revenue and limited sponsorship. Here there is the potential to pay some or all participants part-time, or expenses. Historically, perhaps cricket is one sport where paid and unpaid players might both participate in the same team: a tradition kept alive by having one or more 'professionals' attached to an otherwise amateur (that is, unpaid) team. As outside revenue expands, notably with the sale of television rights and associated revenues, 'expenses' may effectively cover full-time payments so that ultimately the sport is transformed into a professional structure.

The Paid Professional

Further up the diminishing hierarchy are sports or leagues with full-time professional players. At the lowest rung of the professional level, participants are effectively paid their opportunity cost, that is, pay is equal to outside earnings plus forgone earnings in training and any premium arising from the greater career uncertainty associated with professional sports. Teams in leagues such as the lower professional leagues of football (for example, Divisions 1 and 2 in England) pay a wage that, while often exceeding outside earnings, does not represent a large rent to ability. Players are potentially substitutable by others (albeit not without the club incurring training costs or transfer fees) and revenue sources depend on, and are dominated by, the loyalty of the fan base rather than outside sources such as revenue from broadcasting rights.

Still further up the pay pyramid are sportsmen and women who are demonstrably more productive than any potential replacement, and where team revenue sources can be augmented by outside revenues such as sponsorship, merchandising and broadcasting rights. These additional sources of revenue have grown recently in many sports – notably broadcasting revenues.[8] Such players earn a 'rent to ability' and numerous studies have attempted to link individual remuneration to measures of this 'rent to ability' derived from indicators of productivity such as win percentages over the season and other measures of on-field performance. An early and influential study of baseball by Scully[9] calculated these measures of success as 'outputs' in a production function conditioned on inputs such as batting and fielding averages, runs scored and defended, and so on. Such methods have been applied to other similar sports such as cricket.[10] Interestingly, Scully[11] showed that the application of the 'reserve clause' in baseball, which allowed professional teams to make exclusive long-term contracts (see later), discounted individual salaries well below marginal products. Abolition of this clause raised baseball salaries significantly[12] as did, unsurprisingly, the removal of salary caps such as the abolition of the maximum wage in professional football in Britain.

---

[8] Commercial receipts and gate receipts in the English Premier League between 1992 and 2003 both rose by around 300 per cent in nominal terms and account for roughly equal sources of revenue: about 30 per cent each. Revenues from broadcasting rights rose by over 3000 per cent in the same period and accounted for over 40 per cent of total revenues by 2003 (cited by J. Michie and C. Oughton, 'Competitive balance in football: trends and effects', *Football Governance Research Centre, Research Paper*, no. 2, Birkbeck College, London, 2004).

[9] G. Scully, 'Pay and performance in major league baseball' (1974), **64**, *American Economic Review*, 915–30.

[10] J. Schofield, 'Production functions in the sports industry: an empirical analysis of professional cricket' (1988), **20**, *Applied Economics*, 177–93; E. Bairam, J. Howells and G. Turner, 'Production functions in cricket: the Australian and New Zealand experience' (1990), **22**, *Applied Economics*, 871–9.

[11] *Supra*, n. 9.

[12] D. MacDonald and M. Reynolds, 'Are baseball players paid their marginal products?' (1994), **15**, *Managerial and Decision Economics*, 443–57; S. Rosen and A. Sanderson, 'Labour markets in professional sports' (2001), **111**, *Economic Journal*, F47–F68.

Whilst pay may be broadly competitively determined by productivity in such settings, however, the simple paradigm of the atomistic competitive market does not completely hold. Team success is a joint, rather than an individual, output. A revenue-maximizing owner can hire a manager and set of players that optimizes expected team production given the raw materials and budget constraint, and both individual and joint remuneration depends on team performance.[13] Greater success allows the owner of the team to increase overall remuneration and perhaps to supplement the existing squad with new and better players. However, although pay may be differentiated among members of the squad, individually differentiated remuneration based on joint production has its limits: higher pay to the better players in the squad may induce claims for comparability amongst other squad players, and risk-averse players might prefer longer and more stable contracts to pay systems which 'reward' exceptional performance in particular matches. Incentives contracts (such as 'win bonuses') are therefore generally applied at a team level rather than an individual level: players receive extra remuneration for winning an important cup tie, but a bonus is not usually awarded to the 'man of the match'.

With some pooling of rewards and incomplete matching of individual pay to productivity, the standard competitive model of individual remuneration predicts that a worker paid less than his or her marginal product is likely to quit (or ask to be released from contract). In turn, a club should be prepared to release or sell a player if it believes that that player's productivity would be enhanced by moving to another club, since the present value of retaining the player is less than the future earnings and transfer fee, if any, that could be obtained by trading the player. This is an implication of the 'Coase theorem', discussed shortly. However, the difficulties of disentangling individual productivity in a team setting, the uncertainty of measuring future productivity flows in alternative teams, and any residual loyalty to fans or to the club (or, in the opposite case, disenchantment) may induce frictions in the labour market. Clubs retain players even when they appear to have no use for them (this is one sense in which the facts of the *Bosman* case, as opposed to the outcome, might puzzle the economist). Players may move club (or ask for a transfer) even when their club is doing well, or not leave it even though they might do better elsewhere (less commonly).

There are two possible forces at work here. One is uncertainty. Player valuations, whether pay or transfer fees, are not fully certain in alternative settings and may only be revealed after contracts have been negotiated or renegotiated. Indeed, it is sometimes argued as a case for maintaining some control of clubs over contracts (beyond the standard argument that clubs should recoup train-

---

13   See Rosen and Sanderson, *supra*, n. 12.

ing costs) that owners bear the costs of the initial uncertainty as to player performance, which subsequently becomes transparent. Transfer fees permit clubs to extract some of the rent derived from efficient reallocation of players, based on revealed productivity. This is especially true for young players, for whom ultimate performance is less certain.

Second, rather like homeowners who seek to move during house price downturns but refuse to lower their reservation price, owners, and indeed the players themselves, may be reluctant to believe that past expenditures on players are essentially 'sunk costs' and should be ignored in current valuations. Clubs and players' representatives with underperforming players will typically argue that current productivity, or lack of it, arises from other aspects of the team rather than their own player's worth. The fact that there may indeed be some truth to this assertion further complicates the issue.

Superstars

Towards the apex of the pyramid are sportsmen and women who have special and demonstrably irreplaceable talents, and where there is a sufficient revenue base to permit remuneration to far exceed outside earnings. Standard empirical models of remuneration and sporting productivity generally find a very small sub-set of professionals whose remuneration far exceeds any measurable performance-related measure of productivity. The distinction between simple rents to ability and sports 'superstars' lies in the ability of the latter to construct a unique brand affiliation in addition to an observable contribution to team productivity. This affiliation, based on both perceived sporting achievement and high visibility, allows such a sportsman or sportswoman to benefit from the 'personal scale of operations' described earlier. In individual sports such as golf and tennis, where there is huge potential for consumer spending on sport-related products derived from brand identification with certain individuals (for example, Tiger Woods or André Agassi), and, where there are tournaments with explicit individual 'winners', the potential for superstar status is obvious.

In team sports, it is a little harder to identify which individuals will obtain superstar status. It is well documented in cricket, for example, that there are a few individuals who will induce extra crowds to attend sessions of cricket matches or to switch on their televisions: the arrival at the crease of a Don Bradman, Lara, Tendulkar, Viv Richards or, these days, of Freddie Flintoff being illustrations.[14] But, as these cases illustrate, there are also indefinable

---

[14] J. Blackham and B. Chapman, 'The value of Don Bradman: additional revenue in Australian Ashes tests' (2004), **23**, *Economic Papers* (Economic Society of Australia), 369–85.

aspects to 'superstar' status arising from character, media presence (either 'genuine' or carefully manipulated) and other facets that cannot so easily be measured.

EXTENSION OF THE PAY AND REMUNERATION MODEL

Market Imperfections and the Competitive Model

Underlying much of the preceding discussion was a competitive paradigm of the determination of pay of sportsmen and sportswomen. The focus was on individual preferences, differences in measured productivity and the capacity of top stars to exploit their 'personal scale of operations'. True, there are problems of measuring individual productivity in a team setting, and complications to the 'story' induced by various uncertainties, but the basic message was that participants' pay was related in some way to their marginal revenue product.

However, towards the apex of the remuneration pyramid, sport is not organized as a competitive market. Professional sport is organized in leagues, which rarely compete directly with each other. Leagues may be 'closed' (that is, a limited set of franchises compete in the league and the league decides whether to permit additional franchises to enter the sport, as in the United States), or 'open', in the sense that promotion and relegation is permitted from a hierarchy of leagues down to semi-professional lower leagues, as in Europe. Such leagues have joint market power as national purveyors of the sport, and joint monopsonistic power as sole national buyers of talent in that sport. Nevertheless, despite the sports market not being structured competitively, leagues have an interest in maintaining 'competitive balance' among participating clubs as a way of maximizing revenue to the clubs within the league. Which of these structures, the open or closed structure, enhances 'competitive balance', and how this affects pay, is an issue to which we return shortly. For the moment, however, it is sufficient to note that professional leagues do not compete with one another except indirectly (for example, in football, the Premier League and the European Champions League) and that players who aspire to reach the highest echelons in their sport will typically have to enter a single league that is regulated in various ways by its governing body and that may include limits on the structure of remuneration and contracts.

The first limit on the competitive model therefore is the recognition in law that, in certain circumstances and on specific issues, collusive agreements among franchises or clubs within a league are not necessarily anti-competitive, since the 'product' that is being provided is a joint product (or 'joint venture'[15]): namely a competitive sports league. Examples of such collusion could include decisions about who has first choice of newly trained players, as in the National Football League (NFL) where the worst performing teams have first pick of the college draft. Another issue of joint production is the sharing of gate revenue, which is pervasive in US sport but less so in Europe (with exceptions such as the FA Cup)[16] and the sharing of broadcasting revenues, which is much more pervasive globally since negotiations are often carried on at a league rather than a club level.[17]

Other regulations include caps on salary bills, either as an absolute amount or as a proportion of turnover. In the NFL, for example, each team had a basic salary bill cap of $85 million in 2005. In NBA (basketball) the figure was $47 million with some exceptions. In baseball, teams with a high salary bill pay a 'luxury tax' that is redistributed to other teams. In Britain, rugby league teams had a salary bill cap of £1.7 million in 2005 and rugby union a cap of £2 million. Caps on salary bills have been suggested in order to improve 'competitive balance' in professional football in the UK, and also caps on the wage bill as a fraction of revenue as a means of keeping football clubs solvent.[18]

For reasons that have been extensively discussed, regulations, whether designed to enhance 'competitive balance' or simply reflecting an older form of labour contract, have also permitted individual clubs within the league to place various restrictions on pay and contractual conditions of individual employees. As is well known, professional football in Britain enforced a maximum wage of £20 per week, which was not abolished until 1961. More pertinent has been the system of player registration that has operated in several sports and which allows clubs to determine whether or not a player can move between clubs irrespective of whether the player has an agreed contract with that club.

The principle of whether an out-of-contract player was free to move clubs without the consent of the club with which the player was registered was of course fundamental to the *Bosman* case. The 'Reserve Clause' in baseball which effectively ended in 1975–76 had a similar effect in so far as contracts

---

[15] See Flynn and Gilbert, *supra*, n. 4.

[16] See Hoehn and Szymanski *supra*, n. 7.

[17] See R. Cave and R. Crandall, 'Sports rights and the broadcast industry' (2001), **111**, *Economic Journal*, F4–F26.

[18] Dave Whelan, Chairman of Wigan FC, has argued for salary bill caps in the English Premier League of £25–30 million to restore competitive balance as otherwise 'it's Chelsea on their own'. See the interview on http://news.bbc.co.uk/sport1/hi/football/eng_prem on 22 September 2005. Michie and Oughton, *supra*, n. 8, argue that revenues among Premier League clubs (and therefore, presumably, salary bills) have become more unequal over time and suggest that there is a correlation between team revenues and league success (although, of course, the causation can run both ways).

with baseball players stipulated that at the end of a (typically annual) contract, the players could not simply negotiate with another team ('free agency') but had either to negotiate a new contract with the same team or ask to be released, which could be refused. The Reserve Clause was specifically designed to halt a perceived threat of salaries escalating out of control of the owners. The 2004–5 lock-out in the National Hockey League in North America also in part stemmed from a disagreement between owners and players' negotiators about a contractual clause that limited 'free agency' until the player was aged 31 or over.

Overall, these deviations from a competitive market structure would be expected to have an implication of the allocation of resources in sport (that is, the pricing of inputs and outputs relative to marginal cost) and the distribution of resources among participants (notably, as to who receives the rents from the departure of prices of inputs and outputs from marginal cost). In particular, the specific structure of the market in a sport would be expected to affect pay; indeed, some measures such as limits on 'free agency' were explicitly designed to limit 'salary escalation'. Enhancing 'competitive balance' by other measures such as salary bill caps might or might not increase revenues and remuneration.

At first sight, *any* restriction on levels of remuneration might be expected to affect pay levels adversely, especially of those at the top of the remuneration pyramid. A more subtle argument, described shortly, is that measures to improve 'competitive balance' may also affect player incentives. On the other side of the argument, however, advocates of regulation would make two points: first, that greater competition might enhance revenues and thereby indirectly affect the size of the 'cake' that can be shared; secondly, that there is a risk of an 'arms race' in remuneration levels in a 'winner takes all' setting which ultimately reduces the financial viability of the sport in question.

Most fundamentally, the elements of collusion, oligopoly and monopsony in the economics of sport economics can all be linked to the less attractive features of remuneration bargaining and resource allocation in sport: the 'backroom deals' and settlements of remuneration issues outside the public gaze, including cash transfers at motorway service stations.[19] In European football, some club chairmen like to point to the activities of sports agents, to the explosion in pay expectations and greed, and to the threat of financial ruin as a rationale for tightly regulating players' contracts and remuneration levels despite the rapid rise in revenues in recent years. All the same arguments were made in baseball and US sports in the 1920s, and in British football in that

---

[19]   T. Bower, *Broken Dreams: Vanity, Greed and the Souring of British Football*, (London: Pocket Books, 2003).

same period, to justify forms of contractual servitude that are correctly deemed no longer to be acceptable. Moreover, many other industries that have seen large increases in revenues in short time periods in recent years owing to deregulation, privatization and technological changes have also been characterized by rapid increases in remuneration levels at the apex of the pyramid while leaving pay at the base of the period largely untouched. Indeed, it might be argued that those with experience of large revenue windfalls arising from mass privatizations taking place under arbitrary and dictatorial regimes are best qualified to run football clubs, which now inhabit a similar environment.

The Implications of the Coase Theorem, Free Agency and *Bosman*

There is one element to economic theory that has implications for resource allocation even where markets have high levels of imperfection, such as monopsony in the labour market. It implies that rational or profit maximizers may provide the 'correct' resource allocation decisions independently of who *owns* the rights (for example, labour contracts) in the market. This is a version of the Coase theorem applied to sports economics.[20] It is a necessary antidote to the commonly-held view that the 'laws of economics' do not apply to sport, given the amount of collusion and market power held by certain participants.

Coase's theorem relates to the allocation of (and more pertinently, the presence or absence of) property rights. It is commonly applied to environmental issues; for example, the allocation of rights to pollute or not to pollute. In the standard example, if an industrial firm pollutes a river downstream, the marginal cost of clearing up the pollution can be equated to the marginal social cost of the pollution itself so long as property rights exist. If the polluter has the right to pollute, the unfortunate downstream owner of the river pays. If the downstream owner has the right to unpolluted water, the firm pays. The optimum resource allocation should be unaffected by the distribution of property rights, although of course the ex post distribution of income will be affected by the allocation of property rights. It is the *absence* of property rights in the context of pollution that causes the environmental problem.

As hinted in the previous section, this theorem can be applied to the question of 'free agency' in sport. With free agency, the individual sportsman or sportswoman can choose to play for whatever team maximizes his or her

---

[20]   S. Rottenberg, 'The baseball players' labor market' (1956), **64**, *Journal of Political Economy*, 242–58; M. El-Hodiri and J. Quirk, 'An economic model of a professional sports league' (1971), **79**, *Journal of Political Economy*, 1302–19; S. Rossen and A. Sanderson 'Labour markets in professional sports' (2001), **111**, *Economic Journal*, F46–F48; M. Schmidt and D. Berri, 'On the evolution of competitive balance: The impact of an increasing global search' (2003), *Economic Inquiry*, 41.

productivity and remuneration without hindrance. Without free agency, a revenue-maximizing owner of the contract should either offer a contract to the player and use the player, or sell the player to another club that can maximize the player's potential. Failing to release the player and not playing the player is not rational in a revenue-maximizing sense.

Bosman, and moves to free agency in other sports, therefore have implications for the structure of remuneration of players relative to the profits of owners (redistribution), especially in the short run, but not necessarily for the allocation of players or for remuneration in the long run. In particular, application of an efficient bargaining model (which really requires a Coase-type theorem to hold) suggests that the post-*Bosman* framework will lead to a lengthening of contracts and a remuneration package at the existing club that will lessen the pay-off to a potential new club. Out-of-contract players will obviously benefit from free agency, and players offered new contracts will have also benefited immediately since the longer and, most likely, more generous contract offer from the incumbent club will produce increased benefits over the duration of the contract. However, these new terms essentially raise the threshold for any new club bidding for that player and, by reducing the pay-off to the outside offer, ultimately reduce the renegotiation pay-off to the player.[21] For short time horizons (career spans), it is not obvious that this intertemporal trade-off has much impact, so *Bosman* over the relevant time horizon benefits players. For the longer term, the results are less clear although most economic analyses seem to agree unequivocally that the incentives for clubs to engage in training young players, where the uncertainty of ultimate ability militates against any attempts to increase contract durations, is considerably reduced by the ruling in *Bosman*.

Crime and Punishment

The organization of sport into professional associations and leagues inevitably raises the question of how its regulatory structures are able to discipline participants who, in some way or other, fail to obey the rules of that association. There are of course large issues here, such as whether there is a public interest in the way professional bodies regulate themselves and, if so, whether external regulation should supersede self-regulation. As noted earlier, the market structure, organization and remuneration of professional sports have much in common with other markets characterized by high pay-offs to 'winners' and in which many of the transactions (for example, large-scale

---

[21]   E. Feess and G. Muehlheusser, 'The impact of transfer fees on professional sports: An analysis of the new transfer system for European football' (2003), **105**, *Scandinavian Journal of Economics*, 139–54.

financial sales and purchases such as transfers of players, the intervention of third parties such as agents, takeovers and the rest) take place 'behind the scenes', such as corporate finance and equity markets. In general, however, professional sports, at least in Europe, have managed to avoid such interventions, relying on their own investigations into malpractice such as 'bungs' (bribes) in football.[22]

There are broadly three forms of regulatory intervention within professional sports' regulatory bodies that lead to the enforcement of penalties or disciplinary action: the requirement of a solvency condition as a prerequisite for a team's participation in the league, issues surrounding registration and transfers of registrations of players, and issues concerning conduct of players, such as public behaviour on and off the field. Inevitably, there are several tensions in this essentially self-regulated environment: between participants in the league and the regulatory body of the league as to whether alleged misdemeanours warrant punishment and whether such punishments are applied consistently, but also within the league as a whole as to whether 'self-regulation' is publicly seen to be carried out effectively (most notably on issues of 'sleaze') as a way of forestalling outside regulation. Again, sport is not unique in facing these dilemmas and in how it attempts to resolve them.

Solvency tests are generally applied to clubs participating in leagues as a means of ensuring the fulfilment of contracts, fixtures and so on. Such conditions are sometimes underpinned by explicitly redistributive procedures operated at the league level (such as 'parachute payments' or revenue-sharing), which may be designed to protect clubs from adverse shocks to finances, such as relegation. It is often argued that such solvency tests are applied loosely and unequally; that is, more loosely to higher profile participants. The essential difference between sports and other markets in this context is that brand identification and brand loyalty are much stronger in the affiliation to clubs than to products in other markets. Consequently, clubs have some market power in deterring competitors or creditors from driving the club to exit (bankruptcy) and it is unusual to see high-profile professional clubs driven out of professional leagues. This leeway, plus the tournament nature of sport have implications for the financial strategy of league participants. While not justifying some of the more bizarre financial behaviour of football clubs in particular (such as debt overhangs on borrowing to finance the purchase of players that have long since been sold), or contesting the view that normal solvency conditions should apply, the combination of a fall-back bargaining position and high pay-offs to success explains why professional sports clubs adopt more risky financial strategies than firms operating in other markets.

---

[22]   T. Bower, *Broken Dreams: Vanity, Greed and the Souring of British Football* (London: Pocket Books, 2003).

The issue of regulating registration and changes in registrations of players is at the heart of the organization of professional sporting leagues, for the reasons described in the previous sub-sections. Since these rules are central to economic aspects of sport such as 'competitive balance' and thereby affect player remuneration indirectly, it is hard to justify the argument that they lie outside the sphere of economic activities, although professional associations sometimes seek to make that argument. Because of the history of protecting clubs through player registration requirements, it is natural that leagues attempt to exact strong retribution on clubs that overtly challenge these rules. Relegation or points deduction are commonly applied to clubs that field non-registered players, and associations often fine or penalize clubs that transgress in, for example, talking to registered and contracted players with a view to encouraging them to switch clubs, sometimes known as 'tapping up'.

Several points can be noted about punishments for such activities. First, it is obvious to outsiders that such meetings go on all the time. The threat or application of fines seems to be in proportion to the flagrancy of the breach of the rules and the importance (or self-importance) of the offended party (the incumbent club) in the league hierarchy. Second, it might be argued that the league, by enforcing such a rule, is exploiting its dominant market position since clubs ultimately have little choice but to comply with such rules where the league has a monopoly position as the provider of that professional sport in that country. Third, given the steady erosion of this type of restrictions with the shift to free agency, it is arguable that long-term contracts which offer no scope for renegotiation will be (and are) themselves ultimately under threat. For example, unlike contracts in other labour markets, the absence of a clause in many sports contracts allowing a participant to give notice that he or she intends to terminate the contract prematurely in return for appropriate compensation to the other party, or even to talk to a potential outside employer, seems strange from an economic point of view, since again the application of the Coase theorem would suggest that the incumbent club would be better-off selling the player to the suitor at a fee commensurate with the future expected revenue product of that player during the remainder of the contract. In the event of a dispute as to what that sum of compensation should be, binding arbitration (especially pendulum arbitration) would surely resolve the problem.

Finally, there is the range of punishments associated with other forms of conduct that the professional association deems improper: bad sportsmanship, criticizing other participants, including opposing teams, referees and umpires and the league associations themselves. At face value, such punishments (which are usually short suspensions and/or financial penalties) seem to operate on a variety of principles, often simultaneously: the gravity of the offence, the extent of visibility of the offence, whether the offender has 'form', the ability to pay off the club or individual and the threat of legal action (whether retaliatory, or to forestall outside intervention for example, charges of assault or defamation). It is often argued, for example, that professional sportsmen and sportswomen at the apex of the remuneration pyramid have such large incomes that anything but an enormous fine or penalty will have no impact on behaviour, if this character-reforming perspective is indeed the appropriate interpretation of the intent behind punishing the individual.

From an economic point of view, the appropriate model here is the model of *tax incidence* – that is, whether the individual on which the tax is levied effectively ultimately bears the tax – in this case a fine.[23] To illustrate the issue of tax incidence: VAT is levied on the seller of a good, but few believe that anyone other than the consumer bears the tax. Social security contributions are notionally levied jointly on the employer and the employee, and recovered from the employer, but again the notional and effective incidence of each part of the tax are likely to be either on the employee or (if either the firm or worker has some market power) on the consumer.

In the standard analysis of labour markets, where labour supply is not completely elastic because workers have the ability to extract a rent over and above the opportunity cost, part of the tax (fine) should be borne by the person on whom the fine is levied. But again, this takes no account of the inelasticity of the demand for the product (loyalty to the club) and the personal scale of operations, which may allow the person on whom the fine is levied to renegotiate the incidence of the firm onto consumers, such as season ticket holders. To a large extent, the ultimate incidence of these fines in the long run depends on a perception by the most loyal supporters and purchasers of the club's products as to who is the wronged party in the particular setting, a perception that both the professional association and the person concerned will attempt to sway by sympathetic media coverage.

COMPETITIVE BALANCE

As suggested at the start of this chapter, one of the key issues in the economics of sport is the issue of 'competitive balance'. Revenue to professional leagues and thereby levels of remuneration, it is argued, depend in large part on the excitement of the competition generated by teams that are relatively evenly matched. Since the league structure is providing that competition, it is commonly suggested that the league should be treated as a single entity in law

---

[23] See A. Atkinson and J. Stiglitz, *Lectures on Public Economics* (New York: McGraw-Hill, 1980).

rather than each individual club, with implications for the applicability of anti-trust or anti-competitive laws concerning collusive behaviour designed to enhance 'competitive balance'.[24]

As mentioned previously, there are two broad 'models' of the operation of a professional league. The first is the North American variant of a closed league (new entrants or 'franchises' can only be jointly approved in the event of an agreed expansion or the end of an existing franchise) with a self-contained league management structure which negotiates joint broadcasting rights and sometimes shares gate revenue. There are often 'artificial' measures to promote greater competition or to restrict the financial and performance discrepancies between the previous best and worst teams, such as a 'draft' system to feed the best new players into the worst performing teams in the previous session and caps on salary bills (and, in the past, salaries) that may bind on the more successful teams. Since franchises are not infrequently shifted between geographical locations, this structure puts a premium on the national attractiveness of the product as a competitive sport (in terms of tele-vision revenues and national merchandising), with less reliance on local loyalty as a driving force (for example, gate receipts and local merchandising).

The second structure of professional sports organization is where there is an open hierarchy of leagues with competition induced, not just by the possibility of winning, but also by promotion or relegation between leagues. Typically, league organization is through a looser umbrella federation. There are typically no salary bill caps or limits on which teams can recruit which players (although there are restrictions on salary bills in some sports, and both restrictions of salaries and on free agency previously existed). Broadcasting rights are often negotiated jointly but sharing of gate revenues is less pervasive than in North America. In this setting, local loyalties are important and it is unusual, and usually disastrous, for clubs to move geographically. Whilst outside sources of revenue, notably from television rights, have increased dramatically, local affiliation and loyalties are still an important factor in determining club policy. Inevitably, too, governing bodies wield less effective power in such circumstances.

Within the traditional league federation model, there have of course been attempts to break up existing structures and to introduce competitions of top players along more North American-oriented lines. The 'Packer revolution' in cricket was ultimately incorporated into the existing structure of cricket orga-nization but had major impacts on remuneration levels, the structure of domes-tic cricket, and so on (for example, the introduction of 'central contracts' into English cricket). The professionalization of rugby union led some clubs to

---

24   This position is stated by M. Flynn and R. Gilbert, 'The analysis of profes-sional sports leagues as joint ventures' (2001), **111**, *Economic Journal*, F27–F46.

argue for a closed rather than an open structure to the professional league with no promotion or relegation, although this was ultimately defeated. The 'G-14' group in European football (actually 18) and threats to introduce a 'super league', perhaps developing out of the European Champions League, may yet induce changes to the structure of European football.[25] There are several issues that stem from this typology of league structures. Where can the line be drawn as to when interventions by sports' governing bodies are promoting 'competitive balance' or are simply flagrantly anti-competitive? Does greater 'competitive balance' increase revenue and does that get translated into higher remuneration of professional sportsmen and sportswomen? What are the incentive effects of different league structures and how do these affect remuneration?

These issues concerning competitive balance have been considered at length in the literature on the economics of sports. To simplify and condense this discussion, consider the reaction of individual spectators to sporting outcomes in a team sport such as football (or indeed US pro-football). Some spectators may be genuinely impartial over outcomes and would be happy to see a high-scoring game without caring which side wins. At the other extreme, fanatical loyalists would like to see their team trounce every other team by a large score, irrespective of whether the other team make a fight of it or simply 'throw in the towel'. Ideally, perhaps the 'average' spectator would like to see a close high-scoring contest ultimately decided in favour of the team to which that supporter has a perceived affiliation (perhaps bar any particular fierce local rivalries where total humiliation is the perceived objective).

Since contests take place within the league against known rivals with perceived strengths and weaknesses, decisions such as investments in new players have strategic implications. In the 'competitive outcome' scenario, joint investments in better players by a number of teams increase competition, excitement, revenue and potential player remuneration – we can term these investments 'strategic complements'.[26] In the 'fanatical loyalist' scenario, teams will maximize their revenue by investments at the expense of other teams and this scenario sees joint investments as 'strategic substitutes'. Clearly, different weightings of 'competitive balance' and 'win success' in the revenue pay-offs to teams and leagues have implications for league structure: for example, over the value of interventions explicitly intended to maintain 'competitive balance' such as the 'draft' and caps on salary bills.[27]

---

[25]   See Hoehn and Szymanski, *supra*, n. 7.

[26]   Hoehn and Szymanski, ibid., using the terminology and model structure of J. Bulow, J. Geanakopolos and P. Klemperer, 'Multimarket oligopoly: strategic substitutes and complements'(1985), **93**, *Journal of Political Economy*, 488–511.

[27]   Hoehn and Szymanski, *supra*, n. 7, argue that entry into multiple leagues with different potential revenue streams and organizational rules (such as domestic football

Do 'open' or 'closed' leagues increase 'competitive balance'? At first sight, the analysis would suggest that competition is enhanced by explicit measures to equalize teams, such as a 'draft', salary bill caps, and revenue sharing such as occur in 'closed' leagues. In contrast, in 'open' leagues, the richest clubs might be expected to perform better, year-on-year, so that competition throughout the whole league is reduced. Michie and Oughton[28] argue that, during the years in which the English Premiership has existed, and in which broadcasting revenues have accelerated rapidly, the share of tournaments won, and revenues, have tended to become increasingly concentrated among the 'top five' teams, the implication being that, had there been restrictions such as a salary bill cap in existence, a greater degree of competition would have been experienced.[29] However, there have been periods in the past, such as the early 1980s, when one team dominated the then championship in England even though broadcasting and merchandising revenues were much less significant.[30] It is equally true that measures to equalize teams in 'closed leagues' do not guarantee an equal likelihood of wins across clubs.[31] Repeated winning of championships in successive seasons is relatively unusual, whether in an open or a closed league.

Other analyses also question whether 'competitive balance' is enhanced by a closed internally regulated structure to leagues. Noll[32] argues that atten-

---

leagues and the European Champions League) may induce clubs to switch strategies. For example, they argue that growing revenue streams attached to Europe-wide competitions in football may ultimately induce clubs to switch from domestic competition into a closed Europe-wide Super League. It is far from clear that this will happen; a better illustration of the process outlined by the authors may, however, be in cricket, where international contests between the top teams increasingly dominate revenue receipts at the expense of domestic cricket leagues, and where consequently top cricketers may essentially be exempted from playing in domestic competitions through 'central contracts'.

28   J. Michie and C. Oughton, 'Competitive balance in football: trends and effects', *Football Governance Research Centre, Research Paper*, no. 2, Birkbeck College, London, 2004.

29   For a somewhat different 'take' on the data and an alternative test, see S. Szymanski, 'Income inequality, competitive balance and the attractiveness of team sports: Some evidence and a natural experiment from English soccer'(2001), **111**, *Economic Journal*, F69–F84.

30   Between 1975–76 and 1989–90 (15 seasons), Liverpool FC won the English Championship ten times. Between 1992–93 and 2005–06 (14 seasons), Manchester United FC won the English Premiership eight times.

31   For example, in the NFL, three teams (the Raiders, the Redskins and the 49ers) won eight of the Superbowls contested in the 1980s, two teams won five contested in the 1990s (the Cowboys and Broncos, with two Superbowls also won by the Redskins and 49ers), and the Patriots have won three of the five Superbowls since 2001.

32   R. Noll, 'The economics of promotion and relegation in sports leagues: the case of English football' (2002), **3**, *Journal of Sports Economics*, 169–203.

dances, and potentially therefore revenue, investment and remuneration, are higher in leagues that allow promotion and relegation; however, promotion and relegation are likely to be associated with 'strategic substitutability' where newly promoted teams may be 'out of their depth' and have no incentive to make the investments to maintain their position in the league. Forrest and Simmons[33] are among a number of authors that point out that, as 'win uncertainty' increases, in terms of equality of team abilities as a result of 'competitive balance', home advantage necessarily becomes an increasingly important factor in determining outcomes, so that overall results may become more predictable, not less.

The implication of these various findings seems straightforward. Whilst there are basic arguments that suggest that more closely regulated leagues designed to give greater competitive balance *should* produce more evenly matched teams and greater competition, the empirical evidence is far from conclusive. But the rationale for many apparently anti-competitive measures associated with greater internal regulation of leagues is precisely that they foster increased competition. If the evidence suggests that 'competitive balance' is not particularly enhanced by control over players' contracts, levels of remuneration (both in total and of individual players) and other league interventions, relative to the more 'free for all' approach of open leagues, outside bodies such as competition regulators and anti-trust legislators may revise their opinions of what constitutes anti-competitive conduct in professional sports.

The Impact of Competitive Balance on Sports Remuneration

The economic analysis of measures that are sometimes proposed to increase competitive balance gives mixed results. At first sight, caps on salaries or on salary bills would restrict the distribution of remuneration among sportsmen or sportswomen, possibly both the inequality and the average level of salaries. However, if increased 'competitive balance' raises revenues through greater attendance or broadcasting rights, the total 'pot' of money available may increase so that the aggregate salary bill is higher than would be the case were there to be no restrictions on salary levels.[34] On the other hand, inequality will not lessen if, within the overall ceiling, owners choose teams of mixed superstars and mediocre players rather than teams composed of players of roughly similar ability (a choice faced by any participant in a virtual 'Fantasy Football'

---

[33] D. Forrest and R. Simmons, 'Outcome uncertainty and attendance demand in sport: the case of English soccer' (2002), **51**, *The Statistician (JRSS Series D)*, 29–241.
[34] S. Késenne, 'The impact of salary caps in professional teams sports' (2000), **47**, *Scottish Journal of Political Economy*, 422–30.

league). This analysis is of course weakened in so far as 'win success' rather than competitive balance is the prime motivation behind league revenues, and in which a competition among rather similar and average teams generates lower revenues than would the chance to see (and/or support) a sub-set of teams of superstars.

The economic analysis of the sharing of gate receipts also suggests mixed conclusions. If teams have the same 'technology' of converting talent into results, and have a similar support base (revenue-generating function), then gate sharing will have no impact on competitive balance.[35] This result essentially arises because teams jointly maximize profits and allocate talent accordingly.[36] However, revenue sharing will reduce the incentive to win for any given team and therefore reduce the incentive to invest in talent, so that the average quality of players, and the average level of revenue-maximizing remuneration, will fall. Szymanski and Késenne also argue that gate sharing may reduce competitive balance if clubs have unequal 'drawing power' or different intensities of 'win support'. If revenue to any given team depends in large part on its own success, any form of revenue sharing that dilutes the quality of both teams and reduces the win probability of the more strongly supported team will have an adverse impact on gate receipts, which will have a disproportionately adverse effect on the weaker team. Indirectly, the same argument is implied by Szymanski[37] in his evidence that football cup competitions (which do have gate sharing and the possibility of 'upsets' of strong teams) have lower gate revenues than league competitions, where such 'redistributive' rules are not in place.

The desire to enhance 'competitive balance' may therefore seem attractive but it does not necessarily maximize total revenues and therefore remuneration. Leagues composed of teams of roughly equal talent may produce contests of lower quality, with consequently lower joint revenues and remuneration of participants. In contrast, having some teams with a large revenue base and strong and passionate support may be of advantage to the league as a whole, although such teams may be disproportionately successful. However, these types of results from economic analysis rely on assumptions concerning joint revenue maximization in a league setting. It is hardly surprising that individual teams within a league that struggle to win trophies

---

[35]   M. El-Hodiri and J. Quirk, 'An economic model of a professional sports league' (1971), **79**, *Journal of Political Economy*, 1302–19.

[36]   S. Szymanski and S. Késenne, 'Competitive balance and gate revenue sharing in team sports' (2004), **52**, *Journal of Industrial Economics*, 165–77.

[37]   S. Szymanski, 'Income inequality, competitive balance and the attractiveness of team sports: Some evidence and a natural experiment from English soccer' (2001), **111**, *Economic Journal*, F69–F84.

are more vehement in their support of measures that are intended to reduce the inequality of success.

CONCLUSION

This chapter has considered remuneration in sports labour markets, ranging from semi-professional sportsmen and women to superstars. It describes how the competitive model of sports remuneration, which suggests that pay is largely determined by preferences, abilities and the 'personal scale of operations' of sports stars, has implications for the allocative efficiency of the sports labour market in the presence of alternative regulatory structures and distributions of property rights, and for the incidence of 'punishments' levied on players, clubs or leagues.

The economic analysis of remuneration in sports markets has a number of implications. First, departures from a competitive framework by sports clubs and leagues, especially in the treatment of labour contracts and remuneration, have to be very carefully argued: many justifications seem rather spurious or not borne out by empirical analysis of outcomes, especially surrounding the need for measures to enhance 'competitive balance' by limiting salaries, by contractual restrictions or by revenue sharing. That many of these restrictions have been eroded and outlawed over time (notably in the general shift towards free agency) has not eroded 'competitive balance' despite dire warnings to the contrary from within the sport.

Second, there is the issue of joint bargaining and the role of league organizations as coordination mechanisms. It is perhaps oversimplistic to say that, because a sport requires tournaments to have competition, therefore the only relevant legal jurisdiction is the tournament organizer itself (the league or federation). There is a considerable difference in organizational models between the North American closed leagues and the more loosely federated open leagues in Europe. It is a moot point whether the explicit reallocative interventions associated with closed leagues, which have engendered the close interest of anti-trust authorities, really do generate greater 'competitive balance' than the looser regulatory framework of the open league. It may be that European Super Leagues in sports such as football will develop along US lines, but such leagues have to overcome fierce local loyalties and rivalries, and the risk that 'competitive balance' alone is not sufficient to generate the revenues to support such undertakings.

Finally, as suggested at the beginning of this section, there are issues concerning the regulation of financial viability, of penalties for approaching and/or recruiting players who are registered with other teams, and the methods of disciplining or punishing miscreants by league rules, whether officials, managers or players of clubs. At a straightforward level, economic analysis of the incidence of fines and taxes and restrictions on contracts would tell us to be cautious in confusing the notional incidence of these interventions (that is, on whom they are levied) with who actually bears the cost. It also appears hard to justify restrictions (for example, on labour contracts) over and above those that would be applied to participants in other, similar, labour market activities.

PART 3

Sport in the multi-media age

8. Commercial freedom and sport: has sport lost its sporting edge?

Barbara Bogusz

INTRODUCTION

In the twenty-first century the concept of culture has broadened to encompass more populist pursuits such as sport and is no longer confined to just literature and the arts. The development of technology has allowed for cultural pursuits to be disseminated more widely and accessed by consumers at a place and time of their own choosing. The prevalent cultural encoding of sport takes into account the relationship between the consumer, spectator and the sports person. Tensions that exist in the relationship between sport and culture are perhaps most evident in the media rights sales with cultural obligations demanding broad access on a free-to-air basis of some sporting events. By contrast, sports' governing bodies seek to maximize the value of their product through selling rights to the highest bidder. This will readily mean exclusivity of ownership and access by the consumer only through a Pay-TV platform. The growth of new media has also introduced new interpretations of what culture constitutes. Consequently, those sports or events which are designated as 'listed' or 'protected' events and are guaranteed to as wide an audience as possible are being viewed as more cultural than those not on the list.

This chapter adopts the standpoint that the one time spectator of sport has today also become a cultural consumer of sport who demands access to live sporting events. In the light of the technological developments, the amount of sport available to the armchair viewer is beyond comparison with even ten years ago. The increase in economic power of both sporting federations and media organizations has meant that regulators both within the EU and at the national level have placed sport under closer scrutiny. One challenge facing the regulators has been to regulate and preserve the cultural significance of sport while simultaneously recognizing that sporting federations must have the freedom to exploit commercially their most valuable asset.

Exploitation of sport by sporting federations and the athletes dominates as much, if not more, than the pursuit of sporting excellence. One notable spillover from the growth of revenue coming into sport from media rights sales is that individual athletes have become economically empowered, for example through exploiting their image and intellectual property rights. Athletes who achieve on-field success are in a position to develop a lucrative secondary career and will use new media and, where necessary, the courts to protect what they view as being legitimate individual economic rights. This chapter will consider how sport and culture have become intertwined and whether the increased commercialization of sport is undermining its cultural features, and what this means for the regulation of sport as a cultural pursuit.

SPORT AND CULTURE: A EUROPEAN PERSPECTIVE

At the European level since the 1970s, there has been some willingness on the part of the Community to promote cultural matters, despite the lack of a specific Treaty base. The purpose of this has been to promote a sense of European consciousness and to encourage solidarity among the peoples of Europe, and so move towards the notion of a distinct European identity. According to the 1976 Tindemans Report on the European Union, this European identity would be experienced by the citizen on a daily basis and it would improve the quality of their lives. The Report stated that this sense of belonging to the European Union should make itself felt 'in education and culture, news and communications and . . . it must be manifest in the youth of our countries, and in leisure time activities'.[1]

Following the Tindemans Report, the Commission published a number of communications which were intended to stimulate the debate on culture within the European context and which sought to justify the Commission's intervention in this area.[2] The Commission cautiously said that it viewed the Community's role in the cultural sector as complementing and subsidiary to that which was already undertaken at the international level, and that it should not duplicate the work done by the Council of Europe.[3] Yet despite the absence of a clear Treaty base this did not prevent the Commission from pursuing a cultural agenda within its integration strategy. It noted that, although development of cultural policies was not within its area of competence, involvement

---

[1]   L. Tindemans, Report of the European Union Bulletin of the European Communities, 1/76, at p. 12. See also R. Craufurd Smith, 'Community intervention in the cultural field: continuity or change?', in R. Craufurd Smith (ed.), *Culture and European Union Law* (Oxford: OUP, 2004), p. 20.

[2]   Community action in the Cultural Sector COM (77) 560; Stronger Community action in the Cultural sector COM (82) 590; A Fresh Boost for Culture in the European Community COM (87) 603.

[3]   COM (82) 590, p. 2.

in culture should bear the same social and economic responsibilities as it does in other areas of the Treaties. According to the Commission, Community action in the cultural sector is a form of economic and social action which consists of applying the Treaty and Community policies to situations, themselves economic and social, in which culture develops.[4] The underlying sentiment indicates that, despite the lack of competence, the Commission will intervene and promote cultural matters where they are ancillary to the main economic and social objectives.

Culture, as envisaged by the Commission during the 1970s and 1980s, had two dimensions. On the one hand, it was a necessary part of European integration and was requisite to create a sense of solidarity and secure popular support.[5] As part of this approach the Commission envisaged a broader sociocultural dimension which was not limited to literature and arts but went beyond this and included activities such as sport.[6] Alternatively, the Commission viewed the Community's role as a facilitator to the cultural sector, providing favourable socioeconomic conditions for culture to flourish.[7] In this vein the socioeconomic dimension focused, inter alia, on the provision of the free movement of cultural goods and access to culture through different channels such as the mass media. The lack of a Treaty base resulted in a piecemeal cultural policy and frustrated the possibility of devising specific cultural policies. Despite this, from a socioeconomic viewpoint, the Commission has remained enthusiastic to promote a more diverse and pluralistic approach to culture, which is aimed at making culture more accessible and democratic. The Adonnino Report, 'A People's Europe', put forward a number of measures to promote European identity and encourage the sense of belonging for European citizens.[8] Among the many proposals suggested in this report, citizens' access to a wide range of television services was regarded as a means of promoting the cultural wealth of Europe. Adonnino suggested that the integrationist and communicative aspects of sport, which transcends physical and linguistic boundaries, would help to contribute to the development of a European identity and image.

The insertion of a specific Treaty provision on culture into the Maastricht Treaty[9] was indicative of the maturing of the Community. Having established

---

4   Ibid., p. 4.
5   R. Craufurd Smith, see note 1 at p. 23.
6   COM 87 603 at p. 8; COM 77, at p. 25.
7   This approach complements the Court of Justice's judgment in the *Cinéthèque* case which recognized the importance of culture as an exception to the free movement rules, see Cases 60 & 61/84 *Cinéthèque SA* v *Féderation Nationale des Cinémas Francais* [1985] ECR 2605.
8   P. Adonnino, *A People's Europe: Reports from the Ad Hoc Committee* (1985), *Bulletin of the European Communities*, supplement 7/85.
9   Article 151 EC (ex Article 128 EC).

a social and employment strategy and eliminated economic barriers to trade, Europe was ready to pursue integration that was not based exclusively upon the objective of free movement. The formal recognition of culture demonstrates that the EU would need to adopt a proactive stance to culture and employ resources to promote it, following the line of reasoning adopted by the Court of Justice in *Cinéthèque*, where culture, in the form of protecting the French film industry, was recognized as a legitimate exception to the free movement rules.[10] With the aim of creating 'an ever closer union among the peoples of Europe', fostering the European identity through culture and the introduction of European citizenship took the European Union a stage further in its integration process and introduced a social and political dimension.

Under the Treaty, culture is defined broadly; it does not suggest a unification of cultures or cultural identity, rather it seeks to promote pluralism in culture. In line with the approach adopted by the Community from the 1970s, the aim was to continue to complement national policies and so respect the principle of subsidiarity.[11] Although sport is not specifically mentioned within Article 128 (now 151 EC), that does not automatically lead to the conclusion that the development of sporting policies was outside the Community's competence. The development of such policies would have had to come within the scope of the existing Treaty framework, for example, where principles of Community law are triggered once a Community dimension to sport has been established. The case law of the Court suggests that this would occur in situations where an economic activity can be identified, such as the free movement of persons, competition law or State aid.[12] In certain circumstances the public procurement rules will also be triggered where the State is involved in capital expenditure, for example building a sports arena.

Reports such as those by Tindemanns and Adonnino have considered sport as part of the EU's cultural heritage which will also enhance solidarity and cohesion in society. This is reinforced by The Declaration of Sport under the Amsterdam Treaty 1997 which views the role of sport as having a social function of bringing people together and forging identity. This is a formal recognition of the sentiments expressed in the 1970s by Tindemanns and complements the definition of sport adopted by the Council of Europe which includes:

---

[10] See *supra*, note 7.
[11] See Article 151 EC.
[12] See, for example, Case C-36/74, *Walrave and Koch* v *Union Cycliste Internationale* [1974] ECR 1045 and Case C-415/93, *Union Royale Belge des Sociétés de Football Association ASBL* v *Jean-Marc Bosman* [1995] ECR I-4921.

all forms of physical activity which, through casual or organised participation, aim at expressing or improving physical fitness and mental well-being, forming social relationships or obtaining results in competition at all levels.[13]

The Declaration of Sport expressly calls for cooperation between the EU and sporting associations, with special consideration to be given to amateur sports. This vague statement, which is without legal force, signposts amateur sports for special consideration. Arguably, this reference to amateur sport may be an explicit recognition that amateur sports not only have a significant role to play at a social level, fostering social democracy and cohesion, but also form part of our cultural heritage and so need to be nurtured and encouraged. Such a view is reinforced by the Vienna European Council 1998 which acknowledges the social function of sport and called for the Helsinki Council to produce a report 'with a view to safeguarding current sports structures and maintaining the social function of sport within the Community framework'.[14]

The Helsinki Report,[15] published by the Commission, expressed concern over the dilution of sport as a social, popular, educational and cultural activity. The Report identified this as a consequence of the increasing economic dimension to sport arising from its increased commercialization.[16] The Commission attributed the change in the way in which the social function of sport is perceived to several factors. These included the increased popularity of sport, notably through improved participation, an increased number of international competitions and, perhaps most significantly the 'unprecedented development of the economic dimension of sport' which includes the 'spectacular increase in television rights'.[17]

Despite the growth of jobs connected either directly or indirectly to sport, a number of detrimental side-effects produced through the increased commercialization of sport have been flagged up by the Commission. For example, the pressure on sportsmen and women to be successful has undoubtedly increased. Sporting success will often translate itself into financial gain for an athlete through lucrative sponsorship deals. Such pressures and the associated rewards could be identified as one reason for the increase in doping cases. Yet

---

[13] Article 2 of the Council of Europe's European Sports Charter, 1999.

[14] Vienna European Council 1998, at para. 95.

[15] European Commission, Report From the Commission to the European Council with a view to safeguarding current sports structures and maintaining the social function of sport within the Community framework: The Helsinki Report on Sport, COM (1999) 644.

[16] The Report recognized the need for a clearer regulatory strategy in relation to sport. See S. Weatherill, 'The Helsinki Report on Sport' (2000), **25**, *European Law Review*, 282.

[17] COM (1999) 644, at p. 4.

the increase in drug taking among athletes undermines the purpose of sport and how it can be perceived as beneficial for society. Furthermore, the search for lucrative sporting deals could deflect attention away from sports' social function and towards a more commercial approach.

In response to these concerns, the Commission highlighted the importance of the social dimension of sport which not only reflects the Council of Europe's principle of 'social democracy'[18] but also could contribute towards the continued development of a European Social Policy through actions such as promoting equality and combating exclusion, racism and xenophobia. This approach is indicative of the changing face of the EU and a move towards a more social Europe, and arguably sits well with the Lisbon goal of achieving greater social cohesion by 2010.[19] The changing dynamic of sport, whether at an organizational level, or through its social function, or through its economic nature, has provided the Commission with the justification needed to intervene more directly in sport's regulation.

The Commission in its endeavour to be more proactive, has suggested that the European institutions act as a guardian to sport to preserve 'the traditional values of sport, while at the same time assimilating a changing economic and legal environment'.[20] The Commission envisaged the guardianship as a means of encouraging greater dialogue and cooperation between the Community, Member States and sports organizations to promote sport and culture in European society. The Helsinki Report was subsequently endorsed by the Nice European Council in 2000 and, though in the form of a non-legally binding Declaration, it serves as a statement of intent in providing a strategy for the Commission in relation to sport.[21] This strategy has not been without criticism. Weatherill[22] has argued that the Treaty does not provide competence for EU involvement in sport and that regulatory interference should be confined to protecting free movement rights and competition.

---

[18]   'Social cohesion and sport', Clearing House – Sport Division of the Council of Europe: Committee for the Development of Sport, Strasbourg, 1999. See, also, Council of Europe, 'Role of Sport in furthering Social Cohesion', Recommendation no. R (99) 9.

[19]   Presidency Conclusions, Lisbon European Council 2000. The European Council set a policy agenda for the EU of becoming the most competitive and dynamic knowledge-based society with more and better jobs and greater social cohesion by 2010. The aim of the social dimension is not only to improve employment prospects and protection, but also to reduce social exclusion and find different ways of participating in society.

[20]   COM (1999) 644, at p. 7.

[21]   Declaration on the specific characteristics of sport and its social function in Europe, of which account should be taken in implementing common policies; available at http://europa.eu.int/comm/sport/action_sports/nice/docs/decl_nice_2000_en.pdf.

[22]   *Supra*, note 16 above.

PLAYING THE GAME: BUSINESS VERSUS CULTURE?

Article 151 EC is the vehicle for promoting a Community framework for culture. Within this definition there has been a gradual acceptance that sport forms part of a broader cultural/education strategy. In particular, amateur sport is recognized as having a social function. Participation in amateur sport may help to forge a distinct local/regional identity and is one way in which the symbiotic relationship between sport and culture can be expressed. However, as noted in the Helsinki Report, there is a possibility that this symbiotic relationship could erode through the alliance of commercial activities and sport. The symbiosis between sport and culture has, to a certain extent, given way to a tripartite relationship between sport, culture and commercial freedom. The question of whether economic exploitation of sport is detrimental to the development of sport is open to debate. The Helsinki Report recognizes that there is an underlying tension and conflict between sport and the economic dimension which, unchecked, could lead to the economic exploitation of sport overriding its social function. Consequently, sport becomes a new commodity.[23] Giulianotti describes commodification as a 'process by which an object or social practice acquires an exchange value or market centred meaning' which is part of a continuing process. He notes that the 'marked intensification of this process in recent years is of a different order to that which was experienced up until the late 1980s'.[24] If we accept this analysis of sport in the twenty-first century, which has become dominated by commercial agreements, merchandising, advertising and the need to meet the demands of media exploitation, then the assertion of commodification of sport is perceptive. Consequently, it is not surprising that the Commission has kept a watchful eye on sport and in particular activities such as media rights sales.

Giulianotti's observation, made in the 1980s, relates to the rapid commercialization of football, but the argument of commodification may be extended to most, if not all, professional sports. This is largely due to the amount of capital that has entered into the arena through sponsorship, the collective sale of television rights and, in particular, through the exploitation of intellectual property rights. On this latter point, the case of *Arsenal* v *Reed*[25] illustrates the tension that exists between the commercial exploitation of football and the

---

[23]   One sociologist went as far as describing the economic exploitation of sport as 'hypercommodification'; see R. Giulianotti, 'Supporters, followers, fans, and *flaneurs:* a taxonomy of spectator identities in football' (2002), **26**(1), *Journal of Sport & Social Issues*, pp. 26–7.

[24]   Ibid.

[25]   *Arsenal Football Club Plc.* v *Reed (No. 1)* [2001] RPC 46; [2003] RPC 9 (C-206/01); *Arsenal Football Club Plc.* v *Reed (No. 2)* [2003] RPC 39.

'branding' techniques which clubs use, and the emotional allegiance which a fan may feel towards his or her club. The judgment in this case would not surprise commentators such as Giulianotti who consider that football clubs have become competing brands in a sports market rather being competing teams on the pitch. Though the original judgment of *Arsenal* v *Reed* was questionable on grounds of legal certainty, Laddie J made some interesting observations about the relationship between the supporter and the football club. In particular his view that the clubs' symbol was a badge of allegiance suggested that it had some broader cultural significance of binding together the clubs' supporters. Laddie J's statements suggested that ownership of the badge was shared by all supporters and that access and usage could not be restricted. On appeal, the Court of Appeal, rejecting Laddie J's arguments, adopted the Court of Justice's reasoning as based upon a traditional interpretation of the Trademark Directive. The club owned the trademark to the badge and could restrict how and by whom it was used. Furthermore, the judgment settled once and for all any uncertainty that may have existed in relation to the question of how far a football club could exploit the symbols with which its fans were most closely associated. The judgment, not unsurprisingly, recognizes the importance of economic rights and commercial freedom to football clubs.

Commercialization has been taken to a new dimension with the sale of football clubs' equity on the stock market as a means of raising revenue.[26] Though supporters were encouraged to purchase shares and 'own a stake in *their* club', the 2005 sale of Manchester United to an overseas buyer undermines further the argument that local fans have a voice in the way their club is run. Foreign ownership of football clubs, while being beneficial in terms of revenue, may only make a limited contribution to preserving the football club as part of a city's cultural activities. One direct consequence of this form of commercialization is that it has attracted the interest of regulators and the courts.[27] As the commercial rewards have increased, so has the need to control the activities of sporting authorities and their constituent members through the use of legal

---

[26]   A large number of football clubs have been limited companies since the late nineteenth century, owned by shareholders and run by directors. Though commercial exploitation during that era was more localized, directors of football clubs were at that time perhaps more interested in increasing their standing in the local area rather than making a profit from the club itself. See the Sir Norman Chester Centre for Football Research, *Fact Sheet 10: The 'New' Football Economics*, available at http://www.le. ac.uk/footballresearch/resources/factsheets/fs10.html. See generally S. Szymanski and T. Kuypers, *Winners and Losers: the Business Strategies of Football* (London: Viking Press, 1999).

[27]   One example of involvement by regulators was the 1998 decision by the DTI to block the takeover of Manchester United by BSkyB. The DTI was of the view that this would create a conflict of interest when it came to the selling of television rights.

principles, such as competition law. It would perhaps have been unthinkable, even 20 years ago, that the sale of television rights by a sports governing body such as the Premier League would be subject to investigation by the European Commission on the basis that the Premier League has abused its dominant position through collective selling of television rights to a single broadcaster.[28]

Another reason which may be posited for the commodification of sport, though more specifically related to football, is the result of the social change introduced to the sport post-Hillsborough. Lord Justice Taylor's report[29] on crowd control and safety at sports events and the introduction of the Football Association's 'Blueprint for Football' in 1991 were landmarks in the development of football.[30] The expense of fulfilling Lord Justice's Taylor's recommendations, which became legally binding through amendments to the Safety at Sports Grounds Act 1975, placed the burden on clubs. In the light of the prevailing laissez-faire economic environment, this excluded any direct financial assistance from the State. The introduction of all-seater stadia and upgrading of facilities signalled a more reflexive approach towards the sport's attitude to its fans and marked a turning point for football.

The reach of football is far wider and extensive than it has ever been and is perhaps more socially inclusive. The fan base no longer comprises supporters who follow their teams according to locality and having an affinity with their club.[31] The fan base axis has shifted towards middle-class spectators, whose interests lie in family football, the spectacle and skill involved.[32] Most recently it is possible to identify a conscious change of direction towards exploiting the affluent consumer and the so-called 'fashionista'.[33] This realignment of sport on social and cultural grounds is a consequence of a concerted effort over a number of years by directors of football clubs and

---

[28]   See S. Szymanski, 'Collective selling of broadcast rights to sporting events' (2002), *International Sports Law Review*, 3.

[29]   Lord Justice Taylor, *Interim Report into the Hillsborough Stadium Disaster* (London: HMSO, 1989) (CMND 765); Lord Justice Taylor, *The Hillsborough Stadium Disaster, 15 April 1989: Final Report* (London: HMSO, 1990).

[30]   Football Association, *Blueprint for Football*, FA, 1991.

[31]   Traditionally, players were also local heroes who had a strong connection with the local area, and this contributed to and reinforced the participatory culture at the club.

[32]   See I. Taylor, ' "Football mad": A speculative sociology of football hooliganism', in E. Dunning (ed.), *The Sociology of Sport: A Selection of Readings* (London: Frank Cass, 1971, p. 359).

[33]   For example, every football club has its own credit card and financial products and has diversified into creating fashionable clothing which is centred on the club's footballing activities. See, generally, R. Guilianotti, 'Sport spectators and the social consequences of commodification: critical perspectives from Scottish football' (2005), **29**, *Journal of Sport and Social Issues*, 386.

sporting associations to reinvent the presentation of football and their teams through the commercialization of sport and the use of various forms of merchandising and media to exploit it.

BROADCASTING SPORTS EVENTS: WHOSE RIGHTS ARE THEY ANYWAY?

Sport needs exposure and revenue. Post Hillsborough, generating sufficient revenue to pay for the necessary improvements to stadia dominated the English Football Association. Without the maximum level of exposure public interest would be limited and so would revenue. Increased revenue from broadcasters was singled out as the primary mechanism through which to generate the necessary income. Yet, at the same time the broadcasting industry needs sport, which, in the case of Pay-TV, fills endless hours of air time when there is an absence of popular live sport such as football. Sport also contributes to the development of the brand image of the channel provided by the broadcaster. Consequently, this has meant that over the last decade more sports are moving, whether on an exclusive basis or otherwise, to Pay-TV channels. Not all sports attract large volumes of viewers. Football appears to be the most popular sport, particularly in Europe, and so commands greater bargaining power on the part of the rights holders. The additional implication of this is that, not only is the airtime available on Pay-TV greater, but also such channels possess a superior purchasing power.[34] This superior purchasing power can be attributed to its financing through advertising, subscription charges and, in particular, top-up charges where a high-profile football match is being played. In this regard, sport has provided the vehicle for attracting large numbers of viewers who are the targets of advertisers and who in turn will pay television channels a premium to have their product exposed to the armchair viewer.

The superior purchasing power of Pay-TV companies has attracted the interest of competition regulators who are keen to ensure that they do not abuse their position and that access for some culturally significant sports is available for all.[35] On the other side of the equation is the position of the sport-

---

[34]   The Commission made a number of interesting observations in this area in its Decision 2001/478/EC, *UEFA Broadcasting Rules* [2001] OJ L 171/12.

[35]   An example of the monitoring role undertaken by the Commission concerned the acquisition and merger of Pay-TV companies in Italy which would have created a quasi-monopoly; the Commission approved this action, subject to conditions. The Commission suggested that approving this action would be more beneficial to the consumer, otherwise a rejection of this action could have led to small companies

ing federation, which, in the case of football, assigns rights to televised matches on a collective basis rather than each club selling the rights to its own games. If individual clubs want to enter into separate agreements to televise, record or transmit their games via satellite or cable, they must seek permission from the Premier League. The contentious issue surrounding collective selling relates to whether this is anti-competitive and reinforces the dominance of one television company.

In 1999, the Restrictive Trade Practices Court considered the objection put forward by the Director General of Fair Trading (DGFT) to the selling of television rights through collective agreements. The DGFT was concerned that the collective selling arrangement between the Premier League and the broadcaster effectively limited the availability of matches that could be broadcast and excluded other broadcasters. The DGFT further alleged that the collective selling of rights by the Premier League amounted to a cartel and the effect of this could potentially stifle innovation and limited the supply of televised matches. The Restrictive Trade Practices Court took the view that the collective selling arrangement was not contrary to the public interest; on the contrary, it recognized that there were benefits to be gained, such as the redistribution of revenue obtained from the sale of television rights amongst the football clubs.[36]

At the European level the Court of Justice has in a number of judgments reaffirmed that sport, whether professional or amateur, is subject to Community rules where the activities are of an economic nature within the meaning of Article 2 EC.[37] Consequently, this has given the European Commission the opportunity to consider whether collective selling of broadcasting rights infringes competition rules. Though a sporting federation such as the Premier League exhibits many, if not all, of the features of a cartel the Commission recognizes that 'in certain circumstances, joint selling may be an efficient way to organise the selling of TV rights for international sports events'.[38] Where this is the case, an exemption under Article 81(3) EC which allows 'consumers a fair share of the resulting benefit' may be appropriate. A

---

involved in the merger closing, which could have had a disruptive effect on the Pay-TV market in Italy. See Commission Decision 2004/311/EC of 2 April 2003 declaring a concentration to be compatible with the common market and the EEA Agreement (Case COMP/M.2876 – *Newscorp/Telepiù*) [2004] OJ L110/73.

[36] 'Restrictive practice not against public interest', *The Times*, 18 August 1999. See, also, D. Geey and M. James, 'The Premier League–European Commission broadcasting negotiations', **4**(1), *ESLJ*, available at http://www2.warwick.ac.uk/fac/soc/law/elj/eslj/issues/volume4/number1/geey_james/geey_james.pdf.

[37] See note 12.

[38] European Commission, The UEFA Champions League – Background note, MEMO/01/271, 20 July 2001.

recent report[39] examining the process by which media rights for sporting events are sold criticizes the approach adopted by the European Commission towards collective selling. Far from offering consumers the resulting benefit, the report's authors argue that the consumer, as a spectator of sport, is at a disadvantage because of the limited number of live football matches that are on offer over a season. Szymanski argues[40] that exclusivity is somewhat of a red herring. In his view attention should be paid to access by the consumer and not to the fact that the rights are being auctioned off collectively. The outcome of such selling techniques has been consumers having limited choice in the range of matches that they can watch, with only one-third of matches of the Premier League matches being available.

As is the case with many sports governing bodies, the Premier League was reluctant for the Commission to be involved in the rights selling process. Historically, sports governing bodies would view such matters as being part of its regulatory function. The Commission instead has focused on the nature of the activity and whether or not it is to be considered as economic in nature. The application of the test of economic activity, which is fundamental to competition law, would not appear to be problematic in the case of an organization such as the Premier League. In *Höfner and Elser* v *Macroton*,[41] the Court of Justice adopted a broad interpretation of an undertaking and the definition would seem to apply to a sports governing body such as the Premier League. The Court stated that 'the concept of an undertaking, in the context of competition law, covers any entity engaged in an economic activity, regardless of the legal status of the entity or the way it is funded'.[42]

Consequently, the sale of television rights by a body such as the Premier League does amount to an economic activity, and so this could be an anti-competitive practice which *would* come within the scope of Article 81 EC and be subject to regulatory supervision. The European Commission has on several occasions considered whether collective bargaining on the part of the football leagues with broadcasters is anti-competitive. In doing so, the Commission has taken a balanced approach by considering both the need for market access and the provision of consumer choice as well as the need to allow redistribution of revenue from the sales of television rights as stated in the Nice Declaration. For example, the Commission in 2002 issued a statement of objections against the English Football Association Premier League

---

39   D. Harbord and S. Szymanski, 'Restricted view: the rights and wrongs of FA Premier League broadcasting', 2006, available at http://www.market-analysis.co.uk/CAFAPL-SkyReport.doc.
40   Ibid., pp. 17–19.
41   Case C-41/90 *Höfner and Elser* v *Macroton GmbH* [1991] ECR I-1979.
42   Ibid., at paragraph 21.

(FAPL) regarding the collective selling of television rights to Premier League football matches.[43] Several factors concerned the Commission, including, inter alia, that media rights were sold on a collective basis and individual clubs could not negotiate sale of their own media rights; large media organizations tended to acquire and exploit these bundled rights, and consequently competitors were squeezed out; viewers were offered limited choice or no coverage unless they subscribed to Pay-TV; and limited opportunities existed for other platforms, such as third-generation telephones, to compete and obtain media packages.[44]

Although the Commission acknowledged that not all anti-competitive practices are detrimental to the consumer, account had to be taken of the Nice Declaration on the 'Specific Characteristics of Sport and its Social Function in Europe' which should be considered when 'implementing Common Policies'. The Commission highlighted the importance of the redistributive nature of the sale of media rights in sport, particularly as it was viewed as having a beneficial effect on the principle of solidarity between all levels and areas of sport. In this regard the Commission accepted that sport could not be treated like other sectors of the economy. The Commission reached an agreement with the Football Association Premier League whereby live football will be sold in six packages, with no one single broadcaster purchasing the rights to more than five packages. The FAPL has committed itself to providing a greater range of media rights including mobile and internet rights and making these accessible through open competition.[45] Since 1992, BSkyB has been the sole rights holder of all premier league football matches. However, the 2006 agreement with the Commission forced the FAPL to open up the market and this has to some extent alleviated the problematic stance of BSkyB having a monopoly on broadcasting live television rights.[46] The question this raises is whether the

---

[43]   See, also, the European Commission's approach towards collective selling of television rights by the Union des Associations Européennes de Football (UEFA): European Commission, Commission opens proceedings against UEFA's selling of TV rights to UEFA Champions League, 20 July 2001, IP/01/1043 and MEMO/01/271; Commission Decision 2003/778/EC of 23 July 2003 relating to a proceeding pursuant to Article 81 of the EC Treaty and Article 53 of the EEA Agreement (COMP/C.2-37.398 – Joint selling of the commercial rights of the UEFA Champions League) OJL 291, 8.11.2003.

[44]   European Commission, Commission opens proceedings into joint selling of media rights to the English Premier League, 20 December 2002, IP/02/1951.

[45]   European Commission, Competition: Commission makes commitments from FA Premier League legally binding, 22 March 2006, IP/06/356.

[46]   In 2003, to address BSkyB's dominant position in the market place, the Commission required that the matches be divided into four separate packages which included a variety of matches. The objective of this was to bring competition into the bidding process and encourage other television companies to enter the bidding. Despite

Commission's intervention has created a 'real' competitive market in media rights. If the outcome of the Premier League television rights sale is considered, it is debatable whether this has been achieved, in particular as neither of the winning television companies is a terrestrial broadcaster. It could be argued that the rights sales process has entrenched the position of Pay-TV in the market for football rights. A bolder move by the Commission would have been to ring fence a certain number of matches for free-to-air television and would have been consistent with the agreement between UEFA and the European Commission in relation to the sale of rights for Champions League matches. In this agreement UEFA is committed to achieving 'a fair balance between free and pay television'.[47] If the purpose of this agreement is to protect the cultural aspect of European football, which Weatherill has argued,[48] then such a perspective is equally, if not more, relevant, to domestic football.

Sport has proved to be a very powerful tool in the development of Pay-TV services in the EU. The Television Without Frontiers Directive[49] has recognized the importance of developing Pay-TV, but it has also acknowledged the need for wider access to programming and that, in particular, events of cultural significance must be preserved. Consequently, the Directive permits Member States to protect certain sporting events of national significance from the exclusivity of Pay-TV and guarantee access through free-to-air channels.[50] The policy underpinning the Television Without Frontiers Directive is to recognize the cultural significance of certain sporting events through allowing Member States to develop a protected list of events. Though the content of the list varies in each Member State, there is broad agreement that some sporting

---

this, BSkyB successfully retained exclusive control of the television rights by making the winning bid for all four packages. Ultimately, the Commission's intervention made no material difference to the outcome and this is the reason why the Commission in the 2006 bidding process restricted any one broadcaster from owning more than five packages. The Commission's objective was to create, in its own words, 'a meaningful market' in television rights for live premiership football. See, generally, D. Harbord, and S. Szymanski, 'Football trials' (2004), *European Competition Law Review*, 117.

    [47]   TV rights agreement UEFA and European Commission. Available at http://www.uefa.com/newsfiles/25624.pdf.

    [48]   See note 1, Crauford Smith.

    [49]   Directive 97/36/EC of the European Parliament and of the Council of 30 June 1997 amending Council Directive 89/552/EEC on the coordination of certain provisions laid down by law, regulation or administrative action in Member States concerning the pursuit of television broadcasting activities, OJ L 202, 30.7.1997, pp. 60–70.

    [50]   Article 3a, Directive 97/36/EC of the European Parliament and of the Council of 30 June 1997 amending Council Directive 89/552/EEC on the coordination of certain provisions laid down by law, regulation or administrative action in Member States concerning the pursuit of television broadcasting activities, OJ L 202, 30.7.1997, pp. 60–70.

events, such as the Olympic Games and major football events, should be available to all viewers. It will be recalled that the Adonnino Report recognized that sport has a role to play in the creation of a European identity. Though the extent of this role remains debatable, it is important to note that the concept of the protected list of sporting events is enshrined in the Television Without Frontiers Directive. While it remains unclear how, if at all, this has contributed to the creation of a European cultural identity, it is fair to say that recognition in the form of 'hard' law gives the idea a greater legitimacy.

While there are undoubted cultural arguments in favour of such lists the restriction of competition and the commercial freedom of sporting federations cannot be ignored.[51] Revenue from the sale of television rights, which are intellectual property rights, is a major source of income within many professional sports. Interference by the State in relation to the way such rights are exploited raises questions of the extent to which the State or the EU should interfere with the commercial freedom of private organizations. Furthermore, the criteria upon which these lists are formulated lack objectivity and transparency. For the regulator they would appear to be caught between a rock and a hard place. The balance, which is yet to be adequately achieved, is to allow sporting federations to exploit their rights through a competitive rights sale process that maximizes revenue while also ensuring that sporting events are widely available.[52]

Revenue from broadcasting has gone some way to help football clubs improve financial stability. One example already alluded to is the aftermath of the Taylor Report, following which football clubs were faced with the huge financial burden of redeveloping their stadia to comply with safety requirements. In the absence of direct State funding the clubs sought alternative revenue sources, for example, broadening non-football related activities. The growth of television coverage in football coincided with the development of new forms of audiovisual technology. The EU, keen to harness and encourage this development, rather belatedly addressed the need for exploiting this technology to its full potential. It may be argued that football has done more for the Pay-TV market than any other form of 'entertainment'. The Television Without Frontiers Directive embeds the position of Pay-TV while simultane-

---

[51] The Commission has undertaken an in-depth review of the Directive in light of the challenges posed by technological developments and also the provision of audiovisual services in the internal market. The outcome of this is a proposal amending the Television Without Frontiers Directive 89/552/EC (COM (2005) 646 final). For a critique of the recent proposed reforms of the Television Without Frontiers Directive 89/552/EEC, see N. Helberger, 'The "right to information" and digital broadcasting – about monsters, invisible men and the future of European broadcasting regulation' (2006), *Entertainment Law Review*, 70.

[52] See Szymanski, note 28 above.

ously striking the balance between commercial freedom and the broad exposure of key sporting events which are of cultural/national significance.
However, this understanding of cultural and national significance can change
over time; for example, from 2006, cricket is no longer a Category A listed
event which is guaranteed free to air coverage. By contrast, since 2004, all
England football team home matches are shown exclusively live on BBC,
something which had not been the case since 1991. What is apparent from
these examples is that, in a competitive broadcasting environment, there is
scope for several broadcasters to offer a variety of sports to the viewer. If the
notion of cultural events were to be extended, the question that would arise is
how these sports would receive adequate funding.

Revenue from Pay-TV has filled the gap where the State was unable or
unwilling to provide resources to build safe and modern infrastructure for the
sport. The freedom of a sporting federation to obtain the best deal possible for
their sport is undoubtedly correct in a competitive free market environment.
The Television Without Frontiers Directive supports this and, because only a
small number of events are listed as being restricted, it is possible to conclude
tentatively that the cultural significance of sport is confined to only those
events where there is some broad national interest and in which citizens can,
even as armchair enthusiasts, participate. To address the question of whether
sport is special, the Directive would appear, at least in terms of television
access, to offer a qualified 'yes'. Of greater significance is that the Directive
adopts a positivist stance on the development of technology and the access to
information for EU citizens from diverse media sources.

Intervention by the Community in developing an audiovisual policy recognizes both that there are different national standards and the powerful nature
of the communication media. The beneficial relationship between sport and
media was recognized in the Commission's Communication on *Community
Action in the Cultural Sector* as far back as 1977. The Commission noted:

> Sports do at least have one thing in common with the production of certain mass
> media: they have become a spectacle and, what is more, a spectacle with a huge
> audience. For both these reasons they are a means of mass communication and they
> may be one of the channels for promoting European socio-cultural activities. The
> latter should also provide room for the practice of sport, alongside sport for the
> spectator.[53]

Regulation of the audiovisual policy area has attempted to ensure the free
movement of broadcasts, and the ancillary effect of this policy protects
cultural diversity. This goes some way to forming an EU identity linked to EU

---

[53]   See note 2, COM (77) 560, at p. 25.

citizenship. The Commission, in its report *The Digital Age: European Audio-visual Policy*, suggested:

> the role of the media goes much further than simply providing information about events and issues in our societies or allowing citizens and groups to present their arguments and points of view: communication media also play a formative role in society. That is, they are largely responsible for forming (not just informing) the concepts, belief systems and even the languages – visual and symbolic as well as verbal – which citizens use to make sense of and interpret the world in which they live. Consequently, the role of communication media extends to influencing who we think we are and where we believe we fit in (or not) in our world: in other words, the media also play a major role in forming our cultural identity.[54]

In relation to sporting events, national events may reinforce cultural identity and allegiances. For example, at a macro level viewing live football matches in a public house on a large TV screen located in a city centre can replicate, to a certain extent, the same emotional environment and experience of watching a match live at the stadium. With the advent of broadcasting football the affinity at the local level, that is the cultural connection between the fan and the club, has been diluted. The norms that have superseded the traditional subculture of football consciousness have been replaced by a market-driven sport and consumerism. Has this occurred in other areas of sport? It may be argued that football is the exception. Blain states that 'forms of culture that do not depend on the media for their reception and transmission are becoming more and more to resemble curiosities'.[55] A good example of such a sport, which was not covered by the media until the Women's Great Britain team won gold in the Winter Olympics in 2002, is curling. Curling was covered by media, with live broadcasting on the BBC, in the Torino Winter Olympics 2006, but the element of commercialization and consumerism was not at the same level as that found in football.

EXPLOITATION OF COMMERCIAL RIGHTS BY THE INDIVIDUAL ATHLETE

Allied to this rise in television coverage of sport is the increase in associated activities such as merchandising and advertising. Sport and particularly football has become a vehicle through which intellectual property rights are

---

[54] European Commission, *The Digital Age: European Audio-visual Policy – Report of the High Level Group on Audiovisual Policy*, 1998, para.I.1.

[55] N. Blain, 'Beyond "media culture": sport as dispersed symbolic activity' (2002), **5**, *Culture, Sport, Society*, 229.

exploited with brands clamouring to be associated with successful athletes. Television and new media have therefore changed the way in which sport and ancillary products are consumed. Success remains important, but equally so is the exploitation of that success. The change in consumer spending habits and the rise of the 'fashionista' culture has marked a shift from sport as culture to some athletes becoming commercial cultural icons. Stars such as Bobby Moore and Denis Compton were well known for their sporting achievements, whereas the modern athlete can use their sporting achievements as a spring-board to develop their commercial value, through the exploitation of the media, branding and so-called 'celebrity endorsement'. The aggressive exploitation of intellectual property rights by sporting federations has been accompanied by the exploitation of image rights by individual athletes.[56] This has ranged from endorsing a specific product to creating a range of perfumes which bear the name of the athlete.[57] Brands are now becoming symbols of a lifestyle which promote 'a way of living, a way of doing something, a way of being'.[58] Perhaps this is an indication of the consumer culture which has developed so that 'you do not only buy this object: you buy social respect, discrimination, health, beauty, success and power to control your environ-ment'.[59] In some jurisdictions, most notably the United States, athletes have begun to seek intellectual property protection for their 'sports moves' raising questions of what constitutes a specific sporting action and what amounts to nothing more than an ordinary bodily movement. Trademark protection could be considered for moves that indicate a unique source of goods or services. For example, basketball player Kareem Abdul-Jabbar's 'sky hook' was the subject of two trademark applications.[60]

One crucial issue is how far an individual should control the exploitation of their intellectual property rights. Athletes' image rights can be exploited through carefully selected endorsements which are closely controlled by the

---

[56]   More recently there was an attempt by a person associated with sport, Sir Alex Ferguson, to exploit his image through registering his name as a trademark, which was unsuccessful, see *In the Matter of Application No.2323092B in the name of Sir Alexander Chapman Ferguson*.

[57]   See, generally, *Irvine* v *TalkSport* [2002] 1 WLR 2355 ChD; *Irvine* v *TalkSport* [2003] EWCA Civ 423 CA.

[58]   D. Smart, *The State of the World Atlas* (London: Earthscan, 2003, p. 77).

[59]   R. Williams, *Problems in Culture and Materialism* (London: Verso Classics, 1980, p. 189).

[60]   On this issue of sports moves and intellectual property rights generally, see J. Smith, 'It's your move – no it's not!: the application of patent law to sports moves' (2000), *U. Colo. L. Rev.*, 1051; L. Weber, 'Something in the way she moves: the case for applying copyright protection to sports moves' (2000), **23**, *Colum. – VLA J.L. & Arts* 315.

athlete. For example, the law of passing off was extended to include product endorsements. In *Irvine* v *TalkSport*,[61] Eddie Irvine, the motor racing driver, brought an action for passing off for falsely depicting his endorsement of a radio station. In 2000, the commercial radio broadcaster Talk Radio rebranded their radio station and changed their name to TalkSport. As a part of their marketing campaign they had included a brochure promoting their Grand Prix coverage which showed a picture of Eddie Irvine holding a radio on which the station's logo clearly appeared. The picture used in the marketing campaign had been altered to show Irvine listening intently to the radio, giving the impression that he was listening to Talk Radio. Justice Laddie in the High Court noted that the law of passing off was not a static concept and has had to adapt to changes in the commercial environment. He considered:[62]

> It is common for famous people to exploit their names and images by way of endorsement. They do it not only in their own field of expertise but, depending on the extent of their fame or notoriety, wider afield also. It is common knowledge that for many sportsmen, for example, income received from endorsing a variety of products and services represents a very substantial part of their total income. The reason large sums are paid for endorsement is because, no matter how irrational it may seem to a lawyer, those in business have reason to believe that the lustre of a famous personality, if attached to their goods or services, will enhance the attractiveness of those goods or services to their target market. In this respect, the endorsee is taking the benefit of the attractive force which is the reputation or goodwill of the famous person.

Irvine was ultimately successful in his action for passing off as a consequence of TalkSport's false endorsement of their product. Justice Laddie's comments are perceptive and recognize the relationship that exists between an athlete's primary career in their chosen sport and the secondary career they develop when they achieve a significant level of sporting success. This case illustrates the significance of the development of brand association and the growth of business in this area, and the courts' unwillingness to allow this to be undermined. This in itself stimulates consumer demand and expands the reach of an athlete's potential to exploit their own image.[63] Yet it would be incorrect to view this judgment as creating, or even moving in the direction of, a sporting

---

61   [2002] 1 WLR 2355 ChD.
62   Ibid., at para. 39.
63   This was recognized by Laddie J in his judgment when examining the evidence from the trial; see note 25, at paras 40–42. See also, 'Not just famous faces but stars of the boardroom', *The Times*, 20 July 2006. Whether celebrity endorsement actually promotes the product has been called into question in a recent study, which has shown that consumers are more influenced by views from consumer watchdogs and literature on the product. See 'Celebrity endorsements unlikely to sway consumer' *Financial Times*, 19 July 2006.

exception for athletes when protecting their image rights. In many respects the fact that Irvine made his living from being involved in motor racing is irrelevant and it would be expected that such principles would be applied in *any* situation where an individual is protecting the commercial value of their image.

A more recent development in the intellectual property field relates to the registration of a name as a trade mark. Though registration of names has proved controversial, the Court of Justice in *Nichols* v *Registrar of Trademarks*[64] accepted that it could be possible. Nichols plc applied to register NICHOLS as a trademark in the United Kingdom for food and beverages. The registrar refused the application under section 3(1)(b) Trade Marks Act 1994[65] as it was devoid of any distinctive character. The decision was based on the grounds that the food and beverage market included many traders and by using a common surname it may be difficult for consumers to identify the origin of the products. The surname NICHOLS was common because it or its phonetic equivalent 'Nicholls' appeared 483 times in the London telephone directory, and therefore the registrar concluded that it was unlikely that consumers would perceive the mark as an indicator of origin. The Patent Office's practice has been to regard common surnames as incapable of distinguishing goods or services, such as ordinary consumer products, where a large number of traders are involved. The name may not be regarded as devoid of distinctive character for more specialist goods or services, but each case had to be evaluated on its facts.

The Court of Justice, on appeal from the High Court, was asked to consider in what circumstances a trade mark consisting of a single surname should be refused registration as being in itself 'devoid of any distinctive character' under Article 3(1)(b) of the Trade Marks Directive and whether such an application must be or may be refused if it is a common surname in the relevant Member State and has not acquired distinctiveness.

Advocate General Colomer noted that personal names were expressly regarded as registrable trade marks under Article 2 of the Directive.[66] He recognized that any method used to ascertain whether a personal name was devoid of any distinctive character involved some subjectivity. He also noted that the registrar's approach in determining the distinctiveness of surnames differed from the method preferred by the ECJ. The Advocate General went on to state that the issue of whether a surname is capable of being distinctive had to be assessed in the context of the specific market concerned. Ordinary surnames might be commonly used to denote goods or services in one area of

64   Case C-404/02 *Nichols Plc.* v *Registrar of Trademarks* [2004] ECR I-8499.
65   Implementing the Trade Marks Directive: First Council Directive 89/104/EEC of 21 December 1988 to approximate the laws of the Member States relating to trade marks, OJ L 40/1989, p. 1.
66   Opinion of Advocate General Colomer, at para. 32.

trade, but this does not necessarily apply in others. The distinctiveness of surnames must be assessed in the same manner as that of other types of word marks. Advocate General Colomer restated the test established by the Court of Justice which would require an assessment of whether the mark could enable the average consumer to distinguish the product or service from others and conclude that it was manufactured or marketed under the control of the trade mark proprietor, who was responsible for its quality.

The ECJ confirmed that, when assessing the distinctive qualities of a particular surname, it must be assessed in accordance with the specific circumstances of each application. The examination under absolute grounds for refusal (that is, under s. 3 Trade Marks Act 1994) of names must be carried out in the same manner as all other types of trade marks and therefore whether the mark has inherent distinctive qualities or not will depend upon the perception of the relevant consumer, taking into consideration the essential function of a trade mark as being an indicator of origin. The Court stated:[67]

> The criteria for assessment of the distinctive character of trade marks constituted by a personal name are the same as those applicable to the other categories of trade mark . . . In the same way as a term used in everyday language, a common surname may serve the trade mark function of indicating origin and therefore distinguish the products or services concerned.

In its judgment, the ECJ failed to provide the factors to be taken into consideration when assessing the distinctive qualities of common surnames. The Court did state that, although the number of individuals with a similar name, or the number of undertakings using the name in identical or similar services is acceptable, this will only be possible if it applies a less restrictive test of distinctiveness by comparison with other forms of trade mark. The ECJ also confirmed that an application for a surname cannot be refused for the purposes of preventing the applicant from 'advantage' by first registration at the expense of others.

In the light of the Court's judgment this is good news for sports stars who may wish to exploit their name through merchandising and product endorsement in a manner which is separate from any commercial exploitation which their clubs may pursue.[68] The judgment in *Nichols* has given a name, which satisfies the requirements for a trade mark, an economic value. It may also be

---

[67]   See note 54, at paras 25 and 30.
[68]   Though this may be good news, it is apparent that registering a name as a trademark is not easy, as Sir Alex Ferguson experienced when attempting to register ALEX FERGUSON. This application failed as being devoid of distinctive character. See *In the Matter of Application No.2323092B in the name of Sir Alexander Chapman Ferguson*. See, also, *Elvis Presley Trade Marks* [1999] RPC 543.

argued that the decision in *Nichols* and in *Irvine* v *TalkSport*, if applied to athletes, goes a long way to empowering the athlete economically through exploitation of his or her commercial freedom and providing them with a parallel career. Athletes may use intellectual property law to control more directly their careers and how their image is used. This has already featured in the United Kingdom with David Beckham's final contract with Manchester United including a payment by the club for the use of his image in merchandising and advertising. Control over an athlete's name in this way follows a trend first seen in *Bosman*.[69] This judgment has been acknowledged by commentators as empowering the football player to have more contractual and economic freedom. This commercial freedom would now seem to be endless if a popular cultural icon such as Beckham, Rooney or Ronaldo may exploit *their* name for *their* economic benefit. Significantly, as such athletes are now agreeing contracts of employment which include payment for the use of the athlete's image by the employer, legal control of how and by whom that image is used is important, not just for the athlete, but also for their employer.

Sports stars have not been slow to capitalize upon this new found commercial freedom and in developing a secondary career. Even before the *Nichols* judgment it was clear from the David Beckham contract that clubs were prepared to acknowledge the contribution which individual players had made to merchandising success. Many high-profile individuals, such as actors and football stars, have registered their names as domain names either to increase commercial exploitation or to prevent others from domain name squatting.[70] Conversely, there have been a number of cases where high-profile individuals have challenged domain name registrations, for example, Tom Cruise was successful in having the ownership of tomcruise.com transferred to him in a decision by the World Intellectual Property Organization (WIPO). Similarly, Wayne Rooney is also seeking redress with regard to cybersquatting and unauthorized use of his name. WayneRooney has been registered as a domain name since 2002. There are currently eight websites of which only two are fully functioning websites; the remainder are merely holding pages. The case currently before the WIPO Arbitration and Mediation Centre will have to consider whether the website WayneRooney.com should be transferred to

---

[69] Case C-415/93 *URBSFA* v *Jean-Marc Bosman* [1995] ECR I-4921.

[70] The recent introduction of the .eu domain names has caused some disquiet due to the potential rise in cybersquatting; see 'Cybersquatters move in on London.eu', *The Times*, 11 April 2006. The World Intellectual Property Organization Arbitration and Mediation Center has already noted an increased number of cybersquatting cases: in 2005 there was a 20 per cent rise in the number of cases, compared to 2004. No doubt this will continue to rise in the future. See 'Wipo Responds to Significant Cybersquatting Activity in 2005', Press Release 435, 25 January 2006 at http://www.wipo.int/edocs/prdocs/en/2006/wipo_pr_2006_435.html.

Wayne Rooney.[71] Given the approach taken in previous cases involving well-known individuals, it would appear that WIPO is likely to be sympathetic to his cause.

Athletes are in a position to protect their intellectual property rights through established legal rules, but to what extent should the athlete have sole control over, when, how and if they will exploit their rights? One useful mechanism to control exploitation of publicity is through the use of the law of confidence.[72] On the other hand, it is possible to argue that the athlete's commercial exploitation of his or her rights should be curbed and – it is possible to suggest in certain circumstances – be regarded as an essential facility. This would effectively place limits upon the athlete's possibility of exploiting or providing access to their commercial rights. The Court of Justice views the abuse of a dominant position under Article 82 EC through the lenses of fair access for the consumer, promoting market access and competition.[73] The question this raises is to what extent this could apply to an individual who generates income by exploiting their image rights.

It is without question that athletes can and should be able to exploit their intellectual property rights. In this context, developments in technology have facilitated the generation of continued interest in the athlete and consequently the ability to exploit their commercial value. However, where certain sports personalities have reached a particular status whereby they are leaders in their field, for example captain of a team, or an excellence in their area, it may be possible to suggest that some of his or her commercial rights should be viewed as 'public property'. This would entail that the consumer should have access to the athlete, or more specifically images of the athlete, with only limited restrictions. As a practical example, are there any circumstances in which David Beckham, who until July 2006 was captain of the England football team, should be able to restrict any branch of the media from using his image while wearing an England shirt? The interesting issue this raises is whether the courts are prepared to distinguish an athlete *qua* athlete who makes a living from their chosen sport from an athlete who is also commercially active and wants to exploit their image for personal gain? The judgment in *Irvine* v *TalkSport* and the confidence cases would appear to show that, for the time being at least, the advantage lies with the athlete.

Commercial exploitation of intellectual property rights such as trade marks

---

[71]   Case Number D2006-0916, 26 July 2006, pending. See also, 'Rooney's legal fight for website', http://news.bbc.co.uk/1/hi/wales/5207766.stm.
[72]   See *Campbell* v *MGN* [2005] 1 WLR 339; *Douglas* v *Hello!* (No.3) [2006] QB 125.
[73]   See *RTE and ITP* v *EC Commission* [1995] 4 CMLR 718.

is dependent on exposure from the media. For individual athletes who have the financial capabilities, they can now take control of this and use new forms of media to exploit their own persona. The media have an important role to play in sport generally where the event is reported upon, commented upon and analysed. The recipients of this are provided through the available media with an opportunity to view games, but at the same time they are exposed to the sponsors' advertising and celebrity athletes. The by-product of the sporting event is the commercial exploitation of intellectual property rights in the form of advertising of trade marks. Sport has become more than just playing the game or taking part in the race. Sport is about economic freedom for all concerned; that is, sporting federation and athlete.

CONCLUDING REMARKS

The purpose of this chapter has been to explore the interface between sport and culture and demonstrate how commercial considerations are dominating sporting activity. The shift from regional supporter to consumer fan has undoubtedly been facilitated by the growth of a technology and the presence of a regulatory framework which allows for commercial exploitation of sport. Traditional interpretations of sport as a cultural pastime are no longer relevant. The consumer fan has taken sport to a level where sports such as football have, through their television exposure, merchandising and elevation of some players to the status of cultural icon, made football a lifestyle rather than a game. This mainstreaming of sports both in a cultural and regulatory sense has suggested that sport has a contribution to make to the integration process and creation of a European polity. The growth in audiovisual technology has coincided with a time when interest in sport has grown and the two have made for convenient bedfellows. Sport may have lost its sporting edge in a traditional Corinthian sense and as a cultural pursuit the way it is enjoyed has developed, but economic and commercial exploitation of sport and its presence in the media suggest that sport maintains a place in the cultural activity of the nation, even if that activity is as a consumer fan rather than a participant.

9. Fame and its exploitation: the legal protection of celebrity in the United Kingdom

Jennifer Davis

INTRODUCTION: CELEBRITY 'BRANDS' FROM BEST TO BECKHAM

In 2003, David Beckham moved from Manchester United to Real Madrid. The move cost the Spanish football club $43 million. It is generally agreed that this sum was not a simple reflection of the worth of Beckham's footballing skills. Instead, Real Madrid was buying Beckham, the 'global brand'.[1] Beckham personally had marketing agreements with a variety of products, from Adidas to Vodafone to Marks & Spencer, but Real Madrid were banking on the attraction of the Beckham brand not only to cement sponsorship deals from Adidas and Pepsi Cola, but also to gain the club entrée into the Far Eastern market, 'where Beckham is by far the most popular player in the world' and Manchester United was the best known club.[2] Indeed, a year after acquiring Beckham, Real Madrid became 'the biggest earner in world soccer – and probably all sports', a position which had previously been held by Manchester United.[3] As to the values embodied in the Beckham brand, these have been summed up as 'Non-smoking, non-drinking and happily married . . .'[4] Exactly 40 years earlier, George Best, also a football player, got his first professional contract from Manchester United, who that year won the FA cup. Two years later, when Manchester United beat the Portuguese club, Benfica, in the quarter finals of the European Cup, he became the most celebrated footballer in the

---

[1]   R. Starnes, 'Nobody brands it like Beckham', 18 February 2006, Canada.com. The value of the Beckham brand has been put at anything from $370 million to $700 million.
[2]   'Brand it like Beckham', 21 June 2003, rediff.com.
[3]   'Brand it like Beckham', 23 June 2003, *Time*, www.time.com/time/columnist/elliott/article.
[4]   'Brand it like Beckham', rediff.com; see also M. Simpson, 'Beckham, the virus', *Salon*, 28 June 2003, Marksimpson.com.

UK and a style icon, although the values he embodied would present a startling contrast to those represented by the Beckham brand.[5]

Today we are used to sports figures dominating our news and cultural life. Even at the time, it was recognized that George Best represented something new. He was, according the *News of the World* in 1973, 'the man who started the pop-star cult in soccer'.[6] Dubbed 'the Fifth Beatle' by a Portuguese newspaper, Best was perhaps the first British footballer to be followed, not just for his sporting prowess (which arguably was considerably greater than Beckham's) but also for his fashion sense and lifestyle.[7] It is possible to argue that Best was also the first football player, possibly the first sportsman, substantially to supplement his club salary by commercially exploiting his image. According to Best, 'It was inevitable that the commercial world would catch on to a footballer eventually and I just happened to the first'.[8] Indeed, following the Benfica victory, he was 'swamped' with commercial demands. He was 'advertising everything you could think of, from sausages to Brut aftershave'.[9] His first television advert was for Irish sausages, and also featured his mother and baby sisters. As Best noted, 'advertising was pretty basic and a long way from the slick machine that it has become'.[10] He later opened boutiques under his own name, called George Best Rogue. At the height of his earning power, Best might have earned over £1000 from footballing and another £1000 from his commercial activities, 100 times the weekly national wage of £23.[11] Even this sum pales into insignificance when measured against Beckham's own earnings from both playing and exploiting his image, which have been reckoned to total $30 million a year.[12]

It was popular interest in Best as more than a football player which made his image commercially valuable. As we have seen, the same is true for

---

5   By contrast, Best was admired for his womanizing, his cars and his 'pop-star' lifestyle: George Best, Obituary, *The Times*, 25 November 2005.

6   *News of the World*, 23 January 1972.

7   G. Best, *Blessed: the Autobiography* (written with Roy Collins) (London: Ebury Press; 2001, p.99). Interestingly, to the Portuguese he represented a certain sort of 'Britishness' as it was then commonly perceived abroad; a similar point has been made about Beckham, that he is 'an English-speaking aspirational image': 'Brand it like Beckham', rediff.com. Although it is also true that, while Beckham is a global brand, Best never achieved this status; M. Simpson, 'Beckham the virus'.

8   Best, *Blessed*, p. 105. According to Best, 'Actors might have had agents in those days, but players didn't'.

9   J. Lovejoy, *Bestie: a portrait of a legend* (London: Sidgick & Jackson, 1998, p. 154).

10   Best, *Blessed*, p. 103.

11   Lovejoy, *Bestie*, p. 155; Best, *Blessed*, p. 105.

12   Simpson, 'Beckham, the virus'; 'Brand it like Beckham', *Time*.

Beckham. Best's exploits off the field were followed by the tabloid press.[13] By the early 1970s, Best's alcoholism was affecting his playing and stories about him were as likely to concern the fallout from his drinking as his exploits on the field. For example, in January 1973, Best, referred to as 'a celebrity', made the front page of *The Sun* after pleading guilty to assault. Although the press showed a close interest both in his drinking and in his relationships, it appears that, at the time, Best never sought to use legal action to prevent the publication of details of his private life. Indeed, it might be argued that, at the height of his fame, it was precisely Best's affection for both women and drink which gave the Best brand value, as the name of his clothing store suggests. However, it also seems to be the case that the detailed interest in Best's private life which characterized the last few years before his death was not replicated at the height of his fame.[14] The same cannot be said of Beckham, who lives in an age when footballers habitually migrate from the sports page to the front page. Perhaps because Beckham's own image is closely bound up with his clean living and family life, news stories that have threatened this image have also threatened the value of the Beckham brand.[15] Or, as one observer put it, after Beckham was accused of an extramarital affair in 2004, 'Infidelity stories may hit Beckham's brand affairs'.[16] Certainly, unlike Best, Beckham has been assiduous in protecting his image through legal means, as the various actions he has bought against newspapers seeking to publish unflattering information about his private life attest.[17] For example, in April 2005, he sought an injunction to prevent his nanny from disclosing details of his private life in the *News*

---

[13]   See, for example, Lovejoy, *Bestie*, p. 206.

[14]   The story in *The Sun* about the assault took up one column on the front page and a two page spread in the centre of the newspaper, but was not followed up the next day. *The Sun*, 12 January 1973.

[15]   M. Simpson, 'Beckham the virus'.

[16]   T. Datson, 'Infidelity stories may hit Beckham's brand affairs', 4 April 2004, Forbes.com.

[17]   See, for example, *McManus* v *Beckham* [2002] EMLR 40; *Beckham* v *MGN Ltd*. 3 August 2005 unreported and *David Beckham, Victoria Beckham* v *News Group Newspapers Ltd*. [2005] EWHC 2252 (QB). In the latter case, the Beckhams sought to prevent publication of details of their marriage which they claimed were untrue and libellous. The newspaper alleged that 'In order to protect their image and for financial reasons, the Claimants are cynically and hypocritically trying to convince the public that their failed marriage is perfect . . .'. According to 'media lawyer' Mark Stephens, 'They're making a Faustian pact. David and Victoria have created "Brand Beckham" which they desperately want to protect, but if the reality of their lives is at odds with the image, this latest judgment shows that a confidentiality agreement will not be an adequate shield.' Quoted in J. Silverman, 'Does Beckham judgment change rules?' 25 April 2004, BBC News, http://news.bbc.co.uk/go/pr/fr/-/hi/uk/4482073.stm.

of the World, which he alleged would be a breach of confidence. The case was settled before publication.[18]

There seems little doubt that it was, in some measure, George Best who made 'Beckham' the global brand possible. But it is also clear that Best's commercial endeavours occurred at a time when personality merchandising did not have the enormous economic value it carries today,[19] and when football, itself, was not seen as a fertile ground for branding. By the same token, as the value of brands has grown, including those based on celebrity images, so too has the need of those who wish to profit from those images to protect them from being tarnished. A number of jurisdictions have over the past half-century both recognized the commercial potential of personality merchandising and also the ease with which a celebrity's image might be undermined by an intrusion into his or her privacy. As a result, these jurisdictions have developed a variety of legal remedies which, to varying degrees, provide for the protection of the one and the prevention of the other. For example, German law has recognized rights to one's own name and image since the early twentieth century. In 1954, the German Federal Supreme court (BGH) also recognized a general personality right. It has been suggested that these rights were initially intended to be dignitary rights, that is, designed primarily to protect privacy and to prevent the unwanted or unauthorized use of a person's name or image. However, over the years, the German courts have also been increasingly willing to stretch these rights to protect the economic value of those same images.[20] Indeed, in the *Marlene Dietrich* case,[21] in 2000, which

---

[18]   *Beckham* v *Gibson*. See 'Beckham nanny to stop new stories', 29 May 2005, BBC News, news.bbc.co.uk/go/pr/fr/-/hi/uk/4496301.

[19]   There is of course an extensive literature on the rise in the value of the brand as opposed to tangible company assets, see, for example, J. Lindemann, 'The financial value of brands', in R. Clifton and J. Simmons (eds), *Brands and Branding* (Princeton, NJ: Bloomberge Press, 2004, pp. 27–46). This is not to say that branding or image marketing are products of the twenty-first century. Indeed, some of the most important brands emerged at the turn of the twentieth century. So too, in his book, *Celebrity and Power* (Minnesota: University of Minnesota Press, 1997). P. David Marshall places the rise of the modern celebrity in the 1930s, when 'Celebrity status became aligned with the potentialities of the wedding of consumer culture with democratic aspirations' (p. 7). For example, see J. Davis, 'The value of trade marks: economic assets and cultural icons', in Y. Gendreau (ed.), *Intellectual Property: Bridging Aesthetics and Economics – Propriete intellectuelle: Entre l'art et l'argent* (Montreal: Editions Themis, 2006, pp. 97–124).

[20]   H. Beverley-Smith, A. Ohly and A. Lucas-Schloetter, *Privacy, Property and Personality: Civil Law Perspectives on Commercial Appropriation* (Cambridge: CUP, 2005, pp. 94–5). Also, J. Klink, '50 years of publicity rights in the United States and the the never ending hassle with intellectual property and personality rights in Europe', IPWQ (2003), **4**, 363–87.

[21]   *Marlene Dietrich* (2000), NJW 2195 BGH.

concerned unauthorized merchandising of the late actress's name and image, the BGH determined that the economic interests of personality rights might survive after the death of the personality.[22] Nonetheless, it is also generally agreed that the German personality right falls short of offering a general publicity right, a property right in the economic value of one's image such as is available in the United States.[23] In that jurisdiction, there is both a right to privacy and a right to publicity, the latter having been recognized by the Supreme Court in 1977.[24] The right to publicity is seen as concerned with preventing the commercial appropriation of a person's name or image which would cause damage to that image and is treated as a fully assignable property right.[25] The right to publicity has been given a statutory basis in a number of states, including New York and California.[26]

Despite being the home of the most famous and valuable footballer in the world, in the relevant literature the UK is often pictured as an exception to these developments and at the very least a late developer. Certainly, it is the case that the UK boasts neither a right of personality nor a right of publicity, and it is only in the past year that it has been possible to say that the UK has something akin to a right of privacy. Instead, celebrity images, including those of famous sportsmen, are protected by a number of different legal actions, including breach of confidence, passing off and trade mark infringement, in much the same way as would have been the case during Best's heyday in the 1960s. Many observers see the UK's failure to offer greater protection to the commercial exploitation of celebrity as anomalous, and indeed unfortunate. However, these same observers also tend to take the view that the UK must inevitably follow other jurisdictions by developing precisely those rights of publicity and personality which it now lacks, in much the same way that fish emerged from the primeval swamp and developed legs. Thus, in one study of personality and privacy rights, European countries have been described as 'at a more advanced state of evolution' than the UK for the higher level of protec-

---

[22] Klink, '50 years of publicity rights', 382–2. France too has a right of personality, but not a publicity right. See Beverley-Smith et al., *Privacy, Property and Personality*, ch. 5.

[23] Klink, '50 years of publicity rights', Beverley-Smith et al., *Privacy, Property and Personality*, p. 214.

[24] *Zacchini* v *Scripps-Howard Broadcasting Co.*, 433 U.S. 564 (1977).

[25] The person may or may not already exploit his image and may or may not be well known, since in the latter case the exploitation of his image by a third party may give it a value it did not have previously. See H. Beverley-Smith, *The Commercial Appropriation of Personality* (Cambridge: CUP, 2002, p. 181).

[26] In the latter state, the right covers real persons but not fictional characters. For a full description of the publicity right in the US, see Beverley-Simth, *The Commercial Appropriation of Personality*, ch. 7.

tion they give to personality.[27] Elsewhere, the UK approach has been described as 'outdated'.[28]

This chapter will seek to challenge this teleological view. It will also suggest that the UK's failure to develop greater protection for the commercial exploitation of celebrity should not necessarily be viewed as a moral failing. It is true that the UK courts have, since 2004, given increasing protection to the private lives of individuals who may have a public persona. However, it is also the case that the courts have not similarly moved in the direction of giving significantly greater protection to the commercial exploitation of public images and against their misappropriation by third parties. One possible explanation for this is that the issue of privacy is increasingly influenced by European jurisprudence, most particularly case law from the European Court of Human Rights.[29] However, it will be argued here that this is only a partial explanation. For example, it is also the case that UK trade mark law is now a product of European jurisprudence, yet the implementation of the EU Trade Mark Directive[30] in the UK by the 1994 Trade Marks Act has produced more limited protection for celebrity images than observers had expected when it was passed.

In fact, there are a number of reasons why the UK courts have not acted to give extensive protection to the commercial exploitation of celebrity. The next section will look at the development of the right to privacy in the UK. It will suggest that until very recently, the courts have tended to view public persons who have traded on their images as having a lesser right to privacy than those that have not. Although the UK courts may now slowly be abandoning this position, it will be argued that this development reflects a new definition of what is 'private' rather than any significant change in attitude towards the regulation of the commercial exploitation of image. This point will be taken up in the third section, which looks at the way the courts have used the tort of passing off to protect the commercial exploitation of celebrity images. It will be suggested that the limited extent to which the tort protects the misappropriation of image is evidence of the UK court's traditional reluctance to interfere in the free-play of the market, a view which has not significantly changed with the rise of personality merchandising. The final section of this chapter will address the question of whether the UK courts are likely to develop a personality or more specifically a publicity right in the future. It will be argued

---

27   Beverley-Smith et al., *Privacy, Property and Personality*, p. 225.

28   J. Taylor, S. Boyd and D. Becker, 'Image rights', in A. Lewis and J. Taylor (eds), *Sport: Law and Practice* (Butterworths: London, 2003, pp. 635–74).

29   This explanation has been suggested by Beverley-Smith et al. in *Privacy, Property and Personality*; see, for example, p. 222.

30   Directive 89/104/EEC.

that the evidence suggests this will not happen soon. It will point out that the 1994 Trade Marks Act offered the UK courts a clear opportunity to strengthen the protection afforded to celebrity images. But this was an opportunity they chose not fully to take. The general consequences of these developments for sports personalities seeking to profit from their images will then be considered.

PRIVACY AND THE PRICE OF FAME

In 2001, Gary Flitcroft was captain of Blackburn Rovers and married with two children. In that year, he brought an action for breach of confidence against a tabloid newspaper to prevent it publishing two articles detailing his extra-marital affairs with a lap-dancer and a nursery school teacher, who was also named as a defendant in the action. Both women had sold their stories to the newspaper. His wife did not know about the affairs. At the time he brought the action, Flitcroft was known only as 'A', and neither the tabloid nor the women involved were identified.[31] Flitcroft obtained an injunction in the High Court to prevent publication of the articles. The defendants successfully applied to the Court of Appeal to have the injunction discharged.

Sports people are generally known to the public, in that their sporting activities take place in the public arena. Of course, the nature of the sport and its popularity and the success or otherwise of its participants will determine that some individuals will be better known than others and will be of greater interest to the public. Since sportsmen and women have chosen to operate in the public arena, a question arises as to whether and to what extent the public are entitled to know anything further about these individuals beyond the spare details of their sporting biographies and their sporting prowess. Alternatively, despite being public figures, should sportsmen and women be able to control what information about them enters the public domain? Indeed, should this question be answered differently, if the individuals concerned, like Best or Beckham, deliberately choose to exploit their public position for commercial reasons, beyond their sporting activities? It is these questions which will be considered below. It is appropriate to begin with the Flitcroft case, since it can be argued that it represents the high water mark in a strain of judicial thinking which sees the private lives of public figures as a legitimate object of public interest.

The Flitcroft case is notable for laying down some of the key guidelines for the interpretation, and indeed the interrelationship, between Articles 8 and 10

---

[31]   *A v B Plc* [2002] EMLR 7 HC; *A v B Plc* [2002] EMLR 21.

of the European Convention on Human Rights.[32] Among these guidelines was a recognition that a duty of confidence might arise, even without a relationship of confidence between the parties, in a situation where the defendant 'either knows or ought to know that the other person can reasonably expect his privacy to be protected'.[33] Lord Woolf's statement was taken up by Baroness Hale in *Campbell* v *MGN* as constituting 'the starting point' for the balancing exercise between Articles 8 and 10 of the ECHR.[34] However, in the hands of Lord Woolf, the balancing exercise, rather than being forward looking to protect a right to privacy, actually reflected a well-established judicial view of the relationship between celebrity and privacy, in which the former called into question the right to the latter. In *A* v *B Plc*, Lord Woolf held that a public figure was entitled to have his privacy respected in appropriate circumstances; but he also had to recognize that, because of his public position, he must expect and accept that his actions would be scrutinized by the media. Lord Woolf went further and held that, if the public figure was a 'role model' whose 'conduct might be emulated by others' or if he had 'set the fashion' (and the higher the profile of the public figure, the more likely this was to be the case), then that individual might be a legitimate object of public interest *whether or not the individual had courted publicity* (author's emphasis).[35] He concluded that, if there was a public interest in publication, the public had an understandable and so legitimate interest in being informed. The balance in such a case might well come down on the side of publication, because failure to publish might mean fewer newspapers and this was not in the public interest. In the case of Flitcroft, Lord Woolf concluded that the information regarding his affair might well be of public interest. He stated, 'it is not self-evident that how a well-known premiership player, who has a position of responsibility within his club, chooses to spend his time off the football field does not have a modicum of public interest. Footballers are role models for young people and undesirable behaviour on their part can set an unfortunate example'. He also noted that, while Flitcroft (or A) had not courted publicity, 'the fact is that

---

[32]   Article 8 concerns the right of an individual to respect for his private and family life. Article 10 concerns the right to freedom of expression. Both of these rights are qualified rights and each must be read so as not to interfere with the other unless it is 'necessary' to do so.

[33]   *A* v *B* as per Lord Woolf at para.11(ix).

[34]   *Campbell* v *MGN Ltd* [2004] EMLR 15 at paras 134 and 167. Indeed, in the *Campbell* case, it became one of the bases for what is generally recognized to have been a considerable extension of the protection which an action for breach of confidence accords to privacy.

[35]   Although, according to Lord Woolf, if the individual had courted publicity, then he would have less ground to object to press intrusion.

someone holding his position was inevitably a figure in whom a section of the public and the media would be interested'.[36]

In holding that a well-known figure has a lesser right to privacy than a private person, Lord Woolf was certainly following (although he did not cite) the earlier judgment in *Woodward* v *Hutchins* (1977).[37] In this case, the singer, Tom Jones, failed to prevent his erstwhile public relations officer from publishing details of his private life including an extramarital affair. In the Court of Appeal, Lord Denning held that, since the singer had sought publicity of a favourable kind, he could not complain if facts were made public which showed him in an unfavourable light. The public interest in such a case came down upon the side of correcting the false image rather than the protection of confidentiality.[38] The *Woodward* judgment was criticized for, in effect, allowing a celebrity no defence of confidentiality if he had chosen to reveal only certain aspects of his private life.[39] In fact, in *A* v *B*, Lord Woolf seemed to have gone further than Lord Denning. In *A* v *B*, Lord Woolf apparently took the view that well-known individuals who had not courted celebrity might forfeit their right to confidentiality. His judgment would potentially have had a particularly deleterious effects on sportsmen and women who are in the public eye, not because they seek celebrity, but rather because their profession is carried on in public. The truth of this statement is embodied in the *A* v *B* judgment itself, since Flitcroft was not a well-known figure, except on the football field, and perhaps attracted his greatest public attention by bringing and then losing this particular case.

It is submitted that the approach taken by Lord Woolf, which balanced celebrity and the public's right to know, and came down on the side of the latter, is now no longer tenable. That is not to say that the press may not set the record straight when a well-known figure has deliberately lied about unfavourable information. In *Campbell* v *MGN*, the newspaper had published articles exposing the fact that the supermodel was a drug addict and that she was attending meetings of Narcotics Anonymous. The information on her addiction contradicted her earlier claims that she had not used drugs. In the Court of Appeal, the claimant conceded it was legitimate for *The Mirror* to

---

[36] Lord Woolf, at para. 45(vi). Lord Woolf also found the balance in favour of publication because C was held to have a right to freedom of expression. He noted that unlike, for example, the situation between a married couple, in the type of relationship between A and C, it could not be assumed that both parties would expect confidentiality. See, also, *Theakston* v *MGN Ltd.* [2002] EMLR 22.

[37] *Woodward and Others* v *Hutchins and Others* [1977] 2 All ER 751.

[38] *Woodward* v *Hutchins* as per Lord Denning at 752.

[39] F. Gurry, *Breach of Confidence* (Oxford: Clarendon Press, 1991, pp. 99–101); M. Tugendhat and I. Christie, *The Law of Privacy and the Media* (Oxford: OUP, 2002).

publish the fact that she was being treated for drug addiction because she had previously dishonestly claimed that she was not.[40] The House of Lords held that information was confidential where the individual has a reasonable expectation of privacy and that the correct test was to ask whether publication of the information would be highly offensive to a reasonable person of ordinary sensibilities if they were in the same position as the claimant. For the majority, this meant that photographs of Campbell outside NA, taken surreptitiously, and details of her treatment infringed her right to privacy.[41] But, arguably, it is the *Von Hannover* case in the ECHR[42] and the manner in which it has recently been interpreted by the UK court in *McKennit* v *Ash*,[43] which might bring the most comfort to individuals such as Flitcroft who, although they have not courted publicity are, because of the nature of their occupations, nonetheless in the public eye.

In *Von Hannover*, the ECHR broadened the definition of what might constitute a 'private life'.[44] In this case, Princess Caroline, who is a member of the Monaco royal family, sought to prevent the publication of photographs of her private life almost all of which had been taken in public places. The ECHR conceded that Princess Caroline was a well-known person who had received a great deal of public attention although, crucially, she did not exercise any official function.[45] It held that there was a fundamental distinction to be made between reporting information which contributed to public debate, for example about politicians exercising their functions, and reporting details of the private life of an individual who had no official function. The former was a

---

40   *Campbell* v *MGN Ltd.* [2003] EMLR 2 as per Lord Phillips at paras 36 and 53. The House of Lords (HL) agreed that the public had a right to know it had been misled over her drug addiction. The Court of Appeal (CA) also questioned Lord Woolf's sweeping statement that the private lives of role models, even if they have become so unwittingly, are a legitimate object of public interest. According to Lord Phillips, at para. 41, 'For our part we would observe that the fact that an individual has achieved prominence on the public stage does not mean that his private life can be laid bare by the media. We do not see why it should necessarily be in the public interest that an individual who has been adopted as a role model, without seeking this distinction, should be demonstrated to have feet of clay'. On the CA judgment, see R. Calleja, 'Campbell v Mirror Group Newspapers: The Price of Fame', Ent. L.R. 2003, 14(2), 48–50.

41   However, two other Law lords disagreed and, indeed, as we have seen, Lord Woolf used the same standard to find that details of Flitcroft's affairs might be made public. The uncertainty of this test was pointed out by C. Michalos, in 'Image rights and privacy: after Douglas v Hello!', EIPR 2005, 27(10), 384–7 at 386.

42   *Von Hannover* v *Germany* [2004] EMLR 21.

43   *McKennit* v *Ash* [2006] EMLR 10 QB.

44   This point is made by Mr Justice Eady in *McKennit* v *Ash*, at para. 50.

45   *Von Hannover* v *Germany* at para. 65.

vital role for the press and the public had a right to be informed. In the latter case, however, where the purpose of publication was to satisfy public curiosity about the private life of an individual, albeit one who is well known to the public, that individual had a reasonable expectation of privacy.[46]

It can be argued that the principles set out in *Von Hannover* might be of particular comfort to sporting figures, many of whom will be well known, but who exercise no official function and the details of whose private lives would contribute little to public debate of general interest.[47] Mr Justice Eady, in a judgment which was subsequently affirmed by the Court of Appeal,[48] applied the principles of *Von Hannover* in *McKennit v Ash* but went further, in effect calling into question the authority of *Woodward v Hutchins* (and implicitly, *A v B*). Here, the claimant was a folksinger and the defendant was the author of a book entitled *Travels with Loreena McKennitt: My Life as a Friend*. The defendant had been a close friend and a member of the claimant's crew for many years. The claimant alleged that the publication of the book was a breach of confidence. In particular, the claimant objected to information being made public about her personal relationships, her personal feelings and her 'emotional vulnerability'. In defence, it was claimed that either the information was not confidential or the information was in the public interest. It was true that McKennit had released some personal information which 'she felt comfortable with' and 'whose boundaries she could control'.[49] Mr Justice Eady held, following *Von Hannover*, that 'even where there is a genuine public interest, alongside a commercial interest in the media in publishing articles or photographs [of and about well-known figures] sometimes such interests

---

[46]   *Von Hannover v Germany* at paras 76–8. See Michalos, 'Image rights and privacy', 387. The ECHR also appeared to expand the protection afforded by the laws of privacy by holding that activities carried out in public places might still be private if they have no legitimate interest to the public; a ruling which appears to contradict the House of Lords in *Campbell*.

[47]   In their article, 'Phantom intellectual property rights' [2001] IPQ, no. 3 264–285, A. McGee and G. Scanlan present various categories of individuals to whom personality rights might be ascribed, ranging from the private person to the icon. Interestingly, none of their categories involves sportsmen and women. It is submitted that these individuals would fit best into the category of persons 'who are public figures by virtue of their occupation or status'. The authors give the example of, inter alia, backbench MPs. They argue such a person may have less claim to privacy than does an exclusively private person (at 277).

[48]   *Niema Ash and Another v Loreena McKennit and Others* [2006] EWCA Civ 1714 CA.

[49]   *McKennit v Ash*, at para. 7. Mr. Justice Eady, following *Von Hannover*, took the view that its principles applied not just to photographs and not simply in situations where, as was the case with Princess Caroline, she was being 'harassed' by the tabloid press.

would have to yield to the individual citizen's right to the effective protection of private life'.[50] He also held that individuals might have a reasonable expectation of privacy even if the information is trivial.[51] In relation to private information, it may remain confidential even if it has had a limited distribution to the public.[52] There is a difference between what is interesting to the public and what it is in the public interest to know. This is especially true in relation to 'celebrities'. While a claimant has deliberately sought to mislead the public it may be possible to publish confidential information to set the record straight. But in such a case the claimant should be guilty of 'a very high degree of misbehaviour'.[53] He concluded that the principles in *Woodward* v *Hutchins* might now be inapplicable because of developments under the ECHR.[54] The Court of Appeal concurred with Eady J's finding that in assessing an individual's claim to privacy the courts in the UK should have regard to the judgment in *Von Hannover*.[55] In particular, it found that the principles enunciated in *Von Hannover* overrode the interpretation of Arts. 8 and 10 set out, by Lord Woolf, in *A* v *B*. Like Mr Justice Eady, Lord Justice Buxton took issue with the view that just because an individual is of interest to the public, then there is automatically a public interest in allowing information about that individual to be made public. Lord Justice Buxton also expressed his doubts that such a rule would be obviated if the individual was a role model, as Lord Woolf had suggested in *A* v *B*.[56]

In some respects, the judgments in *McKennit* v *Ash* go beyond *Von Hannover*, because, unlike Princess Caroline, McKennit did choose to make some details of her private life public, although in her case it was to publicize a charity. The question remains as to the extent to which the court will protect private information, which relates to well-known figures, indeed celebrities, who seek to profit from public interest in their private lives. This was the issue

---

50   *McKennit* v *Ash*, at para. 57.
51   *McKennit* v *Ash*, at para. 21.
52   *McKennit* v *Ash*, at para. 64 & 81.
53   *McKennit* v *Ash*, at paras 94 –7.
54   *McKennit* v *Ash*, at 105. 'Protection of privacy may extend to relations with other persons. If a person wishes to reveal publicly information about aspects of his or her relations with other people, which would prima facie be private, such revelation should be crafted, so far as possible, to protect the other person's privacy.' 'This is important particularly, of course, in the context of "kiss and tell" stories. It does not follow, because one can reveal one's own private life, that one can also expose confidential matters irrespective of which others are entitled to protection if their consent is not forthcoming. (Para. 77).
55   Indeed, the CA paid 'tribute' to Mr. Justice Eady's judgment at paras. 1 & 88, describing it as 'very skilful'.
56   *Ash* v *McKennit*, paras 64–66, CA.

dealt with by the Court of Appeal in *Douglas* v *Hello! (No. 8)* (2005).[57] In this case, too, the Court of Appeal was willing to take an expansive view of what information should remain confidential. What they were not prepared to do, however, was to follow more 'advanced' jurisdictions in recognizing a right of publicity. The facts of the case are well known. Michael Douglas and Catherine Zeta-Jones agreed that *OK!* magazine should have exclusive photographs of their wedding. A paparazzo crashed the wedding, despite elaborate security arrangements, and took photographs which were subsequently published by *Hello!* magazine. The claimants sued for breach of confidence. In the most recent hearing, the Court of Appeal held, inter alia, that the photographs showed details of the claimant's private life and so fell to be protected by the law of confidence. It also considered the fact that the Douglases sought to profit from the publication of this private information. According to Lord Phillips, a recognition that a celebrity had the right to make money out of publicizing information about his or her private life 'breaks new ground', and, indeed, is reminiscent of the German image right, for example.[58] However, Lord Phillips found authority for protecting such information not in European jurisprudence but in previous UK case law relating to trade secrets. He concluded that where 'an individual ("the owner") has information which he has created or is private and personal and to which he can properly deny access to third parties, and he reasonably intends to profit commercially by using or publishing that information, then a third party who is, or ought to be, aware of these matters and who knowingly obtained the information without authority, will be in breach of duty if he uses or publishes the information to the detriment of the owner'. He added, propitiously, 'We have used the term "owner" loosely'.[59]

If one puts together the judgments in *McKennit* v *Ash* and in *Douglas* v *Hello! (No. 8)*, it might appear that the UK is moving towards a personality right which protects both the dignitary and the commercial aspects of privacy. Certainly, the influence of European case law, particularly from the ECHR, can be seen to have had a significant effect on expanding the circumstances in which an individual will be found to have a right to privacy. However, the *Douglas* judgment also demonstrates the continuing reluctance of UK courts to recognize a broad right to personality or indeed a proprietary right to publicity. In *Douglas* v *Hello! (No. 8)*, the Court of Appeal made clear that it did not consider commercial secrets to be property.[60] An action for breach of confidence continues to provide an equitable remedy which depends upon the

---

57 *Douglas* v *Hello! (No. 8)* [2005] EMLR 28.
58 *Douglas* v *Hello! (No. 8)* at para. 113.
59 *Douglas* v *Hello! (No. 8)* at para. 118.
60 *Douglas* v *Hello! (No. 8)* at para. 120.

conscience of a third party, who receives the information in confidence, being affected.[61] As a result, there was no ownership in the information which could be transferred to *OK!* magazine. The magazine had no proprietary interest in the photographs, and the magazine's own claim for breach of confidence against *Hello!* failed.[62] On an appeal to the House of Lords by *OK!*, the Lords confirmed that confidential information was not property, but by a majority verdict agreed that *Hello!* had breached *OK!*'s confidence under the ordinary rules of commercial confidentiality.[63] Following the recent case law relating to the right of privacy, it is certainly the case that the protection of private information, both for those who unwittingly become objects of public interest, such as Flitcroft, and for those who choose to make certain information about themselves public, such as the Douglases, now attracts far greater protection. Nonetheless, this same case law also demonstrates the reluctance of the UK courts to create, through case law, new rights whether they be free-standing rights of privacy or a proprietary right of publicity. This same reluctance is evident if one turns to the protection which the UK courts accord to personality merchandising.

PERSONALITY MERCHANDISING AND PRODUCT ENDORSEMENT: THE APPROPRIATION OF THE IMAGE

In 2001, Eddie Irvine, the Formula One (F1) racing driver, brought an action for passing off against Talksport Radio.[64] Eddie Irvine was, according to Mr Justice Laddie, 'one of a small group of British drivers who have achieved some success in recent years in that sport'.[65] He had been a runner-up in the 1999 F1 World Championships. Indeed, he had, since 1996, built up a worldwide reputation in the sport, which was accompanied by a growing business in endorsing products. The defendants had, until 1999, been known as 'Talk Radio'. At the end of that year, they had decided to concentrate on live sports coverage and rebrand themselves as 'Talksport'. They initiated a marketing campaign which included sending a number of boxed sets to likely advertisers

---

61   J. Hull and S. Abbott, 'Property rights in secret – Douglas v Hello! in the Court of Appeal', EIPR 2005, 27(10), 379 at 382.

62   For a general discussion, see Hull and Abbott, 'Property rights in secrets', 379–84. See, also, L. Brazell, 'Confidence, privacy and human rights: English law in the twenty-first century', EIPR 2005, 27(11), 405–11; Michalos, 'Image rights and privacy'.

63   *OBG* v *Allen* [2007] UKHL 21.

64   *Irvine* v *Talksport Ltd.* [2002] 32 HC.

65   *Irvine* v *Talksport*, at para. 2.

to promote their Grand Prix coverage. These boxes included a brochure which had a photograph of Eddie Irvine holding a radio, on which the defendant's logo appeared. The picture had been doctored. In the original photograph, the claimant had been holding a mobile phone. The doctored photograph clearly gave the impression that Irvine was listening avidly to the radio, and hence, given the logo, to 'Talk Radio'.

In his judgment in the HC, Mr Justice Laddie noted that the law of passing off 'responds to changes in the nature of trade'.[66] He thought the court should take notice of the fact 'that it is common for famous people to exploit their names and images by way of endorsement. They do it not only in their own field of expertise but, depending upon the extent of their fame or notoriety, wider afield also. It is common knowledge that for many sports men, for example, income received from endorsing a variety of products and services represents a very substantial part of their total income'.[67] In the present case, Mr Justice Laddie took the view that the principles of passing off could apply to an action for false endorsement. The claimant simply needed to show, first, that he had a significant reputation or goodwill at the time of the acts complained of. Second, the claimant had to prove the actions of the defendant gave rise to a false message which would be understood by a not insignificant section of his market that the goods had been endorsed, recommended or approved of by him. According to Mr Justice Laddie, both these elements were present in this case. Irvine was a famous sportsman and, by virtue of his fame, he had been paid to endorse a variety of products. Furthermore, a 'not insignificant' number of those who received the publicity brochure would think that Irvine had endorsed or recommended Talk Radio. As a result, Irvine would suffer damage from the loss of earnings, both for this and for future endorsements. Irvine succeeded in passing off.

There is considerable opinion that personality merchandising is given too little legal protection in the UK, especially in light of its substantial and increasing economic importance. For those who take this view, the judgment in *Irvine* v *Talksport* has generally been welcomed as constituting a significant expansion in the legal protection afforded to personality merchandising.[68] This section of the chapter will consider the extent to which the UK law has protected personality merchandising and will ask whether the *Irvine* v *Talksport* judgment really marks a major 'advance' for those who support the need for greater protection.

---

66 *Irvine* v *Talksport*, at para. 14.
67 *Irvine* v *Talksport*, at para. 39.
68 See, for example, J. Taylor, S. Boyd and D.Becker, 'Image rights', in Lewis & Taylor (eds), *Sport: Law and Practice*, 635–762 at p. 657; also S. Smith, 'The changing face of image protection in sport' (2004), **2** (May), *ISLR*, 37–43.

It is certainly the case that compared to other jurisdictions, the UK has traditionally been parsimonious in the legal protection it has afforded to personality merchandising. There are a number of reasons for this. As we have noted, unlike a number of other jurisdictions, the UK has neither an image right nor a personality right, nor indeed a proprietary right of publicity. This may be explained, in part, by the reluctance of successive governments to introduce such rights through legislation and of the courts to take the initiative in their place. As Lord Justice Walker pointed out in his judgment in *Re Elvis Presley Trade Marks* (1999),[69] as early as 1977 the Whitford Committee 'considered but did not regard as feasible, the introduction of a 'new character right', even though, according to Lord Justice Walker, 'Character Merchandising has been big business for at least 30 years.'[70] And it is certainly the case that traditionally the UK courts have failed to make law where governments have chosen not to do so.[71] Secondly, before the passage of the Trade Marks Act 1994, trade mark registration had offered limited protection for personality or character merchandising, because, under the Trade Marks Act 1938, trade mark proprietors were forbidden to 'traffic' in their marks.[72] Thirdly, if the UK has not developed specific rights to prevent the exploitation of celebrity images, it also lacks a general law of unfair competition, either enshrined in statute or as a species of tort law.[73] Thus there is no general remedy for the simple misappropriation of the value that well-known individuals might have in the commercial exploitation of their personalities, whether or not they have actually sought to realize this potential. From this perspective, the position might be compared with that of Australia, where it has been convincingly argued that, through a series of cases, the Australian courts have been willing to address the unauthorized commercial use of an individual's

---

[69]   *Re Elvis Presley Trade Marks* [1999] RPC 567 CA at p. 580.
[70]   *Re Elvis Presley Trade Marks* [1999] RPC 567 CA at p. 580, Interestingly, in the *Elvis Presely* case, the CA failed to differentiate between personality and character merchandising.
[71]   For the latter point, see *Re Elvis Presley Trade Marks* [1999] RPC 567 CA. Cornish and Llewelyn point out that this reluctance intensified over the course of the twentieth century with the introduction of universal suffrage: W. Cornish and D. Llewelyn, *Intellectual Property* (London: Sweet & Maxwell, 2003, p. 16).
[72]   That is to say, proprietors were prevented from registering famous names or characters as trade marks if their intention was to deal in the marks primarily as commodities in their own right, rather than to identify or promote merchandise in which they were interested. See *Re American Greetings Application* [1984] FSR 199. In the next section, we shall see that the UK courts have not interpreted the 1994 Act to give markedly greater protection to personality merchandising.
[73]   See, for example, H. Carty, *An Analysis of the Economic Torts* (Oxford: OUP, 2001, p. 1) and A. Kamperman Sanders, *Unfair Competiton Law* (Oxford: Clarendon Press, 1997, p. 52).

personality by a third party in terms of 'misappropriation/unjust enrichment'.[74]

It is generally recognized that the key defence against the unauthorized commercial use of a person's name or image in the UK remains an action for passing off, much as it did when George Best was playing for Manchester United.[75] It is true that passing off has sometimes been referred to as unfair competition, most recently by Lord Justice Aldous in *Arsenal v Reed*, when he noted obiter that the 'cause of action traditionally called passing off, [is] perhaps best referred to as unfair competition'.[76] Nonetheless, it is certainly the case that the manner in which passing off has been applied in cases of personality merchandising has not approximated it to a tort of unfair competition. Certainly, until *Irvine v Talksport*, the courts have continued to require the three elements of passing off (goodwill, misrepresentation and damage), whereas, for example in the Australian cases, the courts have arguably dropped the need both for existing goodwill[77] and a misrepresentation.[78] Furthermore, for a considerable period the UK courts also looked for a common field of activity in personality merchandising cases between the claimant and the defendant, since without such a field the courts were unwilling to find that there was an operative misrepresentation.[79] The need for a common field in personality merchandising was introduced by *McCulloch v May* (1947).[80] In this case, Uncle Mac, a children's radio presenter, tried to restrain the defendant from selling a breakfast cereal, also named 'Uncle Mac'. He failed because the court could not find a common field between the claimant and the defendant. A similar result was reached in later cases, involving both character and personality merchandising. Thus the owners of the Wombles copyright were unable to prevent the name of their characters being placed on rubbish

---

[74] See H. Carty, 'Character merchandising and the limits of passing off', *Legal Studies*, **13**(3), November 1993, 289–307. The key cases in this development would be *Henderson v Radio Corporation Pty. Ltd.* [1969] RPC 218; *Hogan v Koala Dundee Pty. Ltd* [1988] 12 IPR 508 and *Pacific Dunlop Ltd. v Hogan* [1989] 14 IPR 398. Canada has also developed a common law tort of appropriation of personality; see Beverley-Smith, *The Commercial Appropriation of Personality*, pp. 115–36.

[75] See, for example, F. Robinson, 'How image conscious is English law' (2004), **15**(5), *Ent. L.R.* 151–6 at 151; Klink, '50 years of publicity rights', IPQ (2003), **4**, 370.

[76] *Arsenal v Reed* [2003] ETMR 73 CA, at para. 70.

[77] *Henderson v Radio Corp*, where the successful plaintiffs did not engage in character merchandising.

[78] As in *Pacific Dunlop v Hogan*.

[79] H. Carty, 'Character merchandising', 295; G. Scanlan, 'Personality, endorsement and everything: the modern law of passing off and the myth of the personality right' (2003), **25**(12), *EIPR*, 563–9.

[80] *McCulloch v Lewis A. May (Produce Distributors) Ltd.* [1947] 65 RPC 58.

skips.[81] The producers of the 'Kojak' television series could not prevent the sale of 'Kojak' lollies[82] and, in *Lynstad v Annabas* (1977),[83] the pop group, Abba, was unable to prevent the unauthorized use of its name on tee-shirts and other merchandise.

The need for a common field in character and personality merchandising apparently persisted even when it had been definitively laid to rest in other areas of passing off.[84] However, it is submitted that, in later cases, the courts were not so much concerned with the need for a common field between the parties, but rather with the fact that, if the claimant did not have a business that involved merchandising, there would be neither a misrepresentation nor damage.[85] The definitive and explicit break with the common field in character merchandising came with the 'Ninja Turtles' case in 1991.[86] In this case the claimants licensed the reproduction of the famous humanoid cartoon characters, but manufactured no goods themselves. The defendants made drawings of humanoid turtles using the same concept (although there was no direct copying) and licensed them for use on clothing. The court granted a pre-trial injunction. According to Browne-Wilkinson VC, the goodwill was located in the claimant's business of licensing the copyright in the drawings, the misrepresentation was that the drawings on the defendant's goods had been licensed by the claimant and damage was to the image of the turtles, which, if placed on inferior goods, would reduce the value of the claimant's licensing rights. In fact, the 'Ninja Turtles' case, while important for character merchandising, arguably did not advance the protection of personality merchandising. The claimant succeeded because its business resided in licensing a piece of intellectual property, its copyright in the drawings. This would not be true in the case of personality merchandising. The claimant also succeeded because the court was willing to assume that the public would believe that the defendants had a license to use the drawings. In later personality merchandising cases, the courts have been unwilling to assume that the public would make a licensing connection.[87] Looking back on the 'Ninja Turtles' decision, Lord Walker noted

81   *Wombles Ltd. v Wombles Skips Ltd.* [1975] FSR 488.

82   *Tavener Rutledge Ltd. v Trexapalm Ltd.* [1975] FSR 479.

83   *Lynstad v Annabas Products Ltd.* [1977] FSR 62.

84   Most notably by Lord Diplock in *Warnink (Erven) BV v J. Townend & Sons (Hull) Ltd.* [1979] FSR 397.

85   H. Carty, 'Character merchandising', 296. For the difficulty of proving damage, see for example *Stringfellow v McCain Foods (GB) Ltd.* [1984] FSR 175. It is arguable that in the 'Abba' case, the court held that the public would not assume that the goods were connected to the pop group.

86   *Mirage Studios v Counter-Feat Clothing Co. Ltd.* [1991] FSR 145.

87   For example, *Elvis Presley TM*, as per Lord Brown, at 598. See, for example, *Halliwell v Panini* [1997] EMLR 94.

in *Elvis Presley* that 'It does not give a green light to extravagant claims based on any unauthorized use of a celebrity's name'.[88]

If it is fair to say that, before *Irvine* v *Talksport*, a 'sports star would have to show he or she was engaged in the actual marketing and selling to the public of products or services endorsed with his or her name or image', to succeed in passing off,[89] it is submitted that, following *Irvine*, the general protection given to personality merchandising has not significantly increased. First of all, in *Irvine* v *Talksport*, Mr Justice Laddie was careful to differentiate cases of false endorsement from merchandising more generally, whether it be character or personality merchandising. The former tells the public that the individual is happy to be associated with the product; the latter involves 'exploiting images, themes or articles' which have become famous.[90] *Irvine* v *Talksport* is generally seen as a breakthrough for personality merchandising because Mr Justice Laddie rejected the need for a common field of activity and applied passing off to famous people, who 'exploit their names and images by way of endorsement'.[91] We have already suggested that the need for a common field of activity had been rejected in earlier cases. Once that is accepted, it is submitted that Mr. Justice Laddie simply went on to apply the classic trinity of passing off.[92] First, Irvine had goodwill in his name because he had used it in the past to endorse products. Secondly, there was a misrepresentation that he had endorsed Talk Radio. Thirdly, he suffered damage because he would ordinarily have charged a considerable sum for making such an endorsement.[93] On that basis, Mr Justice Laddie was willing to find passing off. If his name had simply appeared unauthorized on merchandise (without the representation that he had endorsed the merchandise) or had Irvine not endorsed products in the past, it is submitted that Mr. Justice Laddie would not have reached the same conclusion.[94]

---

[88] *Elvis Presley TM*, at 582.
[89] Taylor, Boyd and Becker, 'Image rights', 651.
[90] *Irvine* v *Talksport*, at para. 9.
[91] *Irvine* v *Talksport*, at para. 39.
[92] Robinson, in 'How image conscious is English law?', also questions the extent to which Mr Justice Laddie moved beyond the traditional limits of passing off (152–3).
[93] The CA subsequently awarded Irvine £25 000 as this would have been his minimum fee for making such an endorsement: *Irvine* v *Talksport Ltd. (Nos. 1 and 2)* [2003] FSR 35. But see A. Michaels, 'Passing off by false endorsement – but what's the damage' (2002), *EIPR* 448–9.
[94] An interesting contrast is the case of *David Bedford* v *The Number (UK) Ltd.* The athlete complained to Ofcom that an advertisement for the operators of a directory enquiry service had breached the Advertising Standards Code by using two characters who appropriated his image (which in the 1970s had involved long hair, a moustache and a distinctive running kit). Ofcom found that the runners did caricature his image, but also

Despite the decision in *Irvine* v *Talksport*, it has been argued here that the UK courts continue to be sparing in the support that they will accord to personality merchandising under the tort of passing off. They have not recognized a proprietary right in a name or image as such. Indeed, this was made clear by Mr Justice Laddie in *Irvine* v *Talksport*, itself, when he emphasized that passing off does not protect property in the word or name 'but property in the trade or goodwill which will be injured by its use'.[95] Similarly, both in character and personality merchandising, the courts have not chosen to stretch the cause of action in passing off to approximate a tort of unfair competition. Unlike the Australian cases, the UK courts will not recognize the simple misappropriation of the commercial value of an individual's name or image.[96] They continue, as was explicitly the case in *Irvine* v *Talksport*, to require an operative misrepresentation. It might be argued that, if the courts are either to fashion a publicity right or apply the principles of unfair competition to personality merchandising, this will inevitably involve a long game, and progress will be made on a case-by-case basis. However, this chapter will conclude by suggesting that, where the courts have had an opportunity to increase the protection afforded to personality merchandising, they have chosen to do so only haltingly. It will illustrate this point by considering how the UK courts have applied the 1994 Trade Marks Act to personality merchandising.

CONCLUSION. THE LIMITS TO THE PROTECTION ACCORDED TO PERSONALITY MERCHANDISING: THE CASE OF TRADE MARKS

In 2003, Sir Alex Ferguson, manager of Manchester United FC, sought to register the trade mark ALEX FERGUSON for, inter alia, printed matter, posters, photographs, transfers, stickers, decalcomanias and stickers relating to football.[97] His initial application was rejected by the Registry and he appealed to the Appointed Person. The appeal was unsuccessful. A trade mark may be

---

found that Bedford had suffered no financial harm as a result, since he did not use his image in marketing. It is submitted that the fact that Bedford did not exploit his image commercially would undermine any action he took in passing off (since there would be no goodwill, misrepresentation or damage). See 'Case comment: David Bedford v The Number (UK) Ltd.' (2004), **2** (May), *ISLR*, 18–21; D. Rose and E. Shaw, 'Misappropriation without misrepresentation', *New Law Journal*, 12 March 2004, 386–7.

[95]   *Irvine* v *Talksport*, at para. 131.

[96]   This is the conclusion reached by C. Wadlow, *The Law of Passing Off: Unfair Competition by Misrepresentation* (London: Sweet & Maxwell, 2004, p. 489).

[97]   He was successful in registering his name for a range of other goods, including computer games, watches and figurines.

refused registration if it is, inter alia, devoid of distinctive character or descriptive.[98] The Appointed Person found that the use of the ALEX FERGUSON name on these goods would be descriptive. In other words, the goods would be mere image carriers. Image carriers are defined in the *Trade Mark Registry Work Manual*. According to the manual (at 21.2): The name of a famous person or group is likely to be perceived as merely descriptive of the subject matter of posters, photographs, transfers and figurines. Names of famous persons or groups are therefore unlikely to be accepted by consumers as trade marks for these goods because they will usually be seen as mere descriptions of the subject matter of the product.

In this case, it was held, inter alia, that the mark ALEX FERGUSON was descriptive of the goods, as the mark would be perceived by potential consumers as defining their subject matter.[99]

When the new Trade Marks Act was enacted in 1994 it was envisaged that both character and personality merchandising would receive more extensive legal protection than under the previous trade mark regime, as the Act for the first time allowed registration of marks for licensing purposes.[100] It is submitted that, had they have been sympathetic to the aim, the UK courts could have interpreted the Act to give more or less open-ended protection to merchandising marks. They chose not to do so. In *Elvis Presley Trade Marks* (1999), the Court of Appeal not only placed considerable limits on the protection afforded to personality merchandising through trade marks registration, they also articulated the reasons why they felt it was justifiable to do so. Elvis Presley Enterprises Inc. was the successor to Elvis Presley's merchandising business. It sought to register the marks 'Elvis', 'Elvis Presley' and the signature mark 'Elvis A. Presley' for toiletries. The application was opposed by Sid Shaw, who had traded in Elvis memorabilia since the 1970s, and had registered the mark 'Elvisly Yours' for a range of goods, including toiletries. In the HC, Mr Justice Laddie[101] found for the opponent and the applicant appealed to Court of Appeal.[102] In his leading judgment, Walker LJ held that the word marks

---

[98]   Trade Marks Act 1994, s. 3(1)(b) and s. 3(1)(c), implementing the Trade Marks Directive (First Council Directive 89/104/EEC of 21 December 1988 to approximate the laws of Member States relating to trade marks), Art. 3(1)(b) and (c).

[99]   The mark was also found to be devoid of distinctive character: *In the Matter of Application No. 2323092B to Register A Trade Mark in Class 16 by Sir Alexander Chapman Ferguson*. For a similar case, see *Linkin Park LLC's Trade Mark Application* [2003] ETMR 17; A. Wood, 'Linkin Park fails to hit a sweet note' (2005), **16**(5), *Ent. LR*. 134–6.

[100]   See, for example, R. Annand and H. Norman, *Blackstone's Guide to the Trade Marks Act 1994* (London: Blackstone, 1994, pp. 213–15).

[101]   *Elvis Presley Trade Marks* [1997] RPC 543.

[102]   The application was made under the 1938 Trade Marks Act, but the CA made it clear that its judgment would remain relevant under the 1994 Act.

lacked the requisite distinctiveness to be registered as trade marks. He asked whether other traders were likely to wish to use that same mark in the course of trade 'without improper motive', and held that they would.[103] In other words, it was held that, by the date of application, the words 'Elvis' and 'Elvis Presley' were so much a part of the language as to be descriptive of the goods rather than distinctive of their source and it would be wrong not to allow other traders the opportunity to use them. In making his judgment he paraphrased Mr Justice Laddie, ' "The commemoration of the late Elvis Presley *is* the product", and the article on which his name or image appears . . . is little more than a vehicle.'[104] It was the idea that the merchandise would be a mere 'image carrier' which of course prevented Alex Ferguson registering his name as a trade mark for printed matter six years later.

In making his argument in support of the applicant, counsel for the applicant invited the court to recognize that, following the 'Ninja Turtles' case, there was now a 'general rule' that a trader should not make unauthorized use of the name of a well-known person or character on his merchandise.[105] Their Lordships disagreed. As Lord Morritt shortly put it, 'I do not accept this submission'.[106] According to Lord Brown, 'the idea that character merchandising is already established and accepted in the public mind as properly the exclusive preserve of the character himself is 'altogether too simplistic a view of the effect of the many authorities in this field'.[107] The Court of Appeal then went on to elucidate two matters of principle which prevented them from recognizing such a general rule of law. First, the government had rejected the idea of a character right in 1977 with the Whitford Committee, and it would be inappropriate for the courts unilaterally to create such a right.[108] The second principle was that to recognize 'a free standing general right to character exploitation enjoyable exclusively by the celebrity' would create an unwelcome monopoly.[109] By making this second point, the Court of Appeal was firmly rejecting the idea that only a celebrity or his successors may properly market or license his own name or image. It appears that, in finding for Mr Shaw, the Court of Appeal had been influenced by the argument of his counsel that Elvis Presley's attraction was not entirely of his own making, but

---

[103]   He was applying Lord Parker's well-known test in *W & G Du Cros Ltd.* [1913] A.C. 624 at 634–5 for the non-registration of descriptive marks.
[104]   *Elvis Presley Trade Marks* (CA), at 565.
[105]   *Elvis Presley*, as per Lord Walker at 583. He went on to argue that 'as a matter of everyday experience, reputable traders do not use the name of a living person in connection with their merchandise without obtain [*sic*] authority'.
[106]   *Elvis Presley Trade Marks*, at 594.
[107]   *Elvis Presley Trade Marks*, at 597.
[108]   *Elvis Presley Trade Marks*, at 596.
[109]   *Elvis Presley Trade Marks* as per Lord Brown, at 597.

rather that he had 'become an important part of popular culture'.[110] It perhaps led to Lord Walker's conclusion that all the products against which the applicants sought to register the marks 'were being marketed primarily on the strength of their bearing the name or image of Elvis Presley'. He took the view, as had Mr Justice Laddie, that the 'real product was Elvis Presley himself'.[111]

Lord Walker, in *Elvis Presley Trade Marks*, identified the crux of the problem which is raised by personality merchandising. According to Lord Walker, 'one of the many paradoxical features of this case, that some celebrities wish to prevent "appropriation of personality" as a means of defending their privacy; others wish to prevent unauthorized appropriation so as to secure a monopoly of commercial exploitation of their names, images and fame'.[112] It is this paradox that the present chapter has sought to address. We began by noting that, generally, the UK is seen to provide relatively little protection for those wishing to exploit commercially their personalities, compared to other jurisdictions. In particular, the UK courts have neither through legislation nor judicial activism developed a personality or an image right, nor a proprietary publicity right. Nor have the courts recognized a tort of unfair competition in relation to the misappropriation of personality. Given the huge increase in the value of personality merchandising over past decades and also the voracious public interest in celebrity lives, fed by the tabloid press, the relatively modest protection given to well-known individuals in the UK to profit from the former and to be protected from the latter is frequently characterized as unsatisfactory and/or likely to evolve towards a more European or North American model.

This chapter wishes to propose an alternative view. It is submitted that the UK courts have achieved a satisfactory balance between the profits and the price of fame. This is particularly the case in relation to sportsmen and women. It has been noted that such individuals are, by virtue of their occupation, public figures. For a great many of these individuals, however, their fame rests exclusively on their sporting exploits. Many of these individuals are interested

---

[110] *Elvis Presely Trade Marks*, at 584.
[111] *Elvis Presley Trade Marks*, at 577.
[112] *Elvis Presley Trade Marks*, at 583. It was admitted by the CA that, as a result of its judgment in *Elvis*, the more famous a person was the harder it would be to register his or her name for merchandise which was unconnected with their fame, such as, in this case, toiletries. Lord Brown noted, at 597, that such a difficulty might be overcome where the goods are connected to the fame of the individuals, such as marketing 'Geoffrey Boycott cricket bats'. Interestingly, the ECJ appears to have taken a similar approach to famous names in *Picasso Trade Mark* (Case C0361/04P) 12 January 2006, when it found that the trade mark 'Picasso' was not particularly distinctive when used in relation to cars, as its primary association for the public would be with the famous artist.

neither in their private lives becoming an object of public interest nor in using their names or images to profit off the field of play. It is submitted that recent developments in the law of privacy in the UK have helped to ensure that such individuals will be able to protect their private lives from public intrusion. Other sportsmen and women have of course opted to exploit details of their private lives commercially. As we have seen, in *Douglas* v *Hello!*, the courts have recognized that such information can receive legal protection. They have done so, not by looking to the European or North American rights-based approaches, but rather by finding that protection of such information can be accommodated under the tort of breach of confidence by analogy to trade secrets.

The UK courts, then, have acted to increase the protection given to the private lives of well-known individuals, including those who choose to exploit commercially the intimate details of their lives. In this respect, the UK is moving along a trajectory similar to that of its European neighbours. The same cannot be said in relation to the legal protection afforded to the commercial exploitation of celebrity names and images. It is suggested that there are two key reasons why this is so. The first concerns the general unwillingness of the UK courts to recognize rights or even new torts, such as unfair competition, if the government is unwilling to do so through legislation. The second reason rests upon a particular judicial view of who manufactures or 'owns' fame and, as a result, who should profit from it. In some jurisdictions, for example Germany, we have seen that protection for an individual against the unauthorized exploitation of his or her personality derives from the court's willingness to protect 'ideal interests'.[113] In the United States, the recognition of a common law right of publicity and its statutory equivalents derives from a belief that a celebrity has a proprietary interest in his or her fame.[114] The UK courts have explicitly rejected both such approaches. Instead, in *Elvis*, they have appeared to take the view that the value of celebrity is not something from which the celebrity alone should profit. From this perspective, celebrity is a joint production of the individual and of the public. It is not simply the actions of the celebrity but also the reaction of the public which gives his or her name or image commercial value. As a result, the public interest does not automatically reside in giving the individual a monopoly over the exploitation of that name or image. It may instead reside in ensuring that competitors will also be able to exploit the commercial value of celebrity. Considered in this

---

[113]   Beverley-Smith et al., *Privacy, Property and Personality*, p. 94. Beverley-Smith likened this right by analogy to a copyright (at p. 214). Interestingly, in the UK, it has long been recognized that copyright favours the entrepreneur rather than the author. See, for example, Cornish and Llewelyn, *Intellectual Property*, pp. 348–9.
[114]   Beverley-Smith et al., *Privacy, Property and Personality*, p. 213.

light, the UK courts may be said to have taken not only a thoroughly post-modern approach to celebrity,[115] but also one which accords with their traditional dislike of monopoly if it is at the expense of competition.[116] While such an approach may cause unhappiness to the owners of the most valuable sporting brands, it is also worth recognizing that, despite the popular interest in sport, very few sportsmen and women seek to exploit their fame in any systematic way. Indeed, of the present English football team, for example, only David Beckham, Rio Ferdinand and Wayne Rooney have registered their names as trade marks. More to the point, if one considers the public complicity in making both Best and Beckham national icons, it seems difficult to demur from this approach.

---

[115] See, for example, R. Coombe, 'Author/izing the celebrity: publicity rights, postmodern politics and unauthorized genders' (1992), **10**, *Cardozo Arts & Entertainment*, esp. 369–70. McGee and Scanlan, in 'Phantom intellectual property rights', argue that the 'Public Person' is shaped to a considerable degree by the media and is 'semi-fictional' and this might affect the amount of privacy he or she accorded (at 267–78).

[116] For a further explanation of this point, see J. Davis, 'Unfair competition law in the United Kingdom', in R. Hilty and F. Henning-Bodewig (eds), *Law Against Unfair Competition – Towards a New Paradigm in Europe* (Berlin: Springer, 2007, pp. 183–98).

10. Exploitation of databases, intellectual property, competition law and the sport industry: a missed goal?

Estelle Derclaye

INTRODUCTION

As the book highlights it, sporting activities are increasingly regulated especially by EU law. One way the sport industry has been indirectly regulated by EU law is through the interpretation of an intellectual property right, the *sui generis* right protecting databases, also called 'database right'. On 9 November 2004, the European Court of Justice ('ECJ') interpreted the right in four related cases concerning football and horse racing fixtures (that is, information[1] relating to the dates, times, places, teams playing in the matches or horses running in the races).[2] Organisers of important sport events like the

---

[1] In the context of this article, the terms 'information' and 'data' will be used interchangeably. For an explanation of the difference of meaning between these two terms, see E. Derclaye, 'What is a database? A critical analysis of the definition of a database in the European Database Directive and suggestions for an international definition' (2002), **5**, *The Journal of World Intellectual Property*, 6, 981–1011, at 1004–1005.

[2] *Fixtures Marketing Ltd* v *Organismos Prognostikon Agonon Podosfairou (OPAP)* (case C-444/02) [2005] 1 CMLR 16 (further referred to as 'OPAP'); *Fixtures Marketing Ltd* v *Oy Veikkaus AB* (case C-46/02) [2005] ECDR 2 (further referred to as 'Veikkaus'); *Fixtures Marketing Ltd* v *Svenska Spel AB* (case C-338/02 [2005] ECDR 4 (further referred to as Svenska Spel) and the *British Horseracing Board Ltd* v *William Hill Organisation Ltd* (case C-203/02) [2005] 1 CMLR 15 (further referred to as 'BHB'), also available on http://curia.europa.eu. Briefly, the facts were that the defendants, several betting organisations, had copied and communicated to the public Fixtures Marketing's and the British Horseracing Board's fixtures without the latter's authorisation. The latter claimed they had database rights in these fixtures and that the defendants had infringed them. For comments on the decisions, see T. Aplin, 'The ECJ Elucidates the Database Right' (2005), *Intellectual Property Quarterly*, 204; M. Davison and P.B. Hugenholtz, 'Football fixtures, horseraces and spin offs: the ECJ domesticates the database right' (2005), *European Intellectual Property Review*, 113; E. Derclaye, 'The ECJ interprets the database *sui generis* right for the first time' (2005), **30**, *European Law Review*, 420–30.

Olympics, football, rugby, cricket, tennis, etc. matches and horse races are therefore affected by law in their ownership rights on information relating to such events. The book aims at examining how and with what effect, among others, intellectual property and competition laws are applied to sporting activities. To this effect, this chapter first gives a general background to the issues (background). Then the chapter explains the main features of the database right as interpreted by the European Court of Justice and examines the effect of the database right on sporting organisations (Section 1). The analysis shows that in most cases, the database right is not of much help to sporting organisations. However, in some cases, sporting organisations can be very well protected, so much so that problems of competition law can occur if the organisation has a monopoly (Section 2). Section 3 then addresses what the sporting industry can do to tackle these problems. Finally, the chapter concludes and outlines future developments in the area (conclusion).

BACKGROUND

Organizing a sporting event, like any event, generates a lot of information. This includes, for instance, information concerning the identity of the sportsmen and women, their coaches, the places, dates and times of events, statistics on sportspersons' performances and results of matches and competitions. Sporting organizations, such as the English and Scottish football leagues and the British Horseracing Board, but also for instance the Rugby Football Union, the British Indoor Cricket Association, the International Olympic Committee, the Women's Tennis Association and so on therefore create databases to record and classify the information they generate to organize events. This information can be classified in three categories: fixtures, results and statistics, and have different consequences at the legal level. These consequences will be explored throughout the chapter. Databases are therefore very important assets for sporting organizations as they generally are the first proprietors of this information. If this information is protected by law, that is, the law gives them property rights on it, they can license their rights to others and thereby make profit by asking for licence fees. In the European Union, databases are protected by intellectual property law.

To understand how databases are currently protected by intellectual property law in the European Union, a short historical review of the evolution of the law is in order. Databases were traditionally protected by copyright law. However, in most European countries (mainly the continental ones),[3] copy-

---

[3]   All except the Netherlands, the Nordic countries, the United Kingdom and Ireland. The latter countries protected the contents of databases either by copyright or by a neighbouring right. See, for example, P.B. Hugenholtz, *Auteursrecht op informatie*

right protected only the structure of the database (the way elements of a database are selected, arranged, classified or presented), not its contents. In addition, copyright protected only original works. Thus databases structured in a banal way, for example alphabetically or chronologically, were not protected by copyright. Most databases were and still are structured in a banal way as it is the most practical way for the user to find the information. Unfair competition, when it was available, was used to fill this protection gap. As the legal protection of databases in Member States radically diverged, the European Commission decided to harmonize the law. The Directive on the legal protection of databases ('the Directive') was enacted in 1996 to do so.[4] Traditional continental copyright was retained but a new right, rather than unfair competition, was created to protect investment in gathering, verifying or presenting databases' contents. This is the database right. What is really important to many database producers, and especially the sport industry, is not really to create an original structure for their database, as this is not very useful (who would want a database classifying towns where matches take place by the personal preference of the database maker for this town?). What matters is the database's completeness, its ease of access (user-friendliness, that is, an easy-to-understand alphabetical or chronological structure, for example) and the information contained in it. Fixtures, sports statistics and sports results are generally not protected by copyright as they are classified by alphabetical, chronological order or by ranking. Therefore, copyright does not really help such database producers. It is the database right that can be useful to the sport industry. The focus of the chapter will therefore be on the extent of its usefulness to sporting organizations.

CHARACTERISTICS OF THE DATABASE RIGHT WITH PARTICULAR APPLICATION TO THE SPORT INDUSTRY

This section concentrates on the features of the database right that are most important to the sport industry and includes a description of the provisions of the Directive as interpreted by the ECJ. The section envisages the features of the right keeping in mind the particularities of the sport industry.

(Amsterdam: Kluwer Deventer, 1989, 41–51, 109–18); G. Karnell, 'The Nordic catalogue rule' in E. Dommering and P.B. Hugenholtz, *Protecting works of fact, copyright, freedom of expression and information law* (Deventer/Boston: Kluwer Law and Taxation Publishers, 1991, p. 67).

[4] Directive 96/9/EC of the European Parliament and of the Council of 11 March 1996 on the legal protection of databases, OJ L77/20, 27.03.1996. Member States had to implement the Directive for 1 January 1998.

Like any intellectual property right,[5] the database right has a subject matter of protection, a protection requirement, rights, exceptions and a term of protection. There are also rules on ownership of the right but what concerns us is not who is the owner of the right but what is a database, under what conditions the right is acquired, what the owner can do with its rights and for how long. The ownership rules are therefore not reviewed.[6]

Subject Matter of Protection

The database right protects, of course, databases. Databases are defined as collections 'of independent works, data or other materials, systematically or methodically arranged and individually accessible by electronic or other means' (art. 1(2)) and can be in any form, for example on analogue or digital media (off or online) (art. 1(1)). This definition is broad[7] as it includes databases in every form and can potentially include collections of tangible objects because of the breadth of the term 'materials'.[8] The latter is not really a matter of concern for sporting organizations since they mainly deal with intangible materials, that is, information.

The three main criteria that restrict this generally broad definition are independence, systematic or methodical arrangement and individual accessibility of the elements. Independence means that the elements of a database 'are separable from one another without their informative, literary, artistic, musical or other value being affected'.[9] This means that, if an element is taken out of the database or is added, this element still makes sense. Examples of inseparable elements are chapters of a novel or images of a film. Novels and films cannot be databases because the value of each of their elements is affected when separated from the whole. In other words, elements of a database must have autonomous informative value.[10] Elements of sports fixtures, as the ECJ has

---

[5]   The intellectual property nature of the database right is not contested. See, e.g., W. Copinger and F. Skone James, *On Copyright*, 14th edn (London: Sweet & Maxwell, 1999, n.18–04); V. Bensinger, *Sui generis Schutz für Databanken, die EG-Datenbank Richtlinie vor dem Hintergrund des nordischen Rechts* (Munich: Beck, 1999, pp. 111ff.); J. Gaster, *Der Rechtschutz von Databanken* (Cologne: Carl Heymanns, 1999, pp. 118 ff., n. 457 ff).

[6]   In most cases, the sports organization will be the owner of the database because it is the person who takes the initiative and the risk of investing.

[7]   Para. 20 (OPAP).

[8]   See, e.g., A. Quaedvlieg, 'Onafhankelijk, geordend en toegangkelijk: het object van het databankenrecht in de richtlijn' (2000), **9**, *Informatierecht/AMI*, 177; D. Visser, 'Carnaval in Oss: Variété, Databank of folkore?' (1999), *Mediaforum*, 374.

[9]   Para. 29 (OPAP).

[10]   Para. 33 (OPAP).

ruled, and sports results by application of this ruling, are independent. Sports statistics (for example, how fast a tennis player's serve is, how many double faults s/he made, how many direct and indirect errors s/he made and so on) are also independent. Systematic or methodical arrangement does not mean that this arrangement must be physically apparent but there must be at least a means, such as an index, a table of contents, or a plan or method of classification that allows the retrieval of any independent material contained within the database.[11] Sports fixtures and results always fulfil this criterion as they are classified alphabetically, chronologically or by ranking. Sports statistics fulfil this criterion as well. The requirement of individual accessibility has not been directly construed by the ECJ and remains unclear to many commentators.[12] Probably, it simply coincides with the previous criterion. In conclusion, sports fixtures, sports results and sports statistics are databases.[13]

Protection Requirement

The database right accrues when a qualitatively or quantitatively substantial investment in the obtaining, verifying or presenting of the materials is proven (art. 7). The investment can be financial, material (acquisition of equipment such as computers) or human (number of employees, hours of work).[14] The Directive does not define substantiality and the ECJ did not venture to give an interpretation. However, many national courts, and the Advocate General in his Opinion in the *Veikkaus* case,[15] interpreted the requirement as being rather low. For example, a few days' work or a few hundred pounds or euros may be sufficient to qualify the database for protection.[16] A quantitatively substantial investment refers to the amount of money and/or time invested in the database while a qualitatively substantial investment refers to the effort and/or energy invested in the database.[17] The alternative requirement set out in the Directive (quantitatively *or* qualitatively) therefore allows protecting a

---

[11]   Para. 30 (OPAP).
[12]   E. Derclaye, n.1 above.
[13]   Para. 36 (OPAP). The judgment only talked of football fixtures but this can be safely extrapolated to sports results and statistics because the criteria of independence and methodical or systematic arrangement are met as well.
[14]   Recital 7 of the Directive.
[15]   Opinion of Advocate General Stix-Hackl, 8 June 2004, case C-46/02 (*Veikkaus*), para. 49, available at http://curia.europa.eu..
[16]   See, e.g., *Sonacotra* v *Syndicat Sud Sonacotra*, TGI Paris, 25.04.2003 [2003] *Dalloz* 2819, comment C. Le Stanc, available at www.legalis.net; *Spot* v *Canal Numédia*, TPI Bruxelles (réf.), 18.01.2001 [2002] *Revue Ubiquité* 95, comment S. Dusollier.
[17]   Para. 43 (OPAP).

database that required only a substantial investment in effort or energy rather than in money. Verifying the elements of a database means ensuring the reliability of the information contained in the database, monitoring the accuracy of the materials collected when the database was created and during its operation.[18] Presenting elements refers to 'the resources used for the purpose of giving the database its function of processing information, that is to say those used for the systematic or methodical arrangement of the materials contained in that database and the organization of their individual accessibility'.[19] Thus 'verifying' and 'presenting' have been given a straightforward dictionary meaning. On the other hand, 'obtaining' the elements of a database exclusively means collecting them. This excludes their creation.[20] In addition, if the substantial investment in the collection, verification or presentation of the materials is inseparable from the substantial investment in their creation, the right will not subsist.[21]

All these requirements do not pose problems to sporting organizations as they generally do invest a lot of money or energy (substantially enough) into obtaining, verifying or presenting their database's materials. However, the fate of sports fixtures on the one hand, and sports results and statistics on the other hand, must be distinguished. As regards sports fixtures, generally, the investment made in obtaining, presenting or verifying the identity of players, dates, times and places of matches or competitions will be inseparable from the investment in their creation. This is what the ECJ held in respect of the sports fixtures lists in question.[22] As the protection requirement is not fulfilled in this case, the sporting organizations are not protected by the database right. This, however, is different for sports results and statistics. Sports results and statistics are not created by sporting organizations but by sportsmen and women themselves. The organizations *record* the results and statistics. This leads us to examine different types of data whose different characteristics influence the subsistence of the right.

There are three types of data: created (also called synthetic), collected and recorded data.[23] Created data is data made by man. These data never existed before. Such data include sports fixtures lists, television listings, event schedules, transport timetables, telephone subscriber data and stock prices.

---

18   Para. 27 (Svenska Spel).
19   Ibid.
20   Para. 24 (Svenska Spel).
21   Paras. 29–30 (Svenska Spel).
22   Paras. 31–6 (Svenska Spel).
23   For more developments, see E. Derclaye, 'Databases *sui generis* right: should we adopt the spin-off theory?' (2004), **9**, *European Intellectual Property Review*, 402–12, at 409ff.

Collected data are pre-existing data.[24] They may have been previously created or recorded by man but they are used at a second stage, that is, the collection comes *after* the recording or creation. Recorded data sit in between created and collected data. They are data existing in nature and recorded by instruments of measure in intelligible form. In this sense, they can also be described as created, since they did not exist in intelligible form before. The difference between recorded and created data is that anyone can record recorded data as they pre-exist in nature. They are not arbitrarily created by only one person. They can be recorded by several persons. However, it can be difficult to determine whether these data are actually created or collected for the purposes of the law. Perhaps they are both collected and created. Despite this quasi-insoluble question, in many cases it will be possible for a sporting organization to claim that a substantial investment went into presenting recorded data in an intelligible form and therefore the database right will accrue. For instance, recording and presenting the results of all football, cricket (and so on) matches held in a given country at a given time would probably consist in substantial investment. Investment in recording and presenting the exact time of the sportspersons' performances (for example of a 100 metres race) could also probably be a substantial investment as specific and expensive computing equipment must be used to do so. The same applies to statistics on sportspersons' performances. Therefore some databases of sports results and statistics may well be protected by the database right.

Rights

The database right grants to the database maker the right to prevent the extraction and the reutilization of a substantial part, evaluated quantitatively or qualitatively, of the contents of the protected database (art. 7). The rights of extraction and reutilization are very similar to the rights of reproduction and communication to the public in copyright law. Both direct and indirect extractions and reutilizations infringe the right.[25] However, extraction and reutilization do not cover mere consultation of the database.[26] A substantial part is not defined but it must represent a substantial investment.[27] A part which does not fulfil the requirement of a substantial part is automatically an insubstantial part.[28] The substantial part evaluated quantitatively refers to the volume of the

---

24   Para. 24 (Svenska Spel).
25   Para. 53 (BHB).
26   Paras. 54–5 (BHB).
27   Para. 45 (BHB).
28   Para. 73 (BHB).

data extracted or reutilized from the database and it must be assessed in relation to the volume of the contents of the whole of the database,[29] while the substantial part evaluated qualitatively refers to the scale of investment in the obtaining, verification or presentation of the contents, regardless of whether that subject (or part) represents a quantitatively substantial part of the contents.[30] Users can therefore extract or reutilize insubstantial parts as long as they do not do this repeatedly and systematically so that the accumulation of insubstantial parts becomes a substantial part.[31]

Sporting organizations are therefore well protected. Their rights are broad; if users extract or reutilize without permission a substantial part of the contents of their database (as long as this part represents a substantial investment), sporting organizations can sue them for infringement. This also means that they can ask for licences for use of substantial parts of the contents of their databases. In the case of sports results, generally, licensees will want to use all of them, and they will not escape the payment of royalties. As mentioned above, the database right's exclusive rights are useless for sports fixtures as the database right does not accrue.

Exceptions

There are three exceptions to the rights of extraction and reutilization: lawful users, that is, those who have acquired a lawful copy of the database,[32] can (a) extract a substantial part of the contents of a non-electronic database for private purposes, (b) extract a substantial part of any database for the purposes of illustration for teaching or scientific research as long as it is not for commercial purposes and the source is indicated and (c) extract and/or reutilize a substantial part of any database for the purposes of public security or an administrative or judicial procedure (art. 9). However, these exceptions are all optional so Member States did not have to implement them. Thus the number of exceptions varies from Member State to Member State. In the United Kingdom, there is no private extraction exception but paragraphs (b) and (c)

---

29   Para. 70 (BHB).

30   Para. 71 (BHB).

31   Article 7(5) and 8(1) as construed by the ECJ, see para. 86 (BHB).

32   No clear guidance is given in the Directive as to who is a lawful user. This is our preferred interpretation as well as that of V. Vanovermeire: 'The concept of the lawful user in the database directive' (2000), *International Review of Intellectual Property and Competition Law*, 62, at 71; U. Suthersanen, 'A comparative review of database protection in the European Union and the United States', in F. Dessemontet and R. Gani, *Creative ideas for intellectual property, the ATRIP papers 2000–2001* (Lausanne: Cédidac, 2002), p. 49, at p. 74 and H. Vanhees, 'De juridische bescherming van databanken' (1999–2000), *Rijkskundig Weekblad*, 1001, at 1007.

of article 9 were implemented.[33] Some countries implemented all three exceptions (e.g. Belgium).[34] The right of the user to use insubstantial parts not
amounting to a substantial part has been made imperative (art. 15 of the
Directive) but not the three optional exceptions. Therefore, database makers
can override these three exceptions using contracts and/or technological
protection measures ('TPMs'). However, as regards TPMs, article 6(4) of the
Copyright Directive[35] must be respected.[36]

Sporting organizations that hold rights on sporting results or other information that could be protected by the database right should not fear these
exceptions as they are very narrow. Persons who wish to use results for their
own private use (for example, a football fan copying football matches results
of his or her favourite team since its creation in a personal notebook) will not
harm the rights of the sporting authorities. The second exception is so narrow
that the sport industry should not worry about it. A teacher or researcher will
not be able to use a substantial part of the results to teach or write an article or
book: this would be prohibited reutilization as it would not fall in the exception. S/he will have to ask for a licence. The only exception that may affect
sporting organizations is the third one. For reasons of prohibited drug-taking
by sportsmen or women for example, sporting authorities may have to disclose
information they hold on those athletes that is protected by the database right
to the police or competent investigating authority. As the exceptions are different in every country, sporting authorities should always check whether each
specific exception exists or not. In any case, when licensing the use of their
protected information, they can override the exceptions so that any use of a
substantial part of their protected database is prevented. If the information is
in electronic format and protected by a TPM, any use can be prevented as well,
although not the use of an insubstantial part, notwithstanding the fact that article 6(4) of the Copyright Directive must be respected.[37]

---

[33]   See regulation 20 of the Copyright and Rights in Databases Regulations of 18
December 1997, SI 1997 n. 3032.

[34]   Art. 23 bis of the 1994 Copyright Act.

[35]   Directive 2001/29/EC of the European Parliament and of the Council of 22
May 2001 on the harmonization of certain aspects of copyright and related rights in the
information society, OJ L167/10, 22.06.2001.

[36]   This provision implies that users may circumvent TPMs for the purposes of
illustration of research and teaching as well as for the purposes of public security and
administrative or judicial procedures if the Member State in question has implemented
them and an agreement to this effect is found with the right holders. If there is no such
agreement, then the state has to provide for this possibility to benefit from the exceptions.

[37]   Para. 4, indents 1–3 of article 6 apply only to copyright law. Para. 4, indent 5,
simply says that article 6 applies also to the database right. However, while it seems

Term of Protection

Databases are protected for 15 years from their completion or their publication (art. 10 of the Directive). Furthermore, each time the database maker reinvests substantially in the obtaining, verifying or presenting of the elements of its database and there is a substantial change, it gets a new term of 15 years. The Directive, however, is unclear as to whether the right applies on the whole new database, which comprises the 'old' elements (those whose term has expired), or only on the elements that have been newly included, verified or presented. The ECJ has not clarified this question and it is therefore possible that constantly updated databases are perpetually protected. Hence, if a sporting authority constantly updates its database of competition results, it may well have a right *ad vitam eternam*.

In conclusion, although the ECJ has considerably reduced some of the excessively protective features of the database right,[38] the right remains very strong: the definition of a database and rights is broad, the protection requirement is low, the exceptions are narrow and the term is potentially eternal. Indeed, the right has been heavily criticized by many, especially because it can give a monopoly on information.[39] And, for at least two features, the scarcity and narrowness of the exceptions as well as the potential perpetual duration of the right, the right can still be criticized.[40]

---

clear that Member States must, if no agreement is found between right holders and users, force right holders to allow users to benefit from the two optional exceptions to the database right (as they are similar to those mentioned in article 6(4), indents 1–3 relating to copyright), it is unclear whether the same solution applies when a TPM prevents users from using insubstantial parts as article 15 of the Database Directive makes this provision imperative only as far as contracts are concerned. But, a fortiori, right holders should be forced to allow lawful users to extract and reutilize insubstantial parts as it would be illogical that this solution only applies to bilateral acts (contracts) and not unilateral ones (TPMs).

[38]   Because many terms, such as obtaining, qualitatively, quantitatively and substantial part, were vague they were often broadly interpreted.

[39]   N. Mallet-Poujol, 'La directive concernant la protection juridique des bases de données: la gageure de la protection privative' (1996), **1**, *Droit de l'informatique et des telecoms*, 6, at 10; J. Reichman and P. Samuelson, 'Intellectual property rights in data?' (1997), **50**, *Vanderbilt Law Review*, 51, at 94; C. Geiger, *Droit d'auteur et droit du public à l'information, Approche de droit comparé* (Litec: Paris, 2004), p. 269, p. 268, n.312 and p. 273, n.316.

[40]   As this author does in her doctoral thesis (*The Legal Protection of Databases*, Cheltenham, UK and Northampton, MA, USA: Edward Elgar, forthcoming, 2007).

HOW THE DATABASE RIGHT AFFECTS THE SPORT INDUSTRY

The Database Right does not generally Protect Sporting Organizations well

As can already be seen, the effects of the database right on sporting authorities and organizations are mixed. On the one hand, there is some good news for sporting authorities: sports fixtures, sports results and statistics are databases. Therefore, they fall within the subject matter of protection of the database right. On the other hand, their protection by the database right depends on the type of information involved. Sports fixtures remain almost certainly always unprotected because the stages of creation, collection, verification and/or presentation of the data are interlinked. Obtaining, verifying and/or presenting fixtures does not require any investment independent of that required for the creation of the data contained in those lists. But sports results and statistics may sometimes be protected. If the sporting authority can prove a substantial investment in the collection and/or presentation of the results and statistics which is separable from the investment in creating the results and statistics, it will be protected by the database right. As mentioned above, the recording of times and performances of sportspersons can be very costly as special equipment (such as software and hardware) and personnel is used to do so. However, as also briefly said above, it is unclear whether recording is actually different from creating. Thus the sporting organization will be protected only if the substantial investment relating to the creation of the results is separable from the substantial investment in collecting or presenting them. In sum, some databases of sports results and statistics may be protected by the database right very well.

Competition Problems may Occur despite Protection

Competition law prohibits, among other behaviours, abuses of dominant position (art. 82 of the European Community Treaty ('ECT')). The compilation of sports fixtures will almost never give rise to a dominant position on the relevant market because the database right will not subsist.[41] Recording the results of certain types of sporting activities, such as football or tennis matches, is simple. It may be made by several entities, such as the spectators, the media and the sporting authority organizing the event. In this case, there is no monopoly as the information is available to collect/record by anyone present

---

[41]   However, see the *Attheraces* case, discussed below.

at the game.[42] In addition, there may often be no substantial investment involved and thus no protection. Therefore, in this case, abuses of dominant position will not exist.

Other types of results, implying specific times, such as races (running, skiing, swimming) and sports statistics such as averages in tennis, may only be recorded by machines and the latter generally belong in exclusivity to the sporting organization. In addition, they may not permit other companies on the site to record the information. In such a case, a natural monopoly on the information automatically arises. Therefore, in this case, sporting organizations are subject to article 82 ECT if they abuse their monopoly, e.g. they ask excessive or discriminatory prices or refuse to license the use of the information. Indeed, there is no compulsory or statutory licence in the Directive requiring the licensing of the information for commercial purposes (that is, apart from the exceptions provided for in the Directive).[43]

WHAT CAN AND MUST THE SPORT INDUSTRY DO?

Sporting authorities can try and address these two types of problems in different ways that have various results.

Lack of Protection of Sports Fixtures and of some Sports Results and Statistics

As to the first problem (lack of protection of sports fixtures), sporting organizations can try and protect their fixtures and some of their sports results and statistics in other ways. There are two main possibilities of doing this: one is to try and attract the database right in other ways; the second is to seek alternative legal protection.

---

[42] This is what happened, for instance, in the American case *National Basketball Association* v *Motorola*, 105 F. 3d 841 (2d cir. 1997). Collecting sports results from television broadcasts or live from the sports arena was not misappropriation.

[43] Such a compulsory licence was envisaged in article 8 of the preceding draft of the Directive but was subsequently withdrawn. It read: '1. Notwithstanding the right provided for in article 2(5) to prevent the unauthorised extraction and re-utilisation of the contents of a database, if the works or materials contained in a database which is made publicly available cannot be independently created, collected or obtained from any other source, the right to extract and re-utilise, in whole or substantial part, works or materials from that database for commercial purposes, shall be licensed on fair and non-discriminatory terms. 2. The right to extract and re-utilise the contents of a database shall also be licensed on fair and non-discriminatory terms if the database is made publicly available by a public body which is either established to assemble or disclose information pursuant to legislation, or is under a general duty to do so'.

There are mainly two other ways to attempt attracting database right protection. A first solution, which some have identified,[44] is to change the way the database is created. The company creating the data would sell its database to another company. This way, the other company, which is buying the database, would make a substantial investment in collecting the data and would attract database right. However, courts may find this operation a bit artificial.[45]

Another way to try and attract database right protection would be to put more money, more time and/or energy into the verification and/or presentation of the database,[46] while of course keeping records of those investments in order to prove them if litigation should ensue. But this may not always be worthwhile commercially speaking. It will depend on the amount the company can recoup from the commercialization of its database. If the amount is small, it does not make sense to spend more money on verifying or presenting the data. In addition, the problem remains: would not this verification and/or presentation be inseparable from the creation of the data?

The second main way for sporting organizations to protect their databases is to use alternative types of protection. One such type of protection would be copyright. Sporting organizations could transform their fixtures and results into original databases and license their copyright on them. However, copyright will not protect against the reutilization of the raw information contained in the database. There would be no copyright infringement if a third party reused the data but in a different order.

Thus copyright is not an alternative protection for the contents of a sporting organization's database. In the United Kingdom,[47] however, there may still be a way of using copyright to protect sports fixtures or results. The category of 'table or compilation' still remains in the Copyright Act alongside the category of database.[48] However, it remains unclear what the difference between

---

[44]　S. Peermohamed and R. Kaye, 'Taking steps' (2005), **154**, *Copyright World*, 17.

[45]　Ibid., at 17; A. Strowel and E. Derclaye, *Droit d'auteur et numérique*, 2001, (Brussels: Bruylant, 316, n.358) were already of the opinion that the acquisition by a second company of a company that makes databases will not constitute a substantial investment.

[46]　Peermohamed and Kaye, n.42 above, at 17.

[47]　But not in Ireland, where tables and compilations have been deleted from the Copyright Act. See s. 17 (2) of the Irish Copyright and Related Right Act 2000: 'Copyright subsists, in accordance with this Act, in –
　(a) original literary, dramatic, musical or artistic works,
　(b) sound recordings, films, broadcasts or cable programmes,
　(c) the typographical arrangement of published editions, and
　(d) original databases.'

[48]　Section 3(1) of the Copyright, Designs and Patent Act 1988 as amended

the two is because a table or compilation is not defined. Nevertheless, the two categories are clearly separate.[49] For this reason, neither a table nor a compilation is a database, so a table or compilation must not have at least one of the requirements of the database definition. As football fixtures and sports results are clearly databases,[50] they cannot be tables or compilations. Therefore, they cannot be copyright protected. However, if sporting organizations were to make elements of their lists or results dependent and/or unorganized, they would not be databases and might fall into the category of table or compilation. But they would not be 'user-friendly' and therefore not , as users will not find the information quickly or maybe at all. Thus this is not a solution for sporting organizations. In any case, it is very unlikely that the retention of the category of table or compilation by the British legislator complies with EU legislation (that is, the Directive).[51]

A second alternative protection is confidentiality contracts. They could be used to protect the contents of sporting organizations' databases. If the data are kept confidential, third parties wishing to use the data will have to ask for a licence. However, if the purpose of the data is to be disseminated to the public, then it must by definition not have confidentiality status and such confidentiality contracts are plainly useless. This is the case for sports fixtures and results and many statistics: their purpose is to be divulged to the broad public. A different type of databases where confidentiality agreements could work would be customer lists, medical data or sensitive news, such as some stock data. Thus one area where sporting organizations may find confidentiality protection useful is their databases covering use of prohibited drugs enhancing sport performance or other sensitive data on sportspersons that are not generally divulged to the public.

A third alternative protection is trade mark law. The use of a trade mark indicates not only the origin of the good or service but also a certain quality that attaches to it and distinguishes the database from other less good (for example, less accurate) databases. However, this will not protect the database owner from reutilizations of the raw data contained in his database. It may

---

('CDPA'), states that 'literary work means any work, other than a dramatic or musical work, which is written, spoken or sung, and accordingly includes –

(a) a table or compilation other than a database,

(. . .)

(d) a database.'

49 See n. 48.

50 Para. 36 (OPAP).

51 For an explanation, see E. Derclaye, 'Do sections 3 and 3A of the CDPA violate the Database Directive? A closer look at the definition of a database in the UK and its compatibility with European law' (2002), **10**, *European Intellectual Property Review*, 466–79.

only entice licensees to pay for the information because of its renowned source.

Last but not least, perhaps the best protection is simply the reality of the industry. Sports fixtures generally need to be known by, for example, betting organizations as soon as possible. Speed of access is therefore crucial. Potential licensees may thus be prepared to pay for the sports fixtures even though they could obtain them at a later date.[52] A recent example of this situation is the *Attheraces* case.[53] In that case, Attheraces ('ATR'), a betting organization, which uses horse racing fixtures to allow users to place bets, was still in need of the 'pre-race' data[54] from the British Horse Racing Board ('the BHB'), even after the ECJ's November 2004 decisions. In reality, if an organization, for its economic survival, desperately needs the information from the organization generating it as soon as it is available, it does not matter whether the organization generating this information has an intellectual property right on it or not. It has power on a product (information) like an undertaking that would sell regular tangible products. The *Attheraces* case has proved this, as will be seen below.[55] This shows that, in the case where the information's time-sensitivity is crucial, and the organization generating it has a monopoly or a dominant position (as is the case for sporting organizations in relation to their fixtures, some of their results and statistics), it does not matter that there is no copyright or database right in the information and sporting organizations are de facto very well protected.

Excessive Protection of Sports Fixtures and Sports Results and Statistics

As has just been seen in the previous section, an undertaking creating information can have a de facto or de jure monopoly in it, and thus have monopoly power. Therefore, its behaviour must comply with competition law and in particular article 82 ECT. Although the undertaking may have a right to charge

---

52   Peermohamed and Kaye, n. 44 above, at 17.
53   *Attheraces v The British Horse Racing Board* [2005] EWHC 3015 (Ch), available on http://www.bailii.org/ew/cases/EWHC/Ch/2005/3015.html.
54   Pre-race data include the place and date on which the race meeting is to be held; the name of the race; a list of horses entered; the list of declared runners (horses competing).
55   Etherton J agreed that the BHB has the right to charge for its data even if it does not have intellectual property rights in them. This is because they are 'a valuable commodity, for which it is entitled to charge'. This is nonetheless disputable as sporting organizations recoup their investments in drawing fixtures by charging a price for entrance at sporting events. The Court of Appeal agreed. *Attheraces Ltd, Attheraces (UK) Ltd v British Horse Racing Board Ltd, BHB Enterprises Plc* [2007] EWCA Civ 38.

for the sports fixtures, be they protected by an intellectual property right or not, it cannot abusively refuse to supply the information or charge an excessive price.[56] The issue of excessive prices is considered in the recent *Attheraces* case, which concerned horse racing fixtures, and is summarized here. As the case mainly concerns excessive prices, this section will first review the law applying to them and then it will review the law relating to refusals to license.

The British Horse Racing Board is the entity that organizes horse races in the United Kingdom and, in this capacity, it creates 'pre-race' data. ATR, a betting organization, pays the BHB for the pre-race data it needs in order to organize its betting activities. ATR claimed that the BHB had a monopoly in the supply of pre-race data and that, by asking an excessive, unfair and discriminatory price, it abused its dominant position in breach of article 82 ECT. This was because the BHB continued asking a price, and a very high one at that, of ATR after the ECJ's November 2004 decisions. The BHB claimed it had copyright and database right on its database to justify this price. Both Etherton J and the Court of Appeal held that the BHB held a dominant position on the relevant product market (UK pre-race data). The data could not be obtained elsewhere so it was an essential facility. At first instance, the judge ruled that the terms at which the BHB proposed to supply the data to ATR were unreasonable and unfair. First, it was so because the BHB claimed an injunction to prevent infringement of copyright and database right by ATR but an intellectual property licence was not warranted. In addition, the BHB never articulated its claim to copyright despite ATR's requests. Second, the BHB's proposed price to ATR was excessive because it was far in excess of the competitive price.[57] The BHB covered its costs nearly four times over. Third, the BHB's price was also discriminatory because it applied a different price to ATR than to another competitor without justification.

However, the Court of Appeal overturned the decision. First, whilst the cost+ approach (cost of producing the product plus a reasonable profit) is a

---

[56] When the owner of an essential facility charges an excessive price it can be a constructive refusal to supply. Thus the concept of refusal to license includes constructive refusal, that is, where the dominant firm subjects supply to objectively unreasonable conditions. See *Deutsche Post AG and British Post Office*, Comp/C-1/36.915, 25 July 2001.

[57] A price is excessive because it has 'no reasonable relation to the economic value of the product supplied'. See *United Brands* v *Commission* [1978] ECR 207, at 250. In other words, according to the European Commission and the Office of Fair Trading ('OFT'), an excessive price is a price that is higher than it would be in a competitive market and there is no effective competitive pressure to bring them down to competitive levels nor is there likely to be. See, e.g., OFT's guideline on 'assessment of individual agreements and conduct', 414, September 1999; *Napp Pharmaceuticals*, No. CA98/2/2001-30.03.2001.

necessary step to determine whether the price is excessive, it is not sufficient. The competitive price is not always cost+. All the relevant circumstances have to be assessed and especially those relating to the product in question. Given the nature of the pre-race data and the basis on which it was marketed, this approach was not right. The judge tied the costs allowable in cost+ too closely to the costs of producing the data. The value of the product to the contracting party is an important factor to take into consideration. Also, even if the BHB sought to take half of what ATR did make, even if this may be unfair, this alone did not constitute an abuse. There must be evidence that competition in the market is distorted by the demands made by the dominant undertaking towards its contracting party. Since ATR's competitiveness was not at risk of being materially compromised, the price charged was neither unfair nor excessive. Second, as the price was neither unfair nor excessive and it was agreed that the BHB could charge for data although it was not protected by intellectual property, the BHB was not abusing its dominant position by refusing to supply pre-race data. Finally, there was no discrimination between ATR and other contracting parties simply because the price the BHB charged was different, even though the transactions were equivalent. Differential treatment is not per se abusive. There must be overcharging, that is, the price differential must go beyond falling more heavily on one buyer than on the other and actually or potentially distorts competition between them.

The ECJ suggested that other ways of proving excessive pricing exist.[58] 'Yardstick competition' is one technique. This compares the performance of one undertaking with the performance of others. Such a comparison can also be made with prices charged in other Member States but only where the Member States are both either high-price or low-price countries. Several methods exist to determine a fair price/royalty for use of an IPR in certain contexts.[59]

Competition law therefore applies and regulates excessive and discriminatory prices for sports fixtures that can be charged by sporting organizations in dominant positions. The same applies for sports results and statistics where the sporting organization is the only one which records them, as it has a monopoly (if speed of access is crucial, which generally will be the case). This will happen with the recording of exact times of sportspersons. When anyone is free to record the results at the same time (spectators, broadcasting organizations), no monopoly arises and there is free competition. This will be the case for the results of tennis, football, rugby and other matches. As a result of the

---

[58] R. Whish, *Competition law*, 5th edn (London: Butterworths, 2003, pp. 690 et seq).

[59] For a description, see M. Dolmans, 'Standards for standards' (2002–3), *Fordham Int'l L.J.*, at 204 ff.

Attheraces decision, it is clear that sporting organizations will have to make sure they do not charge excessive or unfair prices for their sporting data or discriminate unfairly between their customers as to price. However, as a result of this case, it is more difficult than it seemed at first sight to prove that a dominant undertaking commits an abuse in these kinds of situations.

As far as simple refusals to supply are concerned, the law is set in the *IMS Health* case.[60] In that case, IMS Health refused to license its copyright on its database (a structure used to market reports on sales of medicines in Germany) to NDC. The ECJ held that there is abuse when the refusal to license (1) concerns a product the supply of which is indispensable for carrying on the business in question, in that the person wishing to make the product would find it impossible to do so, (2) prevents the emergence of a new product for which there is a potential consumer demand, (3) is not justified by objective considerations, and (4) is likely to exclude all competition in the secondary market.[61] These four conditions are cumulative. This test applies to all intellectual property rights. The *IMS Health* case clarified the law, as previously it was unclear whether the conditions were cumulative or not. The requirement that the refusal prevent the emergence of a new product maintains a good balance between competition and intellectual property law: innovation is not stifled by the obligation to grant a licence to competitors who would just replicate the product. However, the decision did not clarify what it meant by 'new product'. Legal certainty suffers as a result. Similarly, the condition of unjustified refusal to impose the licence has not been defined, leaving the law uncertain. Finally, the decision implies the immediate imposition of the compulsory licence, which can reduce the incentive to create innovative products in the first place. The law should at least provide that the licensee licenses its new product back to the original creator so that the latter can survive in the market. Further developments on this legal issue are awaited in the future *Commission* v *Microsoft* case.[62]

The *IMS Health* decision nevertheless entails that sporting organizations in a dominant position have to immediately license their information to competitors if the latter propose to make a new product out of it. The typical example of a new product comes from the *Magill* case, where Magill proposed to market a comprehensive television guide out of the separate so far existing

---

[60]   *IMS Health GmbH & Co OHG* v *NDC Health GmbH & Co KG*, Case C-418/01 [2004] 4 CMLR 28. For comments, see, e.g., E. Derclaye, 'The IMS health decision and the reconciliation of copyright and competition' (2004), **5**, *European Law Review*, 687–97 and E. Derclaye, 'The IMS Health decision: a triple victory' (2004), **27**(1), *World Competition*, 397–405.

[61]   Ibid., para. 38.

[62]   A decision of the Court of First Instance is awaited in 2007 in this case (Commission decision of 24 March 2004, case COMP/C-3/37.792 *Microsoft*, available at http://ec.europa.eu/comm/competition/antitrust/cases/decisions/37792/en.pdf).

television guides produced by each television channel.[63] It is arguable that a website reproducing sports fixtures in order to place bets is a new product. The *IMS Health* ruling may also apply to situations where the information is not protected by an intellectual property right as it was decided in a line of cases concerning refusals to supply in general. This is not clear-cut though, as information can be viewed as a mere commodity and the 'old test' stemming from the *Bronner* case, not requiring the condition of new product may therefore apply, making a finding of abuse easier.[64] An objective justification sporting organizations could use to refuse to give their information away is that the licensee is a bad debtor.[65] Other objective justifications for refusing to supply information have yet to be developed.

CONCLUSION AND FUTURE PROSPECTS

Sporting organizations are generally not well protected by copyright and the database right. However, when the database right protects them, this protection is very effective, perhaps even too much so, as a result of their monopoly positions. Even where sporting organizations cannot secure intellectual property protection, when speedy access to the information they generate is vital, the simple fact that they have a monopoly on the information protects them well and, again, sometimes too much because of their monopoly power. As the Directive does not incorporate mechanisms to prevent abuses of dominant position by holders of the database right, resort to competition law must be had. Article 82's case law is relatively settled and provides a generally good working framework to prevent abuses such as excessive pricing and refusals to license. However, the recent developments at least in the UK on this issue seem to indicate that it may be an uphill struggle for the claimant to show such abuse exists. Human rights law based on the rights to freedom of speech and to access to information can also provide a means to prevent abuses by monopolists.[66] Nevertheless, as far as the database right is concerned, a better solu-

---

[63]   *RTE and ITP* v *Commission* ('the Magill case'), Case C-241/91 [1995] ECR I-743.

[64]   *Oscar Bronner GmbH & Co. KG* v *Mediaprint Zeitungs- und Zeitschriftenverlag GmbH & Co. KG, Mediaprint Zeitungsvertriebsgesellschaft mbH & Co. KG & Mediaprint Anzeigengesellschaft mbH & Co. KG*, Case C-7/97, (1998) ECR 7791.

[65]   R. Whish, n. 58 above, 611.

[66]   This issue is discussed in E. Derclaye, 'Database *sui generis* right: the need to take the public's right to information and freedom of expression into account', in F. Macmillan (ed.), *New Directions in Copyright Law, Volume V*, Cheltenham, UK and Northampton, MA, USA: Edward Elgar, 2007.

tion would be to incorporate principles of competition law and human rights law within the Directive. This would make the law more certain. A revision of the Directive is therefore mandated, something the European Commission has in mind.[67] In the meantime, the case law applying article 82 ECT (although not yet a perfect tool) plays a crucial role in regulating the sport industry in the area of the licensing of information.

In conclusion, the Directive may have generally missed its goal of protecting database producers such as sporting organizations but even if the law is not helpful, the reality of the industry sometimes provides de facto strong protection. When these power positions are abused, fortunately antitrust law generally does not miss its goal of safeguarding competition.

---

[67]   On 12 December 2005, the Commission handed down a report recommending certain options (e.g. revising or abolishing the *sui generis* right) and requesting comments before taking action. See http://europa.eu.int/comm/internal_market/copyright/docs/databases/evaluation_report_en.pdf; so far, the Commission favours the status quo but it has indicated that it may later on revise the Directive.

Index